Your Service Dog and You

Your Service Dog and You
A Practical Guide

NICOLA FERGUSON

DOGS IN OUR WORLD
Series Editor Brian Patrick Duggan

McFarland & Company, Inc., Publishers
Jefferson, North Carolina

LIBRARY OF CONGRESS CATALOGUING-IN-PUBLICATION DATA

Names: Ferguson, Nicola, 1971– author.
Title: Your service dog and you : a practical guide / Nicola Ferguson.
Description: Jefferson, North Carolina : McFarland & Company, Inc., 2023 |
Series: Dogs in our world | Includes bibliographical references and index.
Identifiers: LCCN 2023026874 | ISBN 9781476690803 (paperback : acid free paper) ∞
ISBN 9781476649122 (ebook)
Subjects: LCSH: Service dogs.
Classification: LCC HV1569.6 .F47 2023 | DDC 362.4/0483—dc23/eng/20230613
LC record available at https://lccn.loc.gov/2023026874

BRITISH LIBRARY CATALOGUING DATA ARE AVAILABLE

ISBN (print) 978-1-4766-9080-3
ISBN (ebook) 978-1-4766-4912-2

Front cover image: © 24K-Production/iStock

Printed in the United States of America

*McFarland & Company, Inc., Publishers
Box 611, Jefferson, North Carolina 28640
www.mcfarlandpub.com*

To Holly and Poppy Bengal.
True love never dies.

Holly and Poppy Bengal, to whom this book is dedicated. Photo by the author (2012).

Acknowledgments

Massive thanks to my editor Brian Duggan, most particularly for putting up with my bad jokes and ensuring this book was the best that it could be. Many thanks also to the team at McFarland that have been incredibly supportive of this book.

Table of Contents

Preface

Service dogs. Haven't we all watched a service dog team in a shop or restaurant, and been full of wonder at the bond between dog and handler? How well behaved the dog was and how simple everything they did together looked? The effortless communication between dog and handler, the love they share there for all to see. I know I marveled at these partnerships and was full of curiosity about them.

I was born with quite severe disabilities, including autism spectrum disorder, osteoarthritis, and autoimmune conditions. Although I was talented academically, all of my life I struggled to hold down a job and live independently. I had always thought a service dog would be beneficial for me, but it wasn't an option where I lived in the UK. Charities only helped autistic children, and none of my other medical conditions qualified for a service dog provided by either a service dog charity or organization. It was not until my mid-forties, when my physical health also started to fail, that my therapist and doctor both suggested I think about training my very own service dog, as they had both seen this done and it was not illegal to do it myself.

I threw myself into researching service dogs; everything from breed selection, puppy training, and finding a good service dog trainer, to the law surrounding these wonderful dogs. Six months later, service dog prospect Mazey arrived. Ten weeks old and with on-fleek brows as befits every Rottweiler (an off breed as service dogs go), she was gorgeous. One service dog trainer even told me to return her to her breeder (!) as Rottweilers are, and I quote, "all vicious." I was very polite and replied with two, short, to-the-point words. I can't recall the exact words I used, but I will leave that to your own imagination. Quickly moving on, I found that even though I had studied veterinary medicine for three years, lived all of my life with dogs and trained a wide variety of other animals, I had a lot to learn about service dogs.

This book is a practical guide to service dogs. It's based on my own experiences authentically living as a disabled person, reliant on Mazey for my health and well-being. Written over five years, it contains all of the valuable research I did before getting Mazey, how I trained her, and the way we live our best life together day to day as a partnership. From the moment your new service dog prospect arrives, you are now living with a Z-list celebrity; I know this was one of the main things that took me by surprise, and which I struggled to deal with.

However, this book is not just for prospective service dog owners. It's also for dog breeders, business owners or people who simply want to learn more about service dogs, providing insight and helpful advice for the next time you meet a service dog team. I also hope the book will be of benefit to dog trainers, even those who currently train service dogs, giving more understanding of what it is to live with a life-changing disability and the tasks and behaviors that don't seem obvious, but are actually incredibly helpful to teach a service dog from a disabled person's perspective.

I think you can tell by now that dogs are my passion—service dogs in particular—though I have to admit to crazy cat lady tendencies too. Shh. Don't tell the dogs! I consider service dogs to be the most wonderful dogs you ever will meet, but there's a lot that goes into their selection, training, upkeep, and working them in public. It's hard being disabled, and a service dog is not for everyone. This book is designed to dish the Darjeeling, to let you learn from my mistakes, and to give you the honest truth about what it is like to own, train, live with, and love a service dog.

I hope you enjoy the book. Woofs and bum scritches for you all.
Nicola Ferguson and Mazey Rottweiler, May 17, 2022.

CHAPTER ONE

The History of the Service Dog (But Not as You Know It)

Service dogs have been around for a long time. A very long time indeed. Longer than me even, despite the fact I have more than a passing resemblance to the Crypt Keeper. On a good hair day. But as we will see, I'm a spring chicken compared to the amazing dogs who first rose to the challenge, earning the coveted title of "service dog" for the wonderful work they did for their disabled owners.

There are already many excellent books and articles narrating the recent history of the service dog, so we're not going to drag out the usual suspects and repeat what's already been documented. How much more interesting to look at the unrecorded history of the service dog, the nooks and crannies of the past which most people gloss over as too unreliable to be true. Poppycock! Hold on to your hat as we soar like a vampire bat, heading straight for the jugular, where we can suck on the juicy bits of history and how it relates to the service dog.

I know many readers may be tempted to flick forward, preferring service dog confirmed sightings to the ramblings of someone it could fairly be said has too much imagination. Stop!!!! History is a living, breathing, ever-changing thing which I liken to our bones. They both may appear boring, dead and hollow, but they're very much alive and underpin how we view and interact with the world around us. As bones can be remodeled, so too is history capable of metamorphosis, revealing different perspectives according to the eye of the beholder. My truth and your truth can be very different, but both can also be correct. Mine the most correct of all. Obviously.

Now, if it's not already clear, I like fun, excitement, thrills and spills myself, so without further ado let's turn our attention to dinosaurs and dire wolves, starting with the domestication of the dog,[1] and therefore the first appearance of the service dog. Humans and dogs started a (platonic) relationship with each other as far back as fifty thousand years ago,[2] during the last Ice Age. The Ice Age!!!! Can you believe it? Ambling around were woolly mammoths, chased by hungry dire wolves[3]—yes, they really were a thing—and as if that was not enough, there were saber-toothed tigers[4] on the scene too. Scary stuff.

At this time Neanderthals had not yet become extinct, with some authors suggesting that the domestication of the dog and their use by humans in hunting expeditions contributed significantly to the Neanderthals' demise.[5] Bad doggy. Well, bad wolfie, or should we say bad proto-dog, since at this time wolves were undergoing the process of domestication, but were not quite there yet. Anyway, my point is, where there's smoke there's fire, or rather in this specific case where there's proto-dogs there's invariably proto-service dogs.

I don't think it's unreasonable to speculate that during the domestication process, proto-service dogs became an unexpected by-product of evolution. In some of the proto-dog litters there would be cute, friendly puppies, well on the way to becoming dogs, engaging with and taking an interest in humans in a way wolves do not. The most intelligent ones would be frantically fluttering their little eyelashes, aiming to tug on human heartstrings, though ideally not literally. Those little proto-dog puppy teeth must have been sharp, sharp, sharp.

Instead of being banished to the freezing cold with the rest of the pack to hunt woolly mammoths, these super cute dog-like puppies would have been retained in the home, or cave as the case may be, carving out very different career paths for themselves. Just as service dogs do today, these proto-dogs would have been capable of tasks such as alerting to ill health, or warning the hard of hearing of an attack from those pesky saber-toothed tigers. Legitimate service dog tasks, performed just as our modern service dogs do to this very day. Well, with the exception of alerting to prowling saber-toothed tigers that have murder in mind.

Now, I'll concede that it's easy to dismiss a fifty-thousand-year-old proto-service dog as the fantasy of a crazy cat lady of a certain age, one with too much time on her hands. After all, say the word "proto-dog" out loud, and it immediately conjures up images of a pack of dire wolves running rampant through the New York Public Library, eating babies for brunch. Dire wolves are to service dogs as Queen Elizabeth II is to Tinder.

But let's look at the facts. In virtually every country in the world you'll see news report after news report of ordinary dogs, of various breeds, start to perform service dog tasks completely on their own initiative. This includes very complex tasks. If the average pet dog can smell a biochemical change in their owner's saliva, understand that this change corresponds with a difference in their owner's behavior and well-being, and lead the dog to find a way to convey this information to their owner, all unprompted, then why not a proto-dog? Why not indeed?

So what are your views? Do you agree with me, or do you want to thump me over the head with this book and knock some sense into my head? Needless to say I'm convinced I'm right. So sure, in fact, that I'll stamp my foot to prove my point, though I draw the line at screaming until I'm sick. My service dogs Mazey and Mina would probably appreciate this. Yes, your eyes did not deceive you: you read right the first time. Mazey and Mina are typical greedy Grottweilers, appreciating any sustenance that comes their way. Yuk. OK, so we can agree that we can't *prove* there were proto-service dogs, but once the dog was fully domesticated, service dogs started to be represented in art, and this is where we will proceed next.

Get your seat belts fastened as we're off to a fiery start, traveling back in time to a sultry morning on the 24th of August, 79 CE, nearly two thousand years ago. Stepping into the shade of the Complesso di Giulia Felice, we admire the Forum Frieze in the Atrium,[6] as behind us we hear the rumble of Mount Vesuvius. Painted on stone we see a depiction of an unkempt man carrying a stick, being led forward by his dog to receive alms. This is one of the earliest depictions of a service dog hard at work.

The majority of early acknowledgments of service dogs are in art, not literature, and it has to be said they almost all comprise guide dogs. Giant breeds that could be used for bracing or counter-balance were not yet employed for this purpose it seems, and tasks such as medical alert or fetching objects that a smaller dog could perform were not easily depicted in art. By contrast, a blind person being led by their guide dog is by far the easiest service dog task to paint or draw, immediately providing context and impact. So for now, it's very much, "guide dogs rule, OK."

Alas, it is almost noon and we must continue our journey, lest we be enveloped by a pyroclastic flow and upset the space-time continuum. Donning our glad rags we travel forward and backward, spinning and twirling through time and space, from country to country, as if on a TARDIS-inspired Grand Tour. We visit China, France, England, Holland and Germany, all of which have art depicting guide dogs for us to admire, including pieces created

This charming illustration shows one of the first guide dogs in action and raring to go. A shoeless blind girl is led by a dog on a path. Sepia stipple engraving by T. Gaugain, after J. Northcote (1785). Wellcome Collection.

by the most renowned of Old Masters, Rembrandt himself, who depicted a guide dog at work.[7]

It's interesting to note that the majority of the guide dogs illustrated in paintings prior to the last hundred and twenty years or so seem to be small dogs of relatively indeterminate breed, being spaniel-sized or less, mostly wearing a collar and lead,[8] not a harness with a fixed handle as we see on guide dogs working today. We do not observe taller dogs until trainers in Germany started using herding dogs, from about 1899 onward, initially using Collies and later German Shepherds.[9]

Although the service dog art of this time is almost exclusively devoted to guide dogs, T.J. Smith produced a picture of a bad-tempered, legless man begging while sitting on a wooden cart.[10] I think we'd all be bad tempered in his circumstances to be fair. He is accompanied by two quite large hounds, both wearing head collars and harnesses (it looks like), indicating these service dogs were used for draft purposes, as were my wonderful Rottweilers and many other service dog breeds back in the day.

Another old photograph I feel a connection to is one of a gallant hound carrying a sick little boy on his back to a hospice, hovering hopefully at the door. This is perhaps more of a rescue, but I would love to know the background of this wonderful dog. Is he owned by the little boy and his family, or is he employed by the

hospice to scour the streets, picking up sick children? I like to think the latter, as the picture is called "The Dog of the Convent."

Clearly people have trained their own guide dogs throughout the ages, but there was no formal training for guide dogs until 1752, when a portrait depicts blind inmates of the Quinze-Vingts Hospital in Paris being guided by their service dogs. Sporadic schools cropped up here and there, but it was not until World War I that the first modern guide dog school was founded in Oldenburg, Germany. After that there was no stopping guide dogs, and today almost every country in the world has working guide dogs, as well as schools for their education and training.

The last piece of art I will mention also includes a deviation from the trend of smaller service dogs. It's a rather alarming 1828 lithograph by Engelmann of a group of blind musicians facing off against a

A rescue dog brings a little boy on his back to a hospice. Image titled *The Dog of the Convent*, date and artist unknown. Wellcome Collection.

rival musician. Their respective pointer-type dogs are about to rip each other apart under their owners' noses.[11] Talk about ending the show just before the climax. This piece of service dog art fascinated me, as I kept wondering what happened next and if fur did indeed fly. I imagine the artist calmly capturing the original scene, no doubt locking it in his mind's eye as chaos ensued, each dog intent on causing major bodily harm to the other.

It's beyond the scope of this book to record in great detail the progression of guide dog's world domination in the service dog sphere, but should you be interested, both The International Guide Dog Federation[12] and also the UK's Guide Dogs for the Blind[13] websites have some fantastic resources, which will keep you occupied on many a rainy weekend.

Without heading off too much on a tangent, I now want to speak a little about service dogs that were never recognized at all, but nevertheless no doubt existed and should not be forgotten. History is a fluid thing, with historical fact more often than

A troupe of blind musicians and their dogs confronting a rival street musician and his dog. Lithograph by Engelmann after M.S. Baptiste (1828). Wellcome Collection.

not being the truth as perceived by the influencers of the time. In those days influencers were not the attractive, scantily clad ladies with a trout pout we follow today, but rather wealthy men together with the all-powerful, all-male clergy.

The church's influence extended for a great many years, the vibe being very much Stepford Wives. Women had to conform, whether they be young maidens, widows, healers, wise women and midwives, old crones, or just women like me who were independent and living their best lives on their own terms. All of these women were in great danger if they stepped out of line. I for one would not have lasted long at all. Would you?

Medicine was not what it is today, and superstition abounded. Those men in positions of power simply would not have believed it possible that a mere dog could foretell illness, and if by chance they were convinced such a thing could occur, it would not have been considered a good thing. The church condemned anything outside its remit and control, particularly where such a happening could not be explained by the rudimentary science of the time. An accusation of witchcraft was a convenient way to deal with wayward women, leading to an almost certain death sentence for both the woman in question and her faithful service dog.

Life was incredibly hard in those days, and any sort of disability was frowned upon, severe deformities treated as the result of a curse or a hex. We know women had a bad deal, but so did many men. Any indication a man was "different" in any way, shape or form, and he would be treated with suspicion, unless of course he was wealthy and in a position of great power and influence. It's a massive leap, I know, but given that keeping of working dogs was so common at the time, I hypothesize that wise women (and men) utilized service dogs to keep themselves safe, breaking the rules while all the time pretending to be meek and mild, incapable of souring milk or curdling cheese.

We've all heard of the Salem Witch Trials that started in February 1692 and ended in May 1693.[14] More than 150 people, almost all women, were accused of being witches. Tragically, nineteen women were hanged, seven women died while in prison and one man died under torture. Quite simply, it was not a good time to be a woman. Yes, men had it bad too, I won't deny that, but women were the main targets of the wrath of their enemies.

But hold onto your broomsticks, girls. These were not isolated incidents, either before or after the events in Salem, with both the U.S. and Europe in the thrall of religious persecution for way too long. In fact, approximately two hundred thousand people, ninety percent of these being women, were murdered in Western Europe between about 1484 and 1750.[15] These were not nice deaths: it was burning, hanging, drowning or good old fashioned torture. It just didn't do to attract attention to oneself. On-point winged eyeliner was definitely out.

But what do witches have to do with service dogs, you may ask, which is a very good question. Well as with proto-dogs, ordinary dogs have been helping us in the capacity of service dogs since time immemorial, taking up this role of their own volition. Witches were usually said to keep a cat as their familiar, typically a pampered puss living rent free in the home, in effect as the witch's pet. These cats were thought to be supernatural spirits embodied within the cat's physical body, which assisted the witch in getting up to no good. But a familiar did not have to be a cat.

On occasion, dogs were also kept in the home instead of being kenneled outside, with suspicion rarely falling onto them in the same way it may have with a cat. I mean, everyone loves dogs, don't they? Dogs at that time had proper jobs, such as herding sheep and cattle. These intelligent, trainable, hardworking dogs would have made excellent service dog prospects for the independent woman about town who may well have chosen a dog to live with to assist in hiding any disabilities she may have had.

Not all dogs flew under the radar, and there were some dogs in recorded history who were accused of being witches' familiars. Looking at their owners and their circumstances, it seems certain those dogs fulfilled a service dog role of some sort. One such case was in England where the Pendle Witches were led by two (very) old ladies,[16] matriarchs of their respective families, both making their living as healers, always a dangerous profession for old matrons. Instead of keeping cats as their familiars, the Pendle witches seemed to have a penchant for dogs.

One such dog accused of being a familiar was poor Tibb. Although his exact fate is not recorded, I doubt he was pampered into a comfortable old age. Tibb belonged to Demdike, an octogenarian and a Pendle witch.[17] The average life expectancy for a woman in 1612 was forty-three, so Demdike, with her herbs and potions bubbling away on the range, managed to live almost twice as long as her peers, which is no mean feat.[18] Given Demdike's great age and the fact Tibb lived in close contact with her, in the home and not the yard, I feel pretty certain Tibb would have carried out at least some basic service dog tasks as many dogs do for their elderly owners to this very day.

House dogs were not common at that time, and Tibb would have had to work for his bed and board in some manner, so why not as a service dog? He could easily have been used to perform simple tasks an old person would appreciate, such as fetching items, helping Demdike undress, assisting her out of bed, not to mention light guiding tasks. If we make a comparison to today and how our life expectancy has been extended by modern healthcare and hygienic living conditions, Demdike would be like, two hundred years old. Yikes! Maybe she *was* a witch after all. Just don't stand in front of the mirror and say her name three times. You just never know....

Demdike has scared me somewhat, and it's time to move on. Quickly. With a few clicks of our glittery red shoes, we arrive in Warwickshire, England. The year is 1945 and it's St. Valentine's Day, but don't let that fool you into thinking this is a sweet and light story. The witchy woo service dog histories are not over yet! Charles Walton, aged seventy-four, was a self-proclaimed wizard who met a very sad end on the most romantic day of the year. Chillingly, his murderer or most probably, murderers, were never found.[19]

So what happened, and where is the service dog in this tale? We know from newspaper reports at the time that poor Charles was crippled with arthritis, using a stick to get around, and therefore in this story his disability was absolutely confirmed and not conjecture on my part. Charles was seventy-four after all, which is a grand old age. Some locals claimed that in addition to a walking stick or crutch, he also relied on the help of a black dog in his day-to-day life, being as he was in the habit of taming wild dogs with his voice.[20] Sounds like a sound guy to me!

In those days there was no Harry Potter, and all wizards were considered to be evil devil worshipers who would curse you as soon as look at you. It has to be said: Charles was playing with fire by boasting so openly about his craft. By and by the locals were thought to have had enough of Charles and his supernatural activities, and he was stabbed through the throat with a pitchfork, pinned to the ground. A cross was then carved into his chest with a sharp blade, making this a ritualistic killing if there ever was one. His familiar, the innocent black dog who was seen to be performing what we now recognize as service dog duties, was found hanging by her collar from a tree several days later, close to where Charles himself was killed. A very sad tale, and surprisingly recent.

You can bet then, if I was alive long ago, or even not so long ago, sitting on a cold, dark winter's night beside the fire with my wee dog on my lap, and she gave me "the look" I would be out of that house and to the privacy of the privy faster than a cheetah on crack before I had a seizure and my puritan husband could accuse me of being a witch, lock me up, torture me, then have me legally bumped off. Afterward he would no doubt plan to remodel the garden, build a new fancy gazebo complete with flowing floribunda in delicate shades of coral and white, all ready for a spring wedding with my younger, prettier replacement. Who would probably be my sister.

Another clickity click of our magic red shoes, and we're home, safe and sound. Mazey and Mina hardly stir, but Izzy and Levi make it very clear that it's time for tea, and my tardiness is unacceptable. As I obediently dish out cat food, I ponder that cats, in contrast to dogs, have never been truly domesticated by humans. Rather, it was the other way around—hence we do not hear of "saber-toothed service cats" or "guide cats for the blind." Perhaps cats saw dogs working hard and decided that being worshiped as a god was more their thing? Who can tell?

In any event, I hope this brief travel though time observing the untold history of the service dog has whetted your appetite, and you'll spend many a pleasant hour or two searching for more unrecognized service dogs of yesteryear. If not, at least you now know dire wolves were a real thing and not a Dungeons and Dragons fantasy. If any billionaires are reading, full of unbridled enthusiasm at the thought of an err dire service wolf, or should it be a service dire wolf?—Don't. Just don't. Leave it be. We all saw how *Jurassic Park* turned out, didn't we now?

CHAPTER TWO

What Defines a Service Dog in Today's World?

We've looked at the history of the first service dogs, so now would be a good time to consider what a service dog actually is in today's world. In the U.S. service dogs are called just that: service dogs. In the UK we call them assistance dogs, but I'll be using the term "service dog" throughout this book, though you'll notice the photographs of my beloved Mazey in her work gear show her labeled as an assistance dog.

To really define a service dog we must turn to the law. In my opinion the U.S. legal system offers one of the most sophisticated legal models in the world, giving

Mazey, dressed and ready to go to work, leaving pesky Mina behind to sulk. Photo by the author (2022).

U.S. service dogs and their handlers unparalleled protection. In comparison, the UK fails miserably. For my sins, I qualified as a Scots law solicitor many moons ago, and spent a little bit of time working in the U.S. I've been retired from law for many years now, and this is not a definitive guide to service dog law and cannot be relied on as such. Nevertheless, in any book on service dogs, I do think it's well worth going over the very basics when it comes to service dogs and the law, whether you live in the U.S. or the UK.

The relevant piece of legislation, which applies across the whole of the U.S. as a federal law, is the Americans with Disabilities Act of 1990 (the "ADA") for which the U.S. Department of Justice (the "DOJ") provides a helpful, concise guide.[1] The relevant UK legislation was enacted somewhat later, being the Equality Act 2010 (the "Equality Act").[2] The Equality Act is much less thorough than the ADA, and offers very little protection for disabled handlers when it comes to themselves and their service dogs, and as such I will examine the Equality Act in less depth later in this chapter.

I'll not repeat the wording of the ADA ad infinitum, but thankfully the definition of a service dog is pretty basic and self-explanatory, being, "a dog that is individually trained to **do work or perform tasks** for a person with a **disability**." I have put in bold the text of particular importance, as there is often some confusion surrounding it.

Before we discuss the ADA definition of disability any further, it's worth noting that individual states may expand upon the ADA's definition of disability, in addition to other provisions in relation to service dogs. However, as a general rule, as the ADA is a federal law, it takes precedence over state enacted legislation by virtue of Article VI, Paragraph 2 of the U.S. Constitution,[3] so for the purposes of this chapter, we will only discuss the ADA in any great detail. Which I'm sure is a relief for the non-legal scholars among you.

Firstly, the person a service dog assists must meet the legal definition of having a **disability** (or a record of a disability) as set out in the ADA, which is, "a person who has a physical or mental impairment that substantially limits one or more major life activity."[4] This is an extremely broad definition, which looks at the effect of a disorder on a person, rather than the individual disorder in and of itself. As such, it covers a great many medical conditions, hinging on the interpretation of the words "substantially" and "major life activity" on which there is no doubt endless case-law, far beyond the scope of this book to discuss.

Let me give you a real-life example. I'm autistic, which is a condition that exists on a spectrum. In my case, currently I struggle to do everyday activities that most people take for granted. I need the assistance of Mazey, and a care worker as and when required, in order to get out of bed, get washed, dressed, and then to prepare and eat breakfast, and that's just the first hour of my day. Therefore it can fairly be said that my autism, in conjunction with my other medical conditions, substantially limits major life activities for me.

On the other hand, there are autistic people who sit very much on the other end of the spectrum, and their lives are more inconvenienced than substantially limited by their autism. At times they may struggle, very much so, but nevertheless they're happily married with kids, enjoying hobbies and interests, in addition to holding down responsible, demanding jobs for years on end, without suffering from a nervous breakdown every six months or so, as I used to when working as a solicitor. We both may have the same medical diagnosis of autism, but in their case the ADA definition of disability is not met, whereas in mine it is.

Now that we know how to interpret what a disability is under the ADA, let's turn our attention to tasks. Within the DOJ guidance is a non-exhaustive list of the tasks or work a service dog may perform, and includes many of the things we all immediately think of when a service dog and their handler pops into our head, namely, "guiding people who are blind, alerting people who are deaf, assisting a wheelchair user, alerting and protecting a person who is having a seizure, reminding a person with mental illness to take prescribed medications, calming a person with post traumatic stress disorder ("PTSD") during an anxiety attack or performing other duties."

This list of tasks is not definitive—rather, it's a guide—so don't worry if the type of tasks you may require from a service dog do not appear in the list. Of particular note is the fact that the ADA only requires that a service dog must *do work or perform tasks*. Essentially this means that the service dog in question only needs to do one task and one task *only* for her handler, since that one task comes under the definition of "work" and thus meets the ADA definition of a service dog.[5] If persnickety about language you could say work does not equal even one task, but I have common sense so I'm going for the interpretation that work includes one task as part of that work.[6]

Understanding that only one task needs to be performed under the ADA is important, as there has long been a common misconception that a minimum of three tasks must be performed in order for a dog to legally meet the definition of a service dog. This probably arose due to international service dog bodies requiring three tasks, as the same myth exists in the UK, despite the Equality Act not specifying how many tasks are required, similar to the ADA.

Before we leave tasks, it's also worth noting that under the ADA the tasks or work a service dog performs for her handler must be directly related to the handler's disability. If you're autistic, and like me have a tendency to dissociate, then one of your service dog's tasks could be to remind you to take your prescribed medication at the correct time. Mazey does this for me, and personally I find it very useful indeed.

After all, there's no point in your dog being task trained to do some random act such as Scottish Country Dancing, since that's not going to be of any help at all as regards your autism, especially if it doesn't even raise the ghost of a smile. If Mazey and Mina started a Reel of Tulloch around the bedroom of an evening, I'd suspect I'd forgotten my medication for a very long time indeed. Either that, or the gourmet mushrooms from the local farmers market were not quite the variety I had bargained for.

But what about emotional support animals ("ESAs"), I hear you cry. Which is a valid point, since ESAs are a massive help to a great many people, a vast proportion of whom suffer from legitimate mental health problems such as anxiety and depression, their ESA having been prescribed for them by a licensed mental health professional.[7] The ADA makes it clear that its provisions and protections do *not* apply to ESAs, being animals, or in the case of this book, dogs who provide comfort or emotional support to their owners, rather than performing tasks for them. So what *are* the practical differences between an ESA and a psychiatric service dog?

As I come from the UK where we do not recognize ESAs, and where we have a very different healthcare system, the issue seems very confusing to me. After all,

from what I can gather, a good many ESAs have an extremely high standard of training and behavior, with some ESAs providing not just comfort and emotional support,
but also performing tasks which are identical to those performed by psychiatric service dogs. Other ESAs are pets with little or no task training at all and, at times, very
questionable behavior.

As with autism being on a spectrum as I described above, so too are other medical conditions. It's not enough to have a diagnosis of anxiety or depression in order to
be entitled to a psychiatric service dog. In all cases the legal definition of disability, as
set out in the ADA, *must* be met, and it's up to a physician to determine this. If a person's medical condition does not meet the ADA definition, then no matter how well
trained their dog is, or the number of actual tasks she has been taught, legally she is
an ESA and not a psychiatric service dog.

Although an ESA does not receive the protection of the ADA in the way a service dog does, there are other legislative provisions that may be useful in some limited areas, for example with housing. The law as it applies to ESAs varies by state and
should be carefully checked in each individual instance. Where you disagree with
a physician's diagnosis of your medical condition and feel your dog should be categorized as a psychiatric service dog as opposed to an ESA, you should consult with
a licensed attorney and quite possibly get a second opinion regarding your mental
health diagnosis.

So, we've covered the ADA, remembering it's an overarching federal law which
applies countrywide, in every U.S. state. However, in addition to federal law, some
states have additional legislation which applies to service dogs and their handlers.
State laws vary vastly and can significantly increase the protection offered by the
ADA.

State laws apply in a number of different areas, including housing, exemptions
to licensing fees and white cane laws. The area I see as most significant and will speak
about in a bit more depth is in relation to the protection given to service dogs from
criminal interference, theft, assault, and death, which at the time of writing applies in
all states with the exception of Alabama, Alaska, Iowa, Montana, and West Virginia.[8]

When dealing with state laws you will need to carefully check the exact law in
your own state, as the legal definitions and protections vary quite considerably, both
in terms of the requirements which must be met in order for the law to be breached,
and also the consequences for doing so. In most states, for a conviction there must be
an intention to harm/steal/kill the service dog in question, or at a minimum, reckless
behavior on the part of the perpetrator.

It may be surprising to learn that in many states it's a crime to deliberately distract service dogs from their work, including service dogs in training. In most cases
distracting a service dog is only a misdemeanor, though it may result in one having to
pay compensation or restitution to the service dog handler. In California, for example, distracting a service dog could send you to the slammer for up to six months or
result in a fine. Or both. Killing a service dog is also taken very seriously and can even
result in a felony charge in some states such as in Arkansas, where purposefully killing a service dog is a class D felony.

State law goes both ways, and the handlers of service dogs are not devoid from
responsibility when working their dog. Always check to see if you meet the ADA criteria, and do not put your pet in a service dog vest simply because she has separation

anxiety and you don't want to leave her home alone. In some U.S. states there are laws prohibiting the fraudulent use of fake service dogs, with penalties varying by state. In general this crime is considered a misdemeanor, though in California you can get six months in jail for it. Breaching these laws can include not only verbally misrepresenting a dog, but also putting on a harness, cape, leash cover, etc., that falsely represents the dog as a service dog.

One major benefit I see U.S. service dog handlers having, by virtue of the ADA, is that service providers are limited in what they can ask a disabled person when trying to determine the legitimacy of their dog. They can ask only (a) is the dog a service dog who is required because of a disability on the part of the handler? and (b) what work or task(s) has the dog been trained to perform? That's it. In the UK, service providers can ask anything they want, no matter how degrading and humiliating.

This is not a legal textbook to debate the rights and the wrongs of the law, to carefully examine the legislation of each state, or to hunt down and peruse case law. All we can look at here are the bare bones of legislative provision. Anyone who wants more detailed and up-to-date information on the law as it relates to service dogs, both nationally and in their state, should contact a legal advice center, particularly one that deals with disability law.

Now let's move across the pond to the UK, where legislation relating to service dogs is primarily contained within the Equality Act 2010,[9] a dismal piece of legislation if there ever was one. Despite definitions quite similar to the ADA, unfortunately the nitty gritty of the Equality Act is nowhere near as comprehensive or as detailed. The act wields gums instead of teeth, offering little to no practical protection for UK service dogs and their handlers. Truth be told, the Equality Act's as much use as a cat flap on a submarine.

The definition of disability under the Equality Act is a physical or mental impairment that has a "substantial" and "long-term" negative effect on that person's ability to do normal daily activities.[10] To be a service dog in the UK the dog must be trained to assist a disabled person, as defined in Chapter One, Section 173 of the Equality Act. There is no mention of task training, simply that the dog must "assist." In general parlance, it's said the dog must mitigate the handler's disabilities. Unlike in many U.S. states, in the UK there is no crime for a dog owner misrepresenting their disobedient pet as a service dog.

As a breach of the Equality Act is a civil matter and not a criminal one, it leaves UK service dog handlers who have suffered discrimination in an extremely poor position with little, if any, recourse should the law be breached. Very few solicitors deal with disability law since awards are minute, and there's no profit to be made. However, if a service dog handler is simultaneously subject to a hate crime while being discriminated against with their service dog, this *is* covered by the criminal law, though the actual law and subsequent penalties do vary between the countries that comprise the UK.

Unlike in the U.S., in the UK a business or service provider may ask any questions they please when a disabled person enters their premises with their service dog, no matter how humiliating, offensive, degrading and invasive those questions are. In short, it's a free for all. The Equality and Human Rights Commission, which sets out the law relating to service dogs, does provide advice for businesses,[11] but as an underfunded organization with no resources, they cannot help with individual cases, no matter how severe the discrimination suffered.

Regarding attacks on service dogs, the only real protection is given by Section 3(1) of the Dangerous Dogs Act 1991, as amended by the Anti-Social Behaviour, Crime and Policing Act 2014, meaning it's now an aggravated criminal offense for a dog to attack a service dog.[12] This can result in up to three years in prison for the dog's owner. In the UK there is no specific crime or punishment for a human attacking or killing a service dog, other than laws which may relate to hate crimes (if applicable in the circumstances), cruelty to animals or damaging another person's property.

Having left behind the sad and sorry state of service dog law in the UK, what are the other legal provisions which are beneficial and broadly similar between the two countries? In both the U.S. and UK people can self-train their own service dogs. It's not essential for a service dog to pass a certain test, or to be registered with a service dog charity/organization. In fact, in both countries there is no such thing as a national, official register of service dogs.

In other countries in the world there are official registers of service dogs and only certain approved trainers, charities and organizations are allowed to train, register and sell/provide service dogs. I don't like this idea. I don't like it one little bit. A restricted, captive market is created and although everyone starts out with the best of intentions, when money is involved it's human nature to act out of self-interest, and disabled people end up losing out, given they are very rarely the ones on the boards of these charities/organizations making the decisions.

Well, that was a very dry introduction to service dog law and what defines a service dog in today's world. My fingers have been quite worn to the bone typing, and my little brain has been frazzled. But never fear, the next chapter should be far more interesting, where we look at the wide variety of tasks our wonderful service dogs can be trained to perform, and the disabilities that these sorts of tasks typically serve. Onwards and upwards, as the saying goes.

CHAPTER THREE

Service Dog Tasks
and Breed Suitability

With the exception of those tasks which depend on brute physical strength and weight, such as bracing, counterbalance and pulling a manual wheelchair, the size of service dog you select tends to be a matter of personal preference. Both small and large dogs are available with varying levels of drive, energy, intelligence and trainability. Although most breeds are capable of being taught the vast majority of tasks, they may not actually enjoy performing them. Since it's essential our service dogs live happy, fulfilling lives, we must always match up the breed we select to the tasks we require.

Now this is a big generalization, but it's more common to select a buzzy, energetic type of dog as a hearing dog, or for most medical alert tasks, and for mobility task-work that involves a lot of retrieving and constantly getting up and down. A quieter, calmer dog is best suited to guide dog work, mobility task-work that requires counterbalance and bracing, and also psychiatric task-work. Both large and small dogs can be found with these characteristics.

We all have our heart dogs, which are very often the breeds we grew up with as kids, but selecting a service dog is very different from finding the perfect pet. It pays to be open minded and put some of our prejudices aside. It can make sense to opt for a vanilla breed of service dog suited to the tasks in question, instead of instinctively going for the breed we've known and loved our entire lives. The job of our service dog is to mitigate our disabilities. Choosing the wrong breed could mean we end up dreading working our dog in public as she's unsuitable for both our tasks and our lifestyle.

As working dogs, most service dogs receive far greater levels of training and intellectual stimulation than most pets do, and in many cases they also get much more physical exercise. As such, when looking at breeds we can often go against some of the perceived wisdom we have been spoon fed over the years when it comes to breed selection, though a lot will depend on each individual's lifestyle and the tasks they require. Different breeds will suit a young man who runs marathons as a hobby versus an older man who has his shopping delivered and rarely leaves his house, even if they both require the same tasks.

To start with, let's explore the relationship between the size of dog and the size of their owner's living arrangements, since haven't we frequently been told many breeds mustn't soil their paws with apartment living? The truth is you don't need to live in Buckingham Palace or The White House to have a large or giant breed of service dog, or an energetic, high-drive breed, provided you make a commitment to meet their needs, as you would with any dog.

Mazey and Mina don't run about playing table tennis, British Bulldog, golf, soccer or any other wild games in my admittedly very small disabled bungalow, a home Bilbo Baggins would describe as, "compact and bijou." Instead, both dogs are expected to lie quietly on their respective beds (ok the sofa) and either chew their bones, quietly play with their toys, or sleep. The house is for resting, appropriate quiet play/enrichment activities, occasional training, and any task-work I require. It's not a place for roughhousing.

Neither does a garden need to be vast acres of lush, rolling pasture. My dogs use the garden for toileting purposes; that's pretty much it. My flowerbeds are (mostly) mine, as is my bird feeder and my small area of grass. True, Mina is fond of gardening, and has kindly offered (without asking) to dig holes for any trees or large shrubs I may want to plant in future. However, she does this in a flowerbed I set aside for that specific purpose, while pretending it was all her idea. Don't tell her!

If you do choose a high-energy breed of service dog, irrespective of size, as an adult they will generally need a minimum of two decent off-lead walks *daily*, between thirty to sixty minutes each. Work as a service dog can be stressful mentally, and dogs do need down time just to be dogs: to sniff, to run, to roll in unmentionable substances, and to play. Even when your service dog has been trailing you around the shops for several hours, they will still want their "me time." A slat treadmill can be extremely useful on the days where your disability prevents you from giving your dog adequate physical exercise, but it shouldn't be the only form of exercise your dog gets.

I highlighted "daily" in the paragraph above, as it surprises me how many dogs now do not get daily exercise. It seems to have become a trend for people to take one or two "days off" per week, meaning on those days their dog is in the house with them all day. At best the dog may get access to a small garden while the owner sits playing on their phone, or uses a ball thrower for five minutes. Personally I feel this is unfair on a high-energy dog, and if your disability means you want several "at home" days per week, ask yourself why you really want a Belgian Malinois.

In addition to two daily off-lead walks, which they have together, I also take time out most days for one-to-one play sessions with both Mazey and Mina individually. These are not necessarily long, but it makes sure we have fun together without the interference of the other dog, and thus I maintain a very strong bond with both of my dogs. On alternate days I will do a bit of obedience training, and tracking, and most days I will do some sort of enrichment activity outside the home.

As with taking several "days off" per week, I really do want to caution against buying a high-energy dog when you're unfamiliar with these sorts of breeds, especially if you don't actually need an energetic, buzzy dog for the task-work you require. High-energy dogs, large or small, are a lot of work. Do not buy a high-energy, high-drive dog in the hope that the dog will somehow spur you into getting more exercise or taking up a sport such as canicross.

Now a dog may very well encourage you to get more exercise, service dog or no, but successfully embarking on a drastic change in lifestyle is a big ask for anyone, particularly someone who's disabled and may frequently be unwell and in a lot of pain. There's also a massive difference between a Terrier dragging you around the block on the tenth day you only walked the dog for five minutes, and a Rottweiler doing so. If you've previously only had small dogs with energy and drive, it's a big transition to a large, powerful one with the same drive and energy levels.

There have been many times I've wished for the convenience of a smaller dog, both when Mazey and Mina were adults, and also when puppies. I was mopping up proportionally bigger puddles of urine, though what could be cuter than a Rottweiler puppy? Do not answer anything other than "nothing, Nicola, nothing at all," if you want us to remain friends.

I love large dogs, can't you tell? However, I also adore small dogs that have a lot of advantages too, so don't write them off, even if your heart lies with large and giant breeds. Do as I say, not as I do…. If it wasn't for the tasks I specifically require, which genuinely do require a large dog, added to my obsession with Rottweilers, I would probably actually go for an active small- to medium-sized service dog for myself. However, who knows what will happen if I ever reach the same age as Demdike?

Having had a very brief consideration of breeds, and how some characteristics better suit some tasks than others, it's now time to examine tasks in more detail. I'm going to split tasks into five main sections: guiding work, medical alert, mobility work, hearing dog tasks and psychiatric tasks. Some dogs such as Mazey perform across several areas, but then, as you may expect, she's a real smarty pants, though don't tell her I said that; she's got a big enough head as it is. Yabba dabba doo, let's go.

Guide dogs. I think it's safe to say that guide dogs are what most people think of when they consider service dogs, being the first service dogs officially trained in service dog programs in Germany, France, the UK and also the U.S. Guide dogs in some programs are trained to understand over one hundred commands, others much less. All programs are different, so I'm just going to give you a rough overview of the work most guide dogs do.

The big oaf Mina at only 20 weeks old looking like an adult dog. What could be cuter, though? Nothing, of course, except for Mazey at the same age. Photo by the author (2021).

In general, guide dogs work in their home area, going to the same shops for victuals, the same parks for exercise, and the same cafes and restaurants for sustenance, so they don't quite work on the initiative you may think they do, rather they guide their handler around very familiar routes. After they graduate from guide dog school together, the partnership learns a series of regular routes with assistance from a trainer when the pair are matched up.

If the handler is in an unknown area, it's much harder for both themselves and their guide dog as neither know which way to go. I know. It's disappointing that guide dogs are not actually reading signs and so forth, bravely going where no dog has gone before. Sorry! However, guide dogs *are* absolutely astounding and use their keen intelligence to improve the lives of their handlers immeasurably.

Guide dogs are taught to stop at pavements, or tell the handler when there is a step up or down. We all know what it's like to think we've gone down the final step in a flight of stairs, then step out into space, or alternatively trip up a step. A person can easily break a foot or a leg in this way. Guide dogs are also taught to lead their handler around puddles since there's no way of knowing what's under the water, including dips or potholes. They're all adept at guiding their handler around people and other obstacles: shop mannequins that move when no one is looking are no match for them.

It's interesting to note that guide dogs are taught to deliberately disobey their handler when necessary. If the handler tells the dog to cross a road, hearing no cars coming but the dog can see cars are approaching and that it's not safe to cross, then the guide dog will stay still and refuse to move forward. This is called intelligent disobedience. Mazey has commented that I have it all wrong, and that *all* intelligent dogs (like her) are disobedient. Hmm. I don't think so Mazey!

Due to the long waiting lists for guide dogs, people are starting to self-train their own. This typically occurs when a person has had a guide dog or two in the past from a guide dog charity/organization and feels they have the confidence and knowledge to now train their own guide dog, since they have a deep understanding of their specific requirements and what best suits them.

With waiting lists of three or more years for a replacement dog, this can be a very good solution, and allows for more choice in breed selection and the tasks to be performed. The dog is also "yours" and you cannot be forced to give her back once she has retired, which sadly is the policy of some guide dog charities/organizations, and which can cause extreme distress to both handler and dog, as you can imagine.

The most common breed of guide dog is the Labrador Retriever. The work requires a relatively low-drive, steady dog, one with a good work ethic who is intelligent but will not take advantage of her handler. This is not an easy combination to find, hence how truly special finding the right guide dog really is.

The photograph below is of a beautiful six-week-old puppy, destined to be a guide dog when she is all grown up. One, two, three, awww. Isn't she gorgeous? Well, I say "she" as I have, on the whole, referred to most dogs throughout this book as a "she" and most people as a "he." In this case, however ... well... I hope I've not offended his masculinity!

The wonderful Labrador Retriever is my absolute number one selection as a guide dog, closely followed by the amazing Golden Retriever. German Shepherds were very popular in the past as guide dogs; however, the breeding of German Shepherds has changed significantly since the heyday of their popularity for guiding work approximately one hundred years ago, so great care must be taken to source the right dog.

Remember, even with a dedicated guide dog breeding program spanning decades, the washout rate is about 40 percent. These guide dog prospects were all selected, trained and worked by professional trainers, and for so few to make the grade and go on to work for a visually impaired person, it's really quite dismal. Consequently, if you're thinking of a nontraditional breed as a guide dog, think very carefully indeed and consider what will happen to the dog should she wash out. You may be an excellent trainer, but without the right dog it's an uphill battle. One that you simply may not be able to win.

Guide dogs were a fantastic start to discussing task-work in this chapter, don't you agree? They're hard to beat in terms of talent, but nevertheless we must move on, and what better dogs to look at next than the wonderful hearing dogs for deaf people.

Working-line Labrador Retriever at six weeks of age, destined to be a guide dog. Photo by Stacy Pick, his breeder (2022). Reproduced by permission of the photographer.

These service dogs comprise a much wider range of breeds, but play just as vital a role in their owner's lives as guide dogs do. Like visually impaired people, there's a range of deafness, so no trash-talk around a hearing dog. Unless, of course, the dog has lifted a leg on your pants, in which case go right ahead and swear as much as you like, my man. Or woman, as the case may be.

Hearing dogs are trained to respond to a wide variety of sounds that their owner cannot hear. The sounds the dog will alert to will very much depend on their owner's requirements. There's no point training a dog to alert to the sound of a baby crying if the dog is going to work for a seventy-year-old confirmed bachelor with no kids or grandkids he would be responsible for. The sounds a hearing dog is trained to alert to would commonly include the doorbell, a knock at the door, smoke or carbon monoxide alarms, the telephone, oven/microwave timers, the kettle whistling, alarm clocks or other specified alarms, the cry of a baby, and also anyone calling out their owner's name. I would probably ditch the last one since the word "recluse" was penned for me.

When a hearing dog does hear the sound she's trained to alert to, she will go to her owner and get his attention. This may be by gently nudging him or getting in front of his line of vision and offering her paw. Once she has his attention, she will then lead him to the place where the noise has come from and indicate to it or leave it to

the owner's imagination, as the noise may demand. A crying baby will look distressed, sporting tearful eyes, wet cheeks and a roaring red mouth. A kettle will be boiling, puffing out steam like a domestic Thomas the Tank Engine (Thomas being a lovable children's TV character). If led to the front door, the owner can check the peephole to see who is there and can pretend not to be at home if desired.

On the whole, most of a hearing dog's work is done in the home, though her alerts may still be important at places of work, for example a fire alarm, or in public, such as if the team are in the supermarket and a friend calls her owner's name from behind them. Most ambient sounds in the general environment outside the home would not require an alert from a hearing dog, though much is going to depend on the team and their specific requirements.

Hearing dogs tend to be quite buzzy dogs who are naturally reactive to noises. An energetic, alert temperament is best as they need to be constantly vigilant and are always on duty, particularly inside the home, where many other dogs prefer to sleep for most of the day. A dog that comes home from her morning walk, gobbles her brunch then reclines on her chaise lounge and is impossible to wake up until teatime simply would not cut it as a hearing dog.

Common breeds that excel as hearing dogs include a variety of Terriers, Poodles of all sizes, Cocker and Springer Spaniels, as well as Doodles and Poos. Labrador Retrievers, and more so Golden Retrievers, do not tend to make the best hearing dogs overall, even from working lines, since they are not breeds which are naturally reactive to noise, being bred to have strong nerves and be steady under gunshot when working in the field.

Some hearing dogs are trained to respond to sign language rather than, or in addition to, verbal cues. As always, it will depend on the handler's own needs, and if you see a hearing dog partnership working together in public it can be quite beautiful to observe them working together in silence.

In today's day and age of technological advancements, there are now a great many hearing aids that can significantly help people with auditory impairments. However, this does not make hearing dogs redundant. They still play a vital role in their owner's lives, many taking on a secondary role as an ESA as do many service dogs with other responsibilities, providing their handlers with comfort, confidence and also companionship.

Having had a brief look at our wonderful friends the hearing dogs, we now move onto the fantastically talented medical alert dogs. They share some of the same characteristics as hearing dogs in that they must always be on the alert to their owner's needs. There is a massive range of medical alerts that a service dog can provide, spanning from low or high blood sugar, to PoTS, to food allergies, to night-terrors, to seizure alerts. Often a medical alert dog can give up to twenty minutes' warning of an oncoming medical incident, allowing their handler to prepare themselves, which could include taking medication or arranging for assistance if required.

Medical alert dogs do their job using their amazing noses. They can actually smell biological changes in their owner's bloodstream. These changes are also present in saliva, so when the owner breathes out, the dog can smell these chemical changes on their breath. Medical alert dogs may also use other parameters to judge their owner's health and the onset of a possible medical emergency including heart rate, breathing rate, any ticks, shaking or other visual or auditory signs.

In general saliva samples, or less commonly blood samples, are collected and used to train medical alert dogs. Sample collection can be difficult, as contaminants present in the sample can confuse the dog, and if the trainer does not know what these are, or there are not enough "pure" samples, training the dog to detect the correct thing can be difficult. We do not want to train our seizure alert dog to detect the scent of garlic just because we ate an excellent garlic bread just before our seizure. Well, unless you're a vampire and you require a garlic alert dog for those pesky humans who like the stuff, you know, before you chow down on them. Better safe than sorry and all that.

Saliva samples can get contaminated very easily. If you've eaten, chewed gum, taken medication, or drank anything besides water within two hours prior to the sample collection, then contamination can very easily occur, such is the sensitivity of a dog's nose. Given that sample collection can be at random, say just after a seizure has occurred, obtaining a sufficient number of quality samples for the trainer to work with can be difficult and take a very long time. Every time a sample is taken, it's bagged, and collection details noted, such as whether the sample was taken just following the onset of a seizure, the date, time and any possible contaminants. Samples are then frozen to preserve them, then defrosted for use when training the medical alert dog.

Medical alert dogs are usually trained specifically for the handler they will be working for, since the training generally involves using a biological sample from that specific person, in addition to the dog using other senses as required. For some medical conditions such as diabetes, generic samples can be used, though this is rare. Other dogs that can be trained separate from the handler are service dogs who will alert not to changes within the handler himself, but to substances that can harm the handler such as gluten in food for those with celiac disease, or peanuts for a handler who has a peanut allergy.

In general, once a service dog prospect has successfully completed her public access training, it will take about six weeks to train her specifically in the scent work required for medical alert tasks. This is if using a professional trainer, or if a service dog charity/organization is doing the training. It can take longer to train your own dog, but there can be many advantages to self-training for medical alert task-work. Taking your time in training can be a good thing. A medical alert dog should have a rate of accuracy that intimidates a Navy Seal sniper. This does not happen overnight.

Mazey performs medical alert for me, and can alert me to the onset of a severe panic attack, allowing me to take my medication to calm myself down before things get out of hand, and I become less Dr. David Banner and more the Incredible Hulk. I mean not in terms of temper but my medical condition going crazy. Okay, so that was a stupid example, but I like it, so there.

Mazey, and more recently Mina, will also properly wake me up from night terrors and sleep paralysis, so I don't fall into a cycle of thinking I'm fully awake, but in reality I'm only half awake, and therefore I fall right back into the nightmare I thought I'd fully woken up from. This very much tends to be more Mina's job now, letting Mazey get a well-deserved full night's sleep.

Different people like their dog to perform different types of alerts, and some dogs will give a two-stage alert. In general a medical alert is unobtrusive, and may be anything from a dog laying her head on her handler's leg, gently nudging her handler or offering her paw. If a handler is not paying attention to the dog, particularly if a handler has a tendency to zone out or dissociate when a medical emergency is imminent, then a second stage alert may be given, which is harder if not impossible to ignore. This could include the dog spinning in circles in front of the handler, or in Mazey's case, a rhythmic bark until I respond to her.

This type of bark when giving a medical alert is a trained behavior, and should not be confused with the yelping, squealing, screeching type of panicked bark I have seen some Tik Tok service dogs giving as an "alert," and which in reality is a very scared dog who's unsure what to do when her handler is lapsing into unconsciousness. Yes, as humans we come first, but it's unfair to force a pet dog unsuited to such a responsible role into service dog task-work, even if they have learned and started to offer a medical alert off their own bat.

Some medical alert dogs not only perform medical alert, but will also perform other tasks, which may or may not be related to their role as a medical alert dog. A related task would be to push a panic alarm, or to go and fetch someone in the house and alert them that something is wrong with their owner. A non-related example of a task would be a medical alert dog who also works as a guide dog. Often it takes two different charities/organizations to train such a dog, as most only have one particular skill set, although occasionally a charity/organization may give the dog's handler permission to train the additional tasks he requires himself.

Exceptionally rarely, and I mean exceptionally rarely, attempts may be made to teach a medical alert dog or a service dog with other duties to leave their handler and to go and find help (if outside the home), leading a rescuer back to their handler. This sounds amazing, but on the whole it's an urban myth. Please remember, there can't be more than one service dog that's a reincarnation of Lassie or Rin Tin Tin.

Unless hiking in the wilderness, by the time a dog has found someone, persuaded them to follow her, then hotfooted it back to her handler's last known location, their handler has almost certainly already been found by someone else, and is lying tucked up in a hospital bed, worried sick about their missing service dog.

Far more often a medical alert dog is taught to stay right beside their handler if they're unconscious or otherwise incapacitated and cannot give the dog commands. Some will be taught to simply sit beside them, some will sit on top of their bag or belongings, and very rarely some will be taught to push their head/neck/body underneath their handler's head, in order to try and support their handlers head and neck. In this way handler and dog are never separated, and when found, the medical alert dog can accompany their handler in the ambulance to hospital, where the handler will rely on their love and support, as well as their dog detecting any further medical alerts.

On the subject of urban myths as they relate to service dogs, yes, our service dogs are absolutely amazing, but they are neither humans nor gods. Dogs do not have opposable thumbs. They do not have the reasoning capacity of an adult human, a teenager or even a tweenie. Dogs certainly do not neatly put a person in the recovery position, nor do they turn them over and lie them on their back, tilting their head just so, opening their mouths and clearing their airway. They cannot give rescue breaths, nor effective chest compressions. Yes, it brings a tear to the eye to see a service dog who loves her owner dearly, desperately trying to lick her owner's lips and revive them, which is a task, but don't confuse this with a dog performing something as complex as CPR. Sorry, but it just isn't.

Far be it from me to rain on anyone's Tik Tok parade, but I have to be truthful, particularly due to recent scams involving service dogs. If you're asked by someone online to finance a service dog prospect for a friend of a friend, invariably at great expense, the dog being trained to do tasks that a human would struggle with in an emergency, never mind a dog, then chances are it's too good to be true.

This neatly leads us onto some unusual behaviors that I'm sometimes asked to consult on, one being training a dog to perform medical alerts/general service dog work alongside being a trained personal protection dog. It's a very sad reflection of today's society that many disabled people are robbed, both while they're conscious and going about their day-to-day life, and more usually when they're unconscious/incapacitated following a seizure.

For this reason, guarding breeds such as the Rottweiler, the German Shepherd and the Belgian Malinois are becoming increasingly popular choices as medical alert dogs, in addition to psychiatric service dogs for conditions such as PTSD. The working lines of these breeds tend to have great noses, plus a "don't mess with me" look and attitude. In 99.99 percent of cases the appearance of these dogs is sufficient deterrent to any but the most determined would-be thief, and in reality they do not need to be trained as dual purpose service/personal protection dogs. Nor is it wise to do so.

When using a guarding breed to work as a service dog, great care must be taken in selecting the right dog. A dog that becomes defensive and starts to work on her own initiative, becoming protective of her handler, barking or growling at anyone that approaches when her handler is incapacitated or feeling vulnerable, becomes a liability. With every service dog it's *essential* that it's safe for paramedics or concerned members of the public to approach the dog and the handler, and to provide assistance to the handler without the possibility of being bitten. This also goes for police or paramedics being able to enter the house safely should the handler dial 911/999 or the dog use a panic alarm in the home.

Guarding breeds for medical alert and other service dog task-work need to have an open and friendly personality, without high levels of defensive drive, or any hint of suspicion or aggression toward strangers. This can be a bit of a hard ask, as these characteristics are the very ones that these breeds were designed to possess. However it is possible, as both Mazey and Mina demonstrate. If I was ever burglarized while I was out for the count, one dog would busy herself packing my pitiful array of valuables, while the other made the burglar a nice cup of tea, followed by a foot massage.

Some service dogs for people with PTSD are taught to perform a house search, where their service dog will enter the home first, turn on lights, and sweep the house for intruders, barking if they find someone where they should not be. However, this task is complex and requires a lot of maintenance and update training in order to be effective. Also consider that almost all violent offenders are known to the victim. If your ex is lurking in the bedroom with a ball/food for the dog and a gun for you, the dog who knows and loves him is not going to give an alert; she will just be happy to see a familiar face she has missed.

Moving on, new types of medical alert are always appearing, and if you have a medical condition which is reflected by biochemical or physical changes, then speak to your physician about whether a medical alert dog may benefit you. Although medical devices for conditions such as diabetes are very sophisticated these days, as with hearing dogs, lots of people still like having their service dog also perform these functions, as they do so much more than just provide an alert. There's nothing more comforting, when ill and waiting for an ambulance, than having your service dog by your side to give love and support. And stop the cats snacking on you should the ambulance tarry.

In addition to medical alert, I have also put service dogs who alert to allergens and other substances which may harm their owner into this category. Labels or verbal confirmation that the substance is not present in food, medicines, makeup and other products should always be checked as a first step, but thereafter a service dog can be exceptionally useful. This is especially the case with allergies. When the handler is eating out, the service dog can be asked to check individual items of food from a plate to ensure there has been no cross contamination in the kitchen of a restaurant or cafe.

With these types of medical alerts it can take longer than the standard six weeks to train a service dog prospect in scent work, particularly if training the dog yourself and hence not doing the task day in day out, as a professional service dog trainer would. This is mainly due to the fact that unlike most medical alert work, where a dog gives an alert when they smell a certain substance, the celiac or allergy medical alert dog must either confirm, "yes," there is gluten (for example) in a sample, or indicate, "no," there is no gluten in a sample. This is more complex than a simple indication that a certain scent has been picked up, as in a standard medical alert.

That's been quite a deviation from pure as the driven snow medical alert dogs! Anyway, as with hearing dogs, medical alert dogs tend to be alert, active dogs who are on duty while off duty (if you get my meaning) and who *love* using their noses. Spaniels and also many working dog breeds can all be wonderful in this role. Again, a lot will depend on whether you want a small dog or a larger one, and any additional tasks you may wish the dog to perform. For gluten or allergen alerts, a more laid-back dog is fine provided they have a good nose and enjoy scent work, since the article in question is being presented to them at random times and they're being asked a specific yes/no question for a very short span of concentration, as opposed to potentially being on duty 24/7.

This is not to say non-working breeds that are not renowned for having a good nose cannot perform medical alert task-work. They can. However, I would not go out and recommend someone buy a French Bulldog, say, as a potential medical alert dog. If you do happen to already own an adorable pet Frenchie that has already started alerting on their own initiative, and is doing a fantastic job, then if everything else required of a service dog is present, then why not use her as such? Just do not buy a Frenchie for this task, then be disappointed when she washes out.

We're all used to seeing service dogs out working in public, but that's only a very small proportion of the work many of them actually do. Strange as it may seem, not all service dogs work outside the home. Being capable of working outside the home in public places is, of course, the ideal, the epitome of what a service dog *should* be, but life is plain weird and some people may have a medical condition that is well controlled, and their service dog only needs to alert a couple of times per month or even per year.

Who are you or I to say that such a dog does not benefit their owner in a meaningful and significant way? A pet turned service dog can work extremely well in such a scenario, even if the dog does not go shopping, out to eat, to the cinema, or accompany their owner to the hospital. The owner may have human company or assistance at these times, or they may simply be uncomfortable working a service dog in public with all that this entails.

When a dog does start putting herself into a role such as giving medical alerts, even if on her own volition, we must carefully consider whether or not it's fair to the dog. Being a service dog is a hard job with a lot of responsibility, and it requires a brave, confident dog who is in good health. With the best will in the world, it's not a job for every dog. Though our wonderful pets may try desperately to help the owner they love, it can be better to bring in another dog to train up for the role of service dog, and give a not-so-suitable pet the chance to excel in the role she was purchased for: to be loved and adored.

Whew, that was a long and hard look at medical alert dogs! Time to move on and cast our greedy eyes over to mobility service dogs, which is another category that has a wide range of breeds, from the majestic Great Dane to smaller dogs bursting with personality, like the versatile Patterdale Terrier. This grouping of tasks is also extremely varied, covering everything from counterbalance and bracing with a giant, powerful dog, to removing socks and other clothing items, which most small dogs are able to accomplish with ease.

Mobility service dogs can often perform as many tasks as their owner can think of. Literally! As with all service dogs, a lot of care must be taken in breed selection, as some tasks typically require a high-drive dog. For other tasks you want a low-drive dog, and never the twain shall meet. For people who are physically very vulnerable, and who require counterbalance and bracing tasks, or help pulling a manual wheelchair, it's important that a dog should not be too high drive. The whole point of having a service dog is to gain support, not to be physically pulled over as the dog spots a different place they would prefer to be.

For dogs constantly being asked to fetch or do things for their handler, particularly in the home where most dogs want to relax and sleep, a higher-drive dog that enjoys buzzing about and retrieving items is usually more suitable than a "go slow or go home" type of dog. Not all dogs enjoy the task of retrieving, even though they may tolerate it on a limited basis. Mazey, for example, will retrieve items I point to, but it's not her bag, baby, as I once heard her mutter. She really hates retrieving items that are cold or things like metal cans that feel odd in her mouth. There goes getting me a drink from the fridge!

Typical at-home tasks for a mobility service dog can include retrieving a phone, fetching and helping put on their own collar and work gear, switching on lights and lamps, opening doors, locating and retrieving a medicine bag, or really bringing any items to their handler which they have been trained to identify. This can be a lot of items. Mobility service dogs are super smart! They can also help to remove items from the washing machine, and assist in removing clothes from their handler, such as socks, or gently pulling/holding the arm of a jumper or pants leg.

For mobility service dogs that provide bracing and counterbalance, helping their handler safely get around the home can be vital, including standing up from a toilet seat, or getting out of the shower or up from a chair or bed. Some dogs may even help their handlers into and out of a wheelchair. And since some wheelchair users have limited use of their legs (at some but not all times), they may walk with the assistance of their mobility service dog, or use her to assist in pulling a manual wheelchair.

Tasks outside the home can be just as complex as those within the home, making it particularly hard for the mobility service dog in a public setting, where lots of distractions abound. Common tasks include bracing and counterbalance work, assisting in pulling a manual wheelchair, handing/receiving a purse/credit card to and from a cashier in a shop, or even retrieving a card from a cash machine. They can pick up dropped items and return them to a shopping cart or basket, and may be capable of picking items off shelves that the handler points to. Mobility service dogs can assist in opening power-assisted doors, they can push the button at crossings, and they can use their nose/mouth/paws in a wide variety of ways.

It may at times seem a waste to teach a mobility service dog one task when the dog can't complete a separate, linked task. For example, a dog may be able to retrieve a card from a cash dispenser and give it back to their handler, but she can't actually put the card in the cash machine slot in the first place, nor can she enter the card's PIN. When you're disabled, what looks like a tiny help on the part of a dog and a bit of a waste is so much more. Often it's actually a **massive** help for the handler.

Haven't you ever thought, "just one more thing and I'll collapse and cry," or counted the steps toward home as you walk exhausted and filled with despair? The same goes for the complete exhaustion and excruciating pain many disabled people experience. That one tiny action on the part of a service dog can be the difference between the handler losing it, or having an okay day. So service dog trainers or bog-standard dog trainers who are venturing into the service dog realm, if you're asked to help train a task like this, one that seems insignificant, don't make assumptions. It may seem minor to you, but it does not diminish the necessity or importance of the task for the disabled person.

Breeds which excel as mobility service dogs will very much depend on the tasks required and can be anything from a Great Dane to a Yorkshire Terrier. The Great Dane is outstanding in tasks which require a very steady, large dog for bracing and counterbalance work. For owners in a wheelchair that require assistance both in the home and while out and about, typically a large to medium breed will do well, including breeds such as the Labrador Retriever and the Golden Retriever, plus Standard Poodles. If the tasks are not dependent on size and strength, but involve a lot of fetching, then medium and smaller breeds that enjoy retrieving may be ideal, including Cocker Spaniels and some of the Terrier breeds.

Having been wowed by the intelligence and ingenuity of mobility service dogs, we come to our final category, the life savers of the service dog world: the psychiatric service dogs. As you can imagine, this is yet another role where breed will very much depend on the tasks required, and in this case not only the tasks, but the handler's state of mind will also be of great importance.

Being a **psychiatric service dog** is a much harder role than you may imagine, as the dog's emotional state and ability to perform task-work can be very much influenced by the handler and his frame of mind. This is one reason why very intelligent but overly sensitive breeds are not ideal, as they can be negatively affected by a handler who is nervous or frequently scared, the handler's fears rubbing off onto the service dog. For this reason, smart, high-strung breeds of dogs such as Poodles, Border Collies and German Shepherds, plus many smaller companion breeds such as Pomeranians and Chihuahuas, may not be suitable, being too loving and switched on to their owner's emotions to be able to cope with their own fears and insecurities too.

A psychiatric service dog may be asked to perform basic tasks such as blocking another person from getting too close to their handler, or standing in front of or behind their handler to physically prevent anyone getting closer. The dog can also be asked to circle them if in a crowd. This is harder than it may sound, as most dogs of every breed inherently give way to people advancing on them, and it takes a lot of training for them to stand their ground if need be.

Many psychiatric service dogs help with grounding their handler should they start to disassociate, or have a panic attack, perhaps licking their hands or face, or nudging/pawing at their handler's legs or arms to help bring them back to the present. They may also do these types of actions in order to disrupt a self-harming behavior on the part of the handler, such as scratching skin, pulling hair, head banging or biting nails. Psychiatric service dogs can be dual purpose dogs, their psychiatric task-work ancillary or in addition to another medical condition, but just as many work solely in this role as it's a very important one.

Just the service dog's presence, there to offer their handler comfort and support in addition to other specific task-work, can immensely increase their handler's confidence and be the difference between a handler being able to leave the house alone without a care worker, or being trapped inside. Although some people may consider this the work of an ESA, nothing could be farther from the truth. All that matters is that the handler's psychiatric medical condition meets the legal criteria to be entitled to a service dog, and that the dog itself is trained to perform one task, which doesn't have to be a complex one, simply a task which helps the handler mitigate the effects of their disability.

When in the home, don't assume that the psychiatric service dog's work is done. As with outside the home, tasks such as deep pressure therapy ("DPT") may need to be performed, as well as grounding. A common task for many psychiatric service dogs is to remind their owner when it's time to take their prescribed medication, including opening a cupboard door and bringing them their medication bag. The dog may well help them to get out of bed in the morning, and can be trained in intelligent disobedience—for example, to pull a duvet off a handler who is depressed and would rather stay warm and cozy in bed rather than get up and out into a cold, cruel world.

For handlers with conditions such as PTSD, a service dog can perform tasks previously mentioned, including grounding, house search, and waking their handler from nightmares, night terrors and sleep paralysis.

I have autism, and autism service dogs are a type of psychiatric service dog that are just as important for adults as they are for children. Get aboard the trigger train: it's time for a rant. Choo Choo! Unfortunately, many autism service dog charities/organizations only provide dogs for children, which does not make sense to me, as autism does not disappear when the clock strikes midnight on the day of your sixteenth birthday. This is not a modern rendition of Cinderella. Autism is a lifelong condition and it's just plain crazy to have the support of an autism service dog removed at a critical juncture of a young person's life, perhaps when stepping out into the world on their own as a young adult going to college or starting a job.

For very young children with autism, the autism service dog can be used as a tether, to stop the child from running off. Children may be faster than their parents, but they will not be faster than a dog! The service dog can comfort the child and physically prevent them from running away until a parent can offer support. I used to run in front of cars as a child, and it's a miracle I got past the age of two or three years old, so I know how valuable this would have been to my own mom. For adults with autism the usual psychiatric service dog tasks will apply, often in conjunction with other tasks such as medical alert, as many autistic people are also prone to seizures.

When it comes to psychiatric service dogs, pretty much anything goes. All sizes of dog, with varying levels of drive are welcome and able to be trained to perform this type of work. Much will depend on the task in question and the medical conditions concerned. As ever, the Labrador Retriever is excellent as a psychiatric service dog, as is the Golden Retriever. Spaniels can make for good medium sized dogs, provided they are not overly sensitive. Many of the Terrier breeds also have the resilience required.

For the right handler, the Rottweiler can be a truly outstanding choice as a psychiatric service dog, with a bold, confident character that is surprisingly sensitive, but that does not allow her handler's fears to become her own. However, great care must be taken as the average Rottie will not hesitate to step in and take charge where she feels her handler is not up to the job.

We are coming toward the end of the chapter now, and people often ask me to give them a list of tasks that a service dog could be trained to perform for them, just for inspiration and ideas. I was going to write out one for this book, until I realized I could be here all day. Service dogs are truly amazing, and it may seem a bit of a cop out, but the scope of tasks they can be trained for is infinite. If you're getting a service dog, remember, you only need one task. One. Don't get hung up on teaching your dog countless tasks, instead concentrate on the essentials.

Think about how your service dog would be categorized, and then what would benefit your life the most. Is that having items fetched for you? Is it help getting undressed at night when exhausted, your muscles weak and cramping, at the end of your tether weeping in pain and exhaustion? Do you have a medical condition which can be expected to degenerate relatively quickly, where your expected needs in three years will be vastly different from what they are now? These are all things to think about.

Obviously for all disabled people, the love and companionship of a service dog is immeasurable. For those people with psychiatric issues, who due to their mental health may have no human friends or family to rely on for companionship or support, a service dog may be the difference between life and death.

Our service dogs really are miracle workers. They are our life savers, large or small. I cannot heap enough praise on them. They give us back our freedom and our independence. No one wants to be consigned to a home or care facility; being disabled should not prevent us from living our best lives. Mazey helps me with this every second of every day, as does little Mina, with significant contributions from our home's feline overlords, Izzy and Levi Bengal.

I owe so very much to my amazing Mazey and the rest of my little menagerie, and they ask so little in return of me: merely for me to love them, and of course to keep the food bowls well topped up. Like every other service dog owner, I'm truly blessed to have my two incredible service dogs. Of course I love Mina, and the kit kits, but it is with Mazey that I have gone through some of the worst days of my life. I love my Mazey Rottweiler unconditionally. She is my everything.

Table of Top Dog Breeds for Each Service Dog Role

Role	*Dog Breeds*
Guide Dogs	First Pick: Labrador Retriever. Highly Commended: Golden Retriever, Standard Poodle. Also Good Bois: German Shepherd
Hearing Dogs	First Pick: Cocker Spaniel. Highly Commended: Poodle, Springer Spaniel. Also Good Bois: Terrier, Doodle, Poos, Labrador Retriever, Golden Retriever, Border Collie
Medical Alert Dogs	First Pick: Cocker Spaniel. Highly Commended: Poodle, Springer Spaniel. Also Good Bois: Terriers, Doodles, Poos, Labrador Retriever, Golden Retriever, Border Collie. Fab with Care: Rottweiler, German Shepherd, Belgian Malinois
Mobility Service Dogs	First Pick: Great Dane, Labrador Retriever, Cocker Spaniel. Highly Commended: Poodle, Springer Spaniel, Terrier, Doodles, Poos. Also Good Bois: Golden Retriever, Border Collie
Psychiatric Service Dogs	First Pick: Labrador Retriever, Golden Retriever. Highly Commended: Cocker Spaniel. Also Good Bois: Terrier, Doodles, Poos. Fab with Care: Rottweiler, German Shepherd, Belgian Malinois, Border Collie, Poodle, Yorkshire Terrier

CHAPTER FOUR

The Big Think—Service Dog Training Ideologies

This is a book about service dogs. Although in no way, shape or form is it a dog training manual, we can't get away from the fact that our service dogs not only need to be trained to perform the tasks we require to mitigate our disabilities, but since the vast majority appear in public they must also demonstrate a far higher standard of obedience than the average pet dog. There are lots of different dog training ideologies about these days, and you may decide that the way you've trained your pet dogs in the past may not be right for training your service dog now.

I've included this chapter pretty early on in the book, as I do need to get a few things off my chest and out in the open. Otherwise, these issues will fester, lurking like an elephant in the room. An elephant with a badly upset stomach. Even should I evade its grabbing, grasping trunk and avoid being stomped on by some extraordinarily large feet, the stench of too many over-ripe melons, having gone in one end and out the other, would floor me eventually.

What I really want to talk about are the appropriate use of corrections and yes, horror of horrors, the use (or not) of punishments in dog training. The vast majority of training you do with your dog should always be with reward-based training, whether that be with food, toys, games, praise or a combination of all these. But what about corrections and punishments?

Only giving a dog rewards and never putting in place boundaries, nor giving a dog direction, is not the most effective, kind way of training a dog in my book. Indeed, ignoring a dog and withholding rewards for not providing the correct behavior, but at the same time never giving the dog appropriate guidance regarding what behavior is right and what is wrong can lead to a very frustrated, unhappy dog who cannot work out what is required of her. This is *not* a kind, compassionate way to train our dogs.

I find that dogs that combine high drive with sensitivity really thrive using play-based training methods and the use of games as their reward during training. Such dogs don't react in a good way to more traditional, harsh training methods that are low on reward and high on force, hence breeds like the Rottweiler gaining an undeserved reputation for being stubborn.

More shy, introverted dogs that would fall to pieces if given *any* sort of firm handling or punishments, can often have their confidence built with food-based games and rewards, as opposed to the type of games that have more rough and tumble, with a high degree of competition. That's not to say corrections cannot be used with such dogs, but as with all dogs, they should only be used kindly and appropriately.

My own view is that training a dog with no corrections, including putting in place no boundaries as regards her behavior, letting the dog do whatever she pleases, is not a recipe for success or happiness, either for the dog or her handler. This is particularly the case for service dogs that are expected to work in public places, with an exemplary standard of behavior and manners. Corrections do not have to be harsh, or even unpleasant. Some can be purely educational, and a skillful trainer can create a great many boundaries during structured play with their dog.

The correction used for a nervous, under-confident dog may be as mild as the word "no" the like of which would not even register on the consciousness of a more hardheaded, confident dog. However, a nervous, flighty dog without any confidence in herself or her handler is not an ideal service dog prospect. It's far more likely you'll end up training a service dog with a more balanced, even temperament that at times very much does want her own way and that will need guidance via a correction, which is perfectly normal, as don't we all like to get what we want in life?

Which dog training ideology, and thus which corrections (if any) are acceptable to you as a handler and trainer, should be considered and decided early on, even before you get your new service dog prospect. This may change once you begin working with your new dog, taking into account her own personality. No dog is perfect and every service dog will at some point perform behaviors that are not acceptable to us. Unless we teach a dog right from wrong, they have no way of figuring it out by themselves, other than by withholding rewards, which as I said above, can lead to a frustrated, confused, unhappy dog.

In the last few years there have been increasingly vocal campaigners trying to push an ideology that there is one way, and one way only, to train service dogs, or indeed all dogs, which is using force-free/purely positive training. Personally I'm not comfortable with being told what I can and can't do, particularly by people who don't share my disability and have no idea what it's like to live with such a disability day in, day out. More importantly, I also don't believe these ideologies are fair to dogs when taken to the extremes.

I live in England, in the UK, where prong collars and e-collars are only "just" legal, but may not be for long. They have now been banned in many Western European countries, including Austria, Germany, Finland, Wales, Norway and Sweden. At the time of writing, the German police force is applying for an exemption to the new welfare law, which, if not granted, will mean the early retirement of many of their operational police dogs.[1]

Don't assume that a service dog in a prong collar, or indeed a police dog in one, has not been properly trained using rewards, or is unsuitable temperamentally for the job in question. When a large, powerful breed of service dog is working for a physically weak, vulnerable person, often the handler can lack confidence. I would too if I felt I could be catastrophically injured with shattered and broken bones should I be suddenly pulled over. A prong collar can be used to psychologically empower such a handler, providing feather-light control, and consequently giving the handler confidence their dog is very unlikely to jerk hard into the prong collar should she see a pigeon looping the loop in the branches of a tree.

For those dog owners or trainers reading who don't use either prong collars or e-collars, why should you care that a ban may be coming your way? Why should I care? After all, a ban would not affect me personally with my own dogs Mazey and

Mina. Not yet anyway, given my current age and state of health. I care because these tools do have a place in service dog training when used correctly, which is in a minimalist fashion, primarily in emergencies. When used incorrectly, then yes, of course prong collars and e-collars will cause pain and fear. So will a flat collar when used incorrectly in the wrong hands. We have laws to ban animal cruelty in place already. We don't need more laws to remove specific tools that when used correctly are both fair and humane, for disabled and non-disabled handlers alike.

I also care because banning one set of tools at the request of a small but vocal group of dog training organizations and animal welfare campaigners that have a very specific agenda (which is not necessarily in the best interests of dogs) and are not scared to play dirty, is the thin edge of the wedge. Who knows which tools could be next to be banned? They may well be ones you and I use and rely on: martingale collars, slip leads, crates, a feeding bowl…. These are what the more extreme animal rights campaigners would like banned. I'm not joking. In some countries in Western Europe, having a door on a crate is now illegal.

The stronger and more prolific these dog training groups and organizations become, the more their ideas will be accepted within mainstream society, irrespective of the wants and needs of disabled service dog handlers, elite competitors in dog sports, and trainers who carry out complex behavioral modification. My worry is that not only will certain tools be banned, but the use of other tools will be made compulsory. In the UK some service dog charities/organizations now enforce the use of head-collars on all dogs trained by them or registered with them. Head-collars are a tool I personally find far more ineffective, harsh and uncomfortable for a dog than a prong collar, and I would only use it on a dog as a last resort. I don't like or use head-collars, that's just me, but I still recognize and agree with the rights of disabled and non-disabled people alike who do use head-collars, and who find them effective on their specific dogs.

So, we've dealt with the banning of certain tools in parts of Europe, which may or may not interest you, and it's time to move onto the use (or not) of corrections and punishments in dog training, plus the dog training ideologies that are starting to take hold in the service dog world. The real meat of this chapter.

When looking at dog training ideologies, first let's have a look at what all these dog training terms are, without getting scientific and discussing classical conditioning or going into the four operant conditioning quadrants: positive reinforcement, negative reinforcement, positive punishment and negative punishment. This is not a technical dog training manual, and in the real world outside the laboratory, I just find there's too much overlap and confusion possible between the quadrants, in a "what came first the chicken or the egg" type scenario.

In addition, and very importantly when it comes to service dog training, as disabled people we have a very special, personal relationship and deep bond of love and respect with our service dogs. They do many tasks as they want to please us. The operant conditioning quadrants take no account of this, of the raw emotion involved when training and loving a dog, especially a service dog that is responsible for saving our lives. For these reasons I'm going to keep everything super simple and use easy-to-understand words and definitions, which are also shorter for me to type. Bonus!

"Reward" is one of the words you'll see me use most often in relation to training, since it's the foundation for everything. Rewards are most commonly used to encourage a dog to repeat a desired behavior. Whether you're training service dogs, narcotics detection dogs, police dogs or pets, you'll primarily be using rewards in your training. A reward is simply something that makes the dog happy, and something that she would like to have more of.

To be most effective, a reward needs to be something *the dog* likes and enjoys, not what we as humans think the dog should like(!) or is most convenient for us to use. For some dogs the very best reward is praise; for others, it's food; for yet other dogs, it may be a game with her handler involving a toy, or it could even be a game that involves food.

My favorite way of rewarding a dog is with play, as this is something we enjoy together as a team, with no measure of coercion involved. I find that when I'm teaching a dog a skill using play as the primary reward, the dog is in a more heightened state of arousal while playing with me than she is while just waiting for me to dole out a piece of food. The dog therefore learns a lot quicker. However, when the behavior has been learned and fully understood, I will start to transition the dog to expect food as the reward for her good behavior, on an intermittent reward schedule. This is because service dogs need to work in public and it's not so easy to whip out a ball or frisbee in the middle of Walmart. I do not reward a dog each and every time she does something I ask her to.

Play can be used both as a reward and also as a method of establishing boundaries. Particularly with rough play such as a game of tug, always make sure your dog does not get over excited. Look for the game to have a good ebb and flow, with changes in body posture in much the same way dogs play with each other. Mazey and Mina may sound like they're trying to kill each other, but there are lots of play bows, pauses to reverse sneeze or to shake their heads, which one does then the other, in order for both dogs to acknowledge to each other that this is a game.

The use of an, "off," or, "out," command during a game of tug between you and your dog is essential, as it ensures you can keep the game under your control, while teaching the dog that games have rules. All games have rules, even Monopoly, and with rules comes the teaching of boundaries. Always make sure the toy is big enough for the dog in question. A small tug toy and a large dog without good aim can result in lost manhood if the dog comes in hard and fast from a distance.

Many dogs much prefer to play with a ball or frisbee than with a tug toy or a ball on a rope. Some dogs want the ball thrown repeatedly and have great fun going back and forward (though watch those joints). Then we have the dog that wants the ball thrown a few times, then would rather carry it proudly about, play with her owner, and be done for the day. Yet others enjoy playing an interactive game of "tag" or "catch me if you can" with her owner, with no toys at all. Some dogs like to shred and rag their toys about. Ideally games should be about interactive play with *you*, the dog always coming back for more, not about letting the dog head off to do their own thing and/or destroy your hard-earned cash in toy format.

I often use games involving food as a reward in order to lower the state of excitement and arousal of the dog. Luring with food can be an excellent training tool and game combined in one. When teaching a service dog to settle, I sometimes like to use food in device similar to the lovechild of a snuffle mat and a feather duster, which allows a trickle of small bits of food, forcing the dog to concentrate on spotting them and then catching them in a calm way. When using rewards, the

Mazey loves all games, including just playing with me without any toys. Photo by the author (2021).

personality of the dog and the emotional state we would like to achieve should always be kept in mind.

Food does not *have to* be used as a reward, though I would say 99.9 percent of dog trainers, even the worst ones, have at some time fed a reward of food while training in order to encourage a behavior. Food can be given either from the hand or thrown down onto the ground, including after a release word is given. Food used as a lure can get amazing results, the dog following our food containing hand until they are in the correct position, when the food can be dispensed as a reward. Some people also trickle feed food as rewards throughout the day instead of bowl feeding, which we shall look at later in the chapter.

We know all about rewards to encourage a behavior. The next term to learn about is a correction. A correction is typically used to teach the dog that a certain behavior is wrong, and not to repeat it. Where a dog already understands that a behavior is wrong, a correction can be used as a punishment to reinforce to her that there will be consequences she does not enjoy if she does not do what is being asked of her. This is not as sinister as it sounds.

A correction is simply a consequence of the dog's actions, which the dog does not like, causing her to not repeat that behavior. Or a correction can be used purely as guidance when teaching a new skill. It can let her know that the answer given was incorrect and to try again. A correction may be slightly physically uncomfortable for her, such as pressure on a lead if she pulls, or it could be as simple as disappointment

All dogs prefer different training rewards. Mina loves scent work and is seen here air scenting, looking for me. I am hidden behind a bush in a non-suspicious manner. Photo by the author (2021).

from withholding a reward. As I mentioned above, withholding a reward can cause frustration and be unfair to the dog, but this is generally where the dog does not understand why her rewards have stopped, as she has never been given any boundaries or shown which behaviors are correct and which are incorrect.

Withholding of a reward can be used effectively as a punishment/learning opportunity in certain circumstances, particularly in the context of a game which has been provided as a reward when training, but where the dog (that fully understands the rules of the game) has chosen to cheat, or play outside the rules, as it were. Simply stopping the game temporarily can be a very powerful motivator for the dog to encourage you to restart the game, usually by repeating the training exercise first. Thus the game, and complying with the boundaries and rules of the game, acts as a motivator for training, since the game is dependent on the successful completion of the training exercise.

When the training restarts, the dog is very motivated to correctly complete the training exercise as she wants to be rewarded with the game. This time around the dog is extremely careful to respect the boundaries of the game, since she wants the game to continue. In such a scenario I would continue the game much longer than usual when using it as a reward, to increase my dog's motivation to play with me (and enjoy her training), while at the same time respecting boundaries.

A correction should always be something that does not hurt the dog or cause her fear, pain, frustration or distress. Nevertheless it should be a consequence that is meaningful to her and that influences her decision not to repeat the undesired behavior, or that indicates to her which direction she should/should not be going in if shaping a behavior. Different corrections will work better or worse on different dogs, and the same correction will have different degrees of severity depending on the dog in question.

When training a dog, we in general should set her up for success, to try as much as possible to prevent her from making poor choices, hence limiting our use of corrections. This is particularly true while learning new skills. However, there comes a time when it may be safer and more desirable to put our dog in a situation where we can set her up to fail, in order to teach her in a fair, safe, controlled way, via a correction, that certain actions are wrong. I know, this goes against everything many purely positive/force-free trainers believe in, but hear me out.

Our service dogs must live and work in the real world. Therefore it's essential that service dogs leave/drop any food items they may find on the street when commanded to do so. Often people discard cooked chicken bones, which could splinter and be fatal if swallowed. Although swapping games are all very well, dogs are not stupid. A chicken bone is particularly high value, and I do not want to find that my dog looks at the chicken bone, knowing all I have in my pockets is kibble, and decide to eat the bone anyway as she knows there will be no repercussions from me for doing so. I would much rather she understand that when I say "leave it" I really do mean "leave it."

When giving a correction, it's important that the timing is right, and that the correction is clear and well understood. If we can, we should *immediately* follow up the correction by marking and rewarding the good behavior, in response to the correction. On top of this we can also follow up by asking the dog for a very simple behavior we know there is a 99 percent chance of her getting right, which we can then lavishly reward, bearing in mind there is a difference between relief (from pressure and release) and reward for a job well done.

When used in the proper way, corrections do not result in a submissive, fearful, shut down dog. All too often we do see dogs that may have been "trained" (and I use the word "trained" loosely) with ears back and tail tucked under, that may be walking on a loose lead, looking like a well-behaved, obedient dog to the inexperienced eye, but that are in reality shut down and in a state of learned helplessness, too scared to do anything at all. Methods that result in a shut down, scared dog are incorrect and are the result of abuse, not training using corrections.

By using minimal discomfort and rewarding a dog abundantly for the right choice following a correction, we avoid emotionally hurting or upsetting the dog. We are able to create a confident dog that understands what is required of her, is happy to learn and be trained, even if that does involve making mistakes at times since our corrections are not inherently bad or to be feared; rather, they enhance her learning and understanding of what we require from her. By setting fair boundaries and using play, we can increase our dog's enthusiasm and motivation to work with us, and to be trained.

Some corrections can cause the dog a high level of discomfort, but this should only be used where absolutely necessary, such as a punishment for a dangerous behavior. Life is not a fairy tale, and if a dog needs to undergo behavioral modification or is about to endanger a person or another dog, then a harsh correction may need to be administered. Such discussions are not within the scope of this book, which is about service dogs, not dogs that have serious behavioral problems and thus are unlikely to go into training as a service dog. Nevertheless I mention such use of more severe corrections for completeness.

When using a correction on a dog that is being disobedient, careful consideration *must* be given as to why the dog is disobeying and the circumstances around the behavior. If we know she understands the request, and we have been clear about what we have asked, and it's a fair thing to ask, then one of the first things that should come to mind is asking whether or not she is in pain. Pain is probably the most common cause for an otherwise well-behaved dog suddenly not wanting to perform simple tasks she knows well. For example, a sudden refusal to sit could be a back problem, or a cruciate ligament in the leg starting to fray and become painful.

Also consider the dog's emotional state, her level of arousal and where her mind is at. Like people, dogs can go to a place in their head where commands are simply not computing, and they cannot think or learn. If you went on *Mastermind* expecting your specialist subject to be the Chernobyl nuclear reactor meltdown of 1986, and you got pop music of 1986 instead, even though you may very well know quite a bit about Bon Jovi, Bananarama and the Bangles, your panic would render you mute anyway.

A good correction needs to be something the dog dislikes sufficiently to be strong enough to reinforce that when you ask her to do something, saying, "no," is not one of her best life choices. I'm not trying to be an alpha, a bully, or assert my dominance over my dog when correcting her. If you object to these words, simply insert whichever word you want to use. My point is that it's in a dog's nature to want to do things that give her the most pleasure in life, and that very well may not be the same things we would like her to do. This is just a fact of life.

Remember, a correction is *never* used in anger, rather to guide the dog in her training or back up and emphasize to her that she needs to listen to me and do as I ask. I do not require anything unreasonable of Mazey and Mina, but they live with me as part of my family, and as such there are certain minimum standards of behavior I expect. I love my dogs. I want them to be obedient, well-mannered service dogs that are a pleasure to be around. More importantly, I want to keep Mazey and Mina safe. I cannot do that without teaching them right from wrong, and that they need to listen to me and do as I ask immediately on being requested to do something.

Increasingly, the world is not a safe place for dogs, particularly any large dog that does not have a near-perfect recall and outstanding manners in public. I do not want to get into a situation where my dog is blamed for something that is not her fault as a result of an entitled person treating her in a way that is not appropriate, and which shows no common sense. All too often people laugh and think it's funny to let their small dog bark, growl, lunge at and yes, even bite and nip my big dogs. If either of my dogs did not listen to me, and retaliated in kind toward the aggressor, biting back, no doubt I would have the police at my door saying my dogs were dangerous and out of control. Therefore, it's essential that your service dog has boundaries and listens to you. If she will not immediately do as she is asked under normal circumstances, you will not have any hope of keeping her under control when she is put in an unfair position that no dog should be placed in, as I described above.

I want to emphasize that there are a great many different types of dog trainers and dog training ideologies out there, so choose wisely. You may be lucky to find a service dog trainer locally who you click with and who can guide you through the whole journey, from puppy to qualified service dog. Or you may initially go with a trainer who can help you develop a well-trained, obedient dog that is then ready to start task-work with a different, more specialized service dog trainer at a later date. The main thing is to find a trainer and method of training that you are comfortable with, and which will achieve the results you *need*. The "must have" tasks for your service dog, if you like.

In my mind, other than the buzzers, the bashers and the yank-and-crank brigade, as long as a trainer is using mostly reward-based training methods, there's no absolute right or wrong ideology when it comes to dog training. It's very much up to each of you to decide what's right for **you**, particularly given any limitations present due to your disability. Some methods will work better for certain dog and owner combinations than others. In addition, each trainer will have their own preferred way of training and type of dog that makes their heart beat faster. I carry a supply of paper tissues since I drool whenever I see a Rottweiler.

Once you find a trainer you like the sound of, ask about their methodology, the tools they use, and how your dog will be treated, particularly if you're considering sending your dog away for a board and train. Don't be shy: there are no stupid questions, so feel free to ask anything. Personally, I would go for a trainer who has a flexible attitude, who is keen to work with you and your dog, and who you're comfortable with. Always go with your gut feeling. Accolades and paper qualifications are meaningless if you and the trainer are not going to see eye to eye.

I would also look for a trainer who has a lot of experience with your breed of dog and who actually *likes* them. I have had a few police dog trainers who do not like Rottweilers. I found training with them, and the unintentional slights, a hard slog. The trainers were extremely knowledgeable, so I took what I needed from them, then moved on. Some obedience classes and puppy classes where I live are for small breeds only, and I had to travel quite a distance to find a good puppy class for Mazey! Puppy classes, and how appropriate they are or are not, are covered in Chapter Ten.

There's no use flogging a dead horse, or trying to change a prejudiced dog trainer. You're never going to succeed. It's always better to travel to find the right trainer with a kind and flexible attitude than put up with the wrong trainer that is local. Indeed, I would say many people travel quite considerable distances to train with the trainer of their choice. In the sports dog world, it's not unusual to travel internationally for seminars and training courses.

Unfortunately, there are still yank-and-crank trainers who immediately put overly harsh tools on any dog they encounter, regardless of her size, disposition or problems, and then proceed to haul the dog about. These types of trainers primarily use severe corrections on dogs to force compliance, with very little, if any, rewards and encouragement used. The dogs are not engaged with the handler, and instead of working as a team, the aim is to break the dog's spirit and force her to toe the line, leaving the dog shut down and scared of making mistakes. If you get anything from this book, it would be to please *never ever* use one of these trainers. Their methods are abusive, pure and simple.

There are also the buzzers, who abuse e-collars, lighting a dog up for the slightest mistake. After a very careful conditioning phase, where used correctly, dogs should not need an e-collar used on them frequently. Other than some sports dog trainers who use incredibly low-level stimulations in very specific, complex ways, an e-collar is only there as an emergency crutch, and that button should not be pressed on a daily, weekly or even on a monthly basis with a well-trained service dog. There are also the bashers, who physically kick and hit dogs. As stated above, *never ever* use any of these trainers. Instead, report them to the police if you have evidence of the abuse.

Balanced training is another term you will see. This is training that uses primarily rewards, but also uses corrections where required. *Great* emphasis should be on the use of reward. If not, then again, I would say the trainer is not so good. If your dog enjoys playing, I would recommend that you look for a balanced trainer who uses a lot of play-based training methods. Trainers who put a heavy emphasis on play will use this to look closely at the personality of the dog, including her strengths and weaknesses.

The last common dog training ideology you'll see advertised is force-free/purely positive dog training, which is based on the notion that the trainers only use reward when training dogs, with no use of corrections. They claim that all of their methods are kind, humane, backed up by science, and will not distress or harm your dog in any way. But this is not exactly the truth; rather, it is more of a marketing ploy.

There are a wide variety of corrections, and some force-free/purely positive trainers will be fine with using one but not another. Often they say a correction is not a correction in order to maintain their force-free/purely positive position. Examples of basic corrections are a disapproving voice, and any restraint placed on the dog, including a collar and leash of any kind. Yes, even a flat collar combined with a lead is a correction, since it's a restraint and will cause pressure and discomfort on the neck/trachea/larynx of the dog if she pulls. Unless, of course, you go wherever the dog demands, keeping the lead slack at all times, which some force-free/purely positive trainers advise. Not easy unless you're nimble as a gazelle. I for one am more of a hippopotamus.

We know a bit about corrections, and that force-free/purely positive trainers do not approve of them. But why? Well, in the past, dog training used to be pretty brutal, mainly based on force, with harsh punishments dispensed for the slightest disobedience. The industry has come a long way since I was a kid, a time when Punk was on the wane, and the New Romantics were fighting the good fight with eyeliner and lace. And that was the blokes.

Almost thirty years on and dog training has come full circle, with force-free/purely positive trainers dominating the market, though thankfully play-based balanced trainers are on the increase. Also, consider the quandary that many balanced trainers of old now call themselves force-free/purely positive, yet are still using the same techniques they always did, which makes things a bit tricky if you value the truth. I always feel very uncomfortable when a trainer calls themselves force-free/purely positive and is either using corrections without admitting it, or will not be honest about what can and cannot be achieved in the training, even if they use only minimal corrections.

A lot will depend on you, your service dog prospect, her basic standard of training, and the tasks you need her to perform. It may be the case that you have an angel of a dog and what you want *can* be done with plenty of treats and minimal corrections. However, the training will take a lot longer if you are not permitted to explain to a dog, via corrections, what is and is not allowed.

A correction does not have to be uncomfortable. It can be educational and motivational, simply by telling the dog whether or not they are going in the right direction and giving them encouragement. Sort of like that game at school when you blindfolded a classmate and they had to find an object, with everyone shouting out "hot" or "cold" depending on the direction they went in. If you could say nothing except "warm" occasionally, we'd still be there forty years later. Or it may be your force-free/purely positive trainer wants to call this type of correction a redirection, or some other phrase. The terminology is not important, more so is the concept that being able to give a dog direction, as opposed to just withholding rewards, can be very valuable.

Also consider that if your dog enjoys a bad behavior more than the offered reward for good behavior, then other than never putting the dog in that situation, which may be impossible, you have a stalemate. What do you do if your dog likes to steal food off shelves in shops? A ham shank tastes far better than a few pieces of kibble, and if you're not allowed to even tell the dog "no" or use lead pressure to stop her from pulling you towards the meat display, then you have a dog that cannot go into food shops, and will wash out unnecessarily in my view.

We all train our dogs differently. If you don't want to use certain corrections, that's fine; don't feel embarrassed, or stupid, or weak. You're not a snowflake, and you don't need to explain yourself or your decisions to anyone. It's your disability, and your service dog. You know her best, and you should never be pressured into doing anything you feel uncomfortable with.

However, if you want to train in an entirely force-free/purely positive way, be prepared for an honest trainer to tell you they can't help you with all the task-work you require and would feel dishonest taking your money for a result they feel you will never get. Or it may be they do feel you can get there in the end, but it will take far, far longer than it should, and this could be considerably more expensive.

Most service dogs are of breeds which have biddable temperaments, and rarely need harsh corrections, no matter the ideology of the trainer. Usually all that is required is to kindly establish a boundary, which the dog will then happily comply with. A mild correction may be required rarely thereafter. Other breeds that are high energy, high drive and have a great deal of self-confidence may have more of a mind of their own due to their genetics, and will need a firmer correction—not often, but it will be required in order for the dog to work effectively and to understand that she is not the one running the show.

I'm a realist. I find that properly administered corrections, performed with good timing, are invaluable in training service dogs and also pets. After all, discomfort and yes, pain, are part and parcel of existence on Planet Earth. I wish it wasn't so, and my ingrown toenails would be but a bad dream. Believe me, they are painful with a capital P, and don't get me started on my hemorrhoids. You'd better not be laughing now; you too will get old one day.

Personally I want a relationship with my dogs based on mutual love, trust and respect. I play with them like a little kid, down on my knees, rolling about in the dirt, sometimes with no toys at all. But I also do set clear boundaries via the use of corrections, and I will use punishment if and when required. I do this to keep my dogs safe, not to be abusive or cruel in any way.

My dogs and cats are my family. We all sleep together on my bed, and we eat at the same time too. Just not the same thing. I devour the local supermarket's brand of value noodles, the cats have whatever their grasping little heart's desire, and the dogs inhale imported Swedish raw meatballs. Such is life.

Does using corrections make me evil? I don't believe so. More and more there's an agenda that a dog is a delicate flower that will have a nervous breakdown if you so much as say "boo" to her. As the equal, no, the superior being in the home, she should have choice and total autonomy in every aspect of her life. If she says "no" to something, then the Princess has every right to do so. She should never be forced to do something she does not want to do. If food lures do not work, then she must simply be allowed to do her own thing, and behave just as she pleases.

If you want to live your life with your dog in this way, I'm fine with that. You do you, I'll do me, and we can agree to disagree. Except that's not what's happening. People like me who use corrections, multitask, and may train dogs for different activities are being called cruel and subject to cancel culture and a great deal of online nastiness and bullying from a tiny minority of extreme trainers, who have an agenda they want to push and will do anything to win, setting their flying monkeys out to do their worst on anyone who may disagree with them.

This is not a one-off. Increasingly, these trainers claim ethical superiority, while acting like high school mean girls, and are being heard and listened to by society at large. This is a cause for concern, particularly surrounding the banning of items such as crates. These trainers say science has proven that their methods are correct, and if anyone does not follow their school of thinking, then they are abusive monsters. Admittedly, I look the part of the Beast rather than Beauty, but the Beast was actually a nice guy if I remember right.

Most people these days own small, desperate to please, very easily trained dogs such as the gorgeous Doodles and Poos that we see everywhere. Consequently, many trainers have never handled a large, energetic working dog. Many never will, since they're scared of them, or if they try and fail, will claim it's not the fault of their methodology or techniques, but pass the buck back to the dog, telling the owner the poor sod has mental health problems(!) and needs either to be drugged into oblivion or euthanized. It's highly unfair to blame a dog for your own failings as a trainer, when her fundamental needs are not being met, including training with fair, consistent boundaries. Dogs also need right type of job to do, enough exercise, intellectual stimulation, and sufficient enrichment activities.

I *really* object to the cry that "science says" anything but reward-only training is unethical and cruel. This makes my teeth itch as there is no credible science to back these assertions up, rather science does confirm that punishment works to reduce unwanted behaviors. To assert reward-only training is the cure for all ills, including effectively preventing confirmed sheep killers from ever chasing sheep again, is make believe. We always want to be fair, kind and ethical, but sometimes decisions must be made. Is it better to use an e-collar and allow a dog off-lead, or to keep a dog on a long line forever? Only a dog's owner can decide this.

By the way, I do still have my very own hair and teeth, you know, making me quite a catch, even if I say so myself. Well, that's what Mazey told me to write, but I think she's biased and wants an extra food dispenser in the house.

One last thing to look out for that spans pretty much every training ideology, and is becoming very popular, and which I have said several times I will cover, is trickle feeding the dog throughout the day, often called the "ditch the bowl" method. The dog gets food only while being trained, or when you want the dog to do something at random times during the day.

This method can get incredible results quickly, particularly with small, fearful dogs, and dogs whose basic needs are not temporarily being met—for example, dogs with pain issues that can't have much play-based activity or exercise at all. These dogs are generally not service dogs.

There is a *big* place for feeding training treats, but my gut instinct doesn't like withholding all food on a "do as I say or you will starve" basis. I'm not a massive fan of coercion, particularly for service dogs that are better off working with you in partnership, which is why I want to quickly mention what to look out for if considering using a trainer who persuades you to give "ditch the bowl" a try.

With a large, deep-chested dog, such as a Great Dane, if pretty much the entire day's food allowance is distributed during training and on walks, when the dog is potentially very active and running around, I would be petrified of bloat. You would also need quite the muscles to heft about a rucksack of food for a Great Dane or several Rottweilers, as in my case. Very active, energetic play and large quantities of food just don't go together, and since I'm really into play-based training, I would feel wary of giving a dog 80 percent of their daily food at one time.

If you're working a service dog and you feed raw or tinned food, it's just not hygienic or fair to other customers to trickle feed in this way while out shopping. Stopping, looking at produce, or even clothes, while your hands are covered in at worst gunge, at best kibble dust, is just plain rude, never mind the impact on other disabled customers with conditions such as celiac disease that could have an allergic reaction to what you've left behind from your manky hands. Also, there's the smell in summer if feeding raw. I'm balking at the thought. You can cook the raw ... but then ... it's not raw, defeating the purpose of feeding raw to begin with.

I also feel that with a service dog, we work them for long periods of time—far, far longer than an average ten- or fifteen-minute training session. Our dogs need to look where they're going when working and be pretty relaxed, not be constantly "up" and trying to catch your eye or maintain a quasi-obedience position as they're hungry, desperate to please and really want some grub. The manager at your local pharmacy won't be amused if your dog topples over the lovingly constructed display of toothpaste tubes, artfully arranged as dominoes, because your dog was looking at you instead of where she was walking. Also consider what happens if you run out of food. Will she still behave, or will she switch off as she's tired and hangry, knowing there's no more food until tomorrow? Will she get demanding in the desperate hope you may have something up your sleeve?

Something about "ditch the bowl" does not feel right to me. Not just the notion of trickle feeding. I simply don't like the idea of withholding food to coerce, or indeed to force, compliance. Food is an essential resource. Would you withhold other essential resources, such as water? Air? Is that the relationship you want with your dog? To be master and servant? No obedience = no food. How many days would you starve your dog until she starts to work hard for the food? Two days? Three? Four? I have seen "as long as it takes" recommended.

If it's for you, go for it. Just be careful, and put a limit on how long you will starve a dog that isn't terribly interested in food rewards, or how long you starve her to reduce her energy levels and predisposition towards being "naughty" where you are not prepared to explain via corrections what the desired behavior is.

We now find ourselves at the end of the chapter. I've tried to show you the various ideologies, and how things are not always as they seem. We're all different, physically and psychologically, and we all own very different dogs, with different needs, with whom we do different things. Remember, an abusive trainer doesn't much care if specific tools are banned or what ideology he says he trains under. He'll continue to abuse those tools behind closed doors regardless, or he can simply use a flat collar, or his fists or feet as weapons.

Be true to yourself, your gut feeling and your dog. Have fun with your training together, no matter the tools, techniques or ideology you use. Play. Be a kid. Just enjoy your dog for the wonderful being she is, with all her emotions and whiskery dog breath as she greets you full of enthusiasm with a forced cheeky snog every morning. Don't let anyone, including me, stuff "their truth" down your throat, or put you off something you think will work for your dog and that you would like to try.

CHAPTER FIVE

Big Bad Bully or Yap on a Strap?
Which Breed Suits You?

This chapter will look at dog breeds most commonly used as service dogs. I will briefly examine the pros and cons of each of the most popular breeds in turn, though I'll try to keep it to service dog related issues, and my own experiences from speaking to owners and handlers of these breeds. I'll look at some of the up-and-coming breeds, and of course, no discussion is complete without examining those breeds which *can* be amazing service dogs, but are perhaps not recommended for most handlers, either due to their health issues or their temperament. How else am I going to wax lyrical about the Rottweiler?

The general description of each dog breed can be found on the American Kennel Club[1] or UK Kennel Club[2] websites, so that's a good place to start if you're debating whether a certain breed is for you in terms of height, weight, coat type, exercise requirements, etc. This chapter is designed to be the real lowdown on each breed as regards whether they make good service dogs, and the tasks each breed is most suited to. For convenience, I include at the end of this chapter tables which summarize each breed and what their good boy skills are.

It has to be recognized that being a service dog is not an easy job, and there are good reasons why the fab four, and in particular the Labrador Retriever, dominates the service dog world. No, not the Beatles, silly, though I do live beside Liverpool! That's not to say other breeds don't excel too, and breed selection *must* take into account the handler's disability and specific needs. Getting the right breed really stacks the cards in your favor towards your dog being good at certain types of task-work, but dogs will always be individuals. Mazey is the biggest love-bug in existence, as is Mina, despite most Rottweilers being a bit aloof with strangers.

Traditionally, the vast majority of service dog charities and service dog organizations have been totally inflexible, training only one breed of dog, typically Labradors, in a very generic manner. This can result in a service dog that may in reality be quite unsuitable for the disabled client the dog is partnered with, trained for tasks the disabled person does not need, and not trained for the tasks they do need.

In part, this is why owner training has become so popular, as it puts the disabled person in control of their own destiny, including the ability to choose their preferred breed of dog, and to specify the tasks their service dog will perform. I see this as an extremely positive thing. My own service dogs are Rottweilers. When we're out and about I'm frequently asked why I chose this breed. On occasion people are clearly wondering if I'm Damien's evil twin. People look at Mazey and don't immediately see a service dog, imagining her working as a police dog instead.

Well, I need this type of breed as every day I walk alone in the forest, the beach, and yes, even the graveyard beside my home, where I can sit in solitude and contemplate my life. I don't venture out during the day much, but prefer to wait for nightfall, where the world is quiet, peaceful and dark. This is the main walk of the day for myself and the girls, being my primary source of exercise, and simply giving me and the girls the sheer enjoyment of being alive. I do get called stupid and irresponsible for going out at night, but this is a feature of my disability. No, not vampirism, but my love of solitude as brought about by my PTSD and autism.

I feel safe when out after dark, more so now I have Mazey and Mina by my side. I definitely wouldn't be so confident if I owned a Labrador Retriever. Even though

One of the fab four is the Border Collie. How could anyone resist those intelligent, gorgeous eyes? Photo by Marion Burgess, her owner and trainer (2022). Reproduced by permission of the photographer.

Mazey's everyone's best friend, to a potential jeeper creeper she looks more Cujo than Lassie. I have had some scary experiences, such as when a man with a powerful flashlight was shining it in my face and advancing on me, refusing to reply when I repeatedly called out "hello." When I recalled Mazey to my side, he shone the light on her and the torch suddenly went off. If I'd been with Mazey Labrador, or Mazey Miniature Poodle, I'm not sure I would be writing this book (from the no gun-carrying UK).

Hopefully you now see that although Labradors are fantastic service dogs, they do not meet the varied needs of every disabled person, hence this chapter. But before we look to any individual breeds, I want to start with tackling the difficult topic of working lines v. show lines. This is not an issue with every breed, and is not something everyone will even acknowledge in the breeds it does apply to, since it can be controversial with fault on both sides of the divide. We have to be fair here, or at least try to be.

I use the word "controversial," but World War I and World War II combined have nothing on the vitriol a great many show-line breeders have for working-line breeders

and vice versa. I have heard of people breaking into kennels and clipping hair off show dogs before a major show, and also padlocks to kennels, cars and houses super-glued shut during the night, so the exhibitor is late for a trial/show and misses their class. Not that I'm trying to give you ideas, you understand!

On the whole, when looking for a service dog prospect, I would advise most people to start by looking at show-line breeders and/or pet breeders. If it's an exceptionally popular breed for service dog work, such as the Labrador Retriever, you may be lucky enough to find a breeder that tries to breed dogs for that specific market. Often such dogs are show lines crossed with working lines, producing a variety of puppies within the litter, some of whom will make fantastic service dogs, others great pets, and yet others still who would be best suited to a working career, per their breed's heritage.

The main difference, we tend to see, is that *good* show-line dogs have a far more placid, easy, biddable temperament. They typically will not need as much exercise as a working-line dog, and depending on breed, will not be as excitable in public. In general, and this is a real generalization, a show-line dog is easier for an inexperienced handler to train, and will make an overall better service dog prospect for such a handler. Working lines can be a handful, especially when young, and without enough stimulation and exercise they will invariably start amusing themselves with your slippers, glasses (always a favorite), sofa or even kitchen cabinets and drywall.

The breeds of dog we see a real divide in when it comes to show versus working lines are the Rottweiler, the Belgian Malinois, the German Shepherd, the Springer Spaniel, the Cocker Spaniel, the Labrador Retriever and the Golden Retriever. As you can see, many of these are very popular choices as service dogs, and as I've said before, selecting the wrong dog can be a disaster. This is particularly true with a rambunctious, large, adolescent dog. Unless you want to compete in IGP, Field Trials or run marathons, I would recommend looking to a pet or show-line dog of these breeds.

Having survived the suggestion that show-line dogs are often a better choice for service dog work, and before angry breeders start poking me with ricin-loaded umbrellas, I need to clarify that sourcing a show-line dog needs to be from a good breeder that temperament tests their breeding stock. The best show breeders may often breed dual purpose litters that can work in addition to excelling in the show ring. Some show breeders breed only for looks and not for temperament, with their dogs being beautiful nervous wrecks, a disaster for a service dog prospect.

Also consider which sex of puppy you want and the matter of spaying and neutering. In the absence of task-work that requires a tall, heavy dog, where the male in the breed is significantly larger, then sex is mainly a matter of personal preference. Most suitable service dog breeds show no great difference between the sexes in terms of trainability or temperament, so sex is really up to you.

However, and I'm going to be controversial here, certain breeds do not do well when neutered/spayed at a young age, or at all, and you may want to keep your service dog intact for his/her entire life. This can be inconvenient with a bitch that will come into heat twice a year as Mazey and Mina do. They are not spayed and I have no intention of having them spayed, at least not unless it becomes a medical necessity—for example, in the event of a pyometra which requires surgical intervention.

Most (un-castrated male) service dog owners, and also service dog trainers of a certain age or mindset, will by now be hyperventilating and require a paper bag. Deal with it. I love my dogs, and I will not compromise their health by spaying them without good reason. Rottweilers have a much greater incidence of cancer when spayed at a young age, as do Golden Retrievers, an extremely popular service dog breed.[3]

Hormones have a profound, lifelong effect on our bodies and our brains. This applies to bitches but also to male dogs too. Both sexes can suffer from anxiety, a lack of confidence and subsequently behavioral issues following castration/spaying and the removal of their hormones. With a small, underconfident breed this may be a very important consideration. More often than not it's small male dogs which become sex pests with pillows, other people's legs, etc., and whose owners turn towards castration in order to fix this issue, sometimes successfully, sometimes not.

Before I go on to discuss the individual breeds, there are some breeds I recommend only with a *great* deal of caution, including Rottweilers, Belgian Malinois, German Shepherds and Pitbull Terriers. To be honest, in many cases I was tempted to just give an outright "no" to these breeds, but that would be hypocritical of me, given I own two Rottweilers. In the right hands and for the right tasks, some of these breeds can be outstanding. However, there are many more failures than successes, and ignore genetics at your peril.

If you've lived with one of these breeds all your life, are an expert in handling them, are fully familiar with the problems inherent within that breed and are prepared for a dog to potentially wash out and end up as your pet, then it would be foolish of me to say go for a Labrador Retriever when your own favorite breed could be a much better match, as Mazey is with me.

However, if you have never owned a breed of the type I have issued warnings about, and your experience of them is limited to watching movies or saying hello to the shining example of that breed in the park, then stick with an easy, reliable breed of service dog. This is particularly the case where you may have owned one of these more difficult breeds years ago but have never trained or worked a service dog before and are plunging back into dog ownership after a break. In such a case, for your first service dog, stick with an easy, biddable breed and do not set yourself up for potential failure.

So which breed is first in our list? We're going to start big and go down in size, so topping our list of giant service dogs is none other than the Great Dane.[4] This majestic, statuesque breed is commonly used for psychiatric task-work, but her most important role as a service dog is providing bracing and counterbalance for her handler as a mobility service dog. Her height, weight and strength mean she can perform mobility tasks like no other breed.

In general, it's recommended that a service dog performing counterbalance or bracing tasks be a minimum of 40 percent of the handler's height and 60 percent of their weight. This can make the Great Dane just perfect for the vast majority of handlers, since male dogs can grow up to about 32 inches in height and weigh approximately 175 lbs. Bitches are shorter and lighter, but could still be a good choice for many people, particularly shorter women. This is according to the KC breed standard. Many dogs will grow taller and weigh more than this.

To give some context, I am 5 ft. 8 inches tall and 154 lbs. (Did you say "liar," Mazey????? I do hope you're looking forward to fasting tonight.) Anyway, for counterbalance I would need a Great Dane about a minimum of 28 inches tall and weighing no less than 94 lb., meaning I could look at a male or female puppy. If I were a 6 ft. tall, 200 lb. man, although a female puppy would probably be fine, a male puppy would be a better choice. The female might not grow as tall as expected, or the gentleman in question could put on weight, which is easy to do when you have mobility issues, and when weight gain is a side effect of many medications.

We know she's big and strong, but don't let the Great Dane's powerful build and strength fool you into thinking she'll be difficult to handle and control. Nothing could be further from the truth. Once mature and fully trained, the Great Dane is a cool, calm and collected service dog. However, she may not be the easiest dog to train for complex task-work that requires quick reflexes and a sharp response. This is not disobedience or stupidity on her part, simply that she has an inherently laid-back nature, and sees no point faffing about at 100 kph, doing exercises that she sees as a bit pointless and not terribly fun.

The Great Dane does not attempt to take advantage of her handler, but instead is reliable, patient and devoted, though expect a bit of back-chat at times as she can be talkative (in a nice way). As this is a breed that loves to be close to her owner, you will never use the bathroom alone again, lest a wormhole opens and swallows you up, tossing your remains into the cold darkness of space. What self-respecting Great Dane would allow that?

In addition to mobility task-work, a Great Dane makes a good psychiatric service dog .Her size alone may make her handler feel safe and give him confidence while out in public, despite the fact she's a gentle giant and not inherently defensive. A solid and affectionate dog, that sheer physicality can be extremely comforting. Small dogs are wonderful, but when everything goes wrong in life, there's nothing like putting your arms around a human-sized dog for a hug. As with other big dogs, the Great Dane is under the misconception she's the perfect size to be a lap dog. If she sits, she fits.

One thing to be aware of, if looking for a Great Dane as an autism service dog, is that they are prone to ... flatulence. Yes, this in part down to correct feeding, but irrespective of good diet, many Great Dane owners will confirm that flatulence is a thing. I have a lot of sensory issues myself due to my autism, and this may be a problem for other people similarly affected, if they cannot tolerate strong (foul) smells. Also bear in mind Great Danes slobber. The slobber can end up everywhere and could get on the nerves of the excessively house proud.

It's the extremely kind nature of the Great Dane which can make her a very good choice for disabled children, particularly those with balance or bracing requirements, as the Great Dane can be easily controlled by a child where a more excitable, higher-drive dog could not. Able to curl themselves into a surprisingly small, unobtrusive package, Great Danes have been known to accompany their junior handlers to school.

As the Great Dane does not have a high prey drive, she is not easily distracted by moving objects such as cats or squirrels, which may dance the Macarena at the most inopportune moments. This means that once trained she is unlikely to rush off and pull over a vulnerable handler or drag them out of a wheelchair. Her exercise requirements are lower than may be anticipated. She does not require hours of off-lead running per day, though she will want her five minutes of zoomies, which can knock over adults like skittles, never mind children. On the subject of children, the Great Dane is patient and good with kids and with other animals in the family.

Great Danes cope well with temporarily being under house arrest, should her handler be ill and unable to walk her for several days. In such a situation the Great Dane will prefer to stay by the side of her handler and not pine for miles of trail walks. The Great Dane's good nature means that anyone can easily pick up the lead and take her out for a walk or a toilet break, which can be very important if her handler is incapacitated for a long time or has to stay in the hospital.

Due to her calm nature, the Great Dane is not the type of service dog that excels in tasks that involve rushing here, there and everywhere. Traditionally she has not been used as a guide dog, as a hearing dog or for scent-work that requires continuous checking up on the handler, such as the majority of medical alert tasks. That is not to say individual dogs with a specific talent in this area cannot do this, but it's rare, and care would be needed to find the right breeder and bloodlines, in addition to accepting in advance that the dog may wash out as a medical alert service dog.

A well-bred Great Dane that has received the proper handling and environmental socialization as a puppy will have strong nerves, but some poorly bred Great Danes may be neurotic, hard to train and have unusual fears that are just odd. I have heard more than once of Great Danes being afraid of the dark or everyday objects they may never have encountered, such as umbrellas (with no ricin), stairs, the noise of a flushed toilet, and the little slats in wooden footbridges, where you can see the water rushing down below. Who knew trolls really lived underneath bridges? Therefore, even with a well-bred dog, take no chances and give her exposure to as many different environments, people, and objects, as possible as a puppy.

Your Great Dane service dog will attract attention when you're out working her, and she will need a large car to be transported comfortably. As with other giant breeds, Great Danes are expensive to insure and buy beds, toys, harnesses, etc., for, since off-the-rack items may not exist, and therefore your service dog gear will come at a high cost. Also make sure counter surfing never becomes a habit, particularly due to their preponderance to bloat. Their height can be used for bad purposes as well as good. Lastly, watch out for that happy wagging tail, which is strong and thin like a whip. You don't want to be smacked in the face with it, that's for sure.

The worst thing about a Great Dane as a service dog is their short working life, bearing in mind you must ensure they are physically mature (at about eighteen months old) before starting any training for counterbalance or bracing work, let alone physically taking heavy loads as a real working responsibility, which should not be until two years of age. Once started, the Great Dane will learn the work quickly, plus there are many other tasks that can be taught before this, such as opening doors, pulling off socks and shoes, etc.

Some Great Danes may only have four or five years of working life following completion of service dog training. Many pass away before the age of ten, which is heartbreaking. On the flip side of the coin, Great Danes can do things the vast majority of other service dog breeds cannot do, so don't let her short longevity and working life put you off if the breed ticks all of your boxes otherwise. As the saying goes, "it's better to have loved and lost a Great Dane, than never loved one at all."

We'll leave the Great Dane relaxing beside us on the sofa as we look to other giant breeds of service dog. I won't cover all of the things that are going to be the same between the giant breeds, including their high cost of upkeep, short longevity, tendency to drool(!) and many health issues by virtue of their size. Instead I'll look to the individual characteristics of these breeds that may help you make a decision between them.

The next candidate on our list of giant service dogs shares all of the Great Dane's excellent characteristics, but has a totally different frame and coat. A true working dog, if you're lucky you may meet her on duty as a lifeguard in Italy. Don't swoon in the water, pretending to drown, hoping for a *Baywatch*-style rescue by hunky human lifeguards. It never works. Trust me. You'll just end up swallowing salt water and being put off your dinner. So who is she, then? She is the beautiful Newfoundland, of course.

In general the Newfoundland is several inches shorter than the Great Dane, but she has a more powerful and substantial build. Bear in mind her height ideally needs to be 40 percent of yours for counterbalance, so although she will suit many women, the average man will be too tall to use her for this type of work. Unlike the Great Dane, the Newfoundland enjoys carting. Once trained and conditioned, she's suitable to pitch in and help pull a manual wheelchair where required—for example, up hills. Just make sure you have good steering; otherwise, I think we all know how that could turn out.

The Newfoundland is a *big* fan of water, even having webbed feet. Her double coat is straight and is of medium length, being oily and water resistant. If you don't enjoy daily grooming, then the Newfoundland is not for you. I have arthritis in my hands, and I could not look after the coat of a Newfoundland. Definitely consider the coat care aspect, and any physical limitations you may have with respect to grooming, including bending over for long periods. She also sheds her coat. A lot. And don't forget the drool. There will be rivers of it.

Slightly calmer and more docile than the Great Dane, once she's fully trained and understands what is being asked, she's unlikely to run off and pull over a vulnerable handler who is using her for bracing and counterbalance work, which she excels at. She's also a fantastic choice for a giant, mega hairy psychiatric service dog, though in general she's not as touchy feely as the Great Dane, appreciating, "me time," on her own, not requiring constant skin-on-skin contact with her owner.

Some Newfoundlands can be suspicious of strangers; therefore, choose a breeder with care. If she is to succeed in service dog work, particularly given this dog's size, any reactivity to people would be a big disqualifying factor for working her in public. She *is* a true working dog, and the vast majority of Newfoundlands are temperamentally sound. With her family, there are no doubts: she is incredibly sweet and good natured, including with children and pets.

The Newfoundland does not deal well with heat and humidity, though she has a good tolerance of colder climates. Bear in mind where you live and are likely to travel to and work her. In hot climates, often the coolest places can be in air-conditioned stores where she may primarily be working, plus a journey in your car to get there, so that could pose little problem. She will need off-lead exercise daily, which can be hard if you live in a tropical, or hot and dry climate, where evenings may be too warm for running about. A desert would not fill her with unadulterated joy, a milder climate with plenty of safe swimming spots would be far more to her taste.

The intelligence of the Newfoundland is great, and she genuinely enjoys having a job to do. She does have a better nose, with more of an affinity to scent work than the Great Dane, although she would not be a top pick for scent-work tasks on their own. Should you need a giant breed for counterbalance and psychiatric task-work, and like massive, hairy dogs (and who doesn't?) then she would be an excellent pick as a service dog.

My two top picks then for giant service dog breeds are the Great Dane and the Newfoundland. Other dogs that get an honorable mention are the Leonberger and the Bernese Mountain Dog, both of whom are large and hairy, but with slightly different personalities. A similar height to the Newfoundland, these breeds could also be used for women of an average height who are looking for a mobility service dog to provide bracing and counterbalance. However, please consider carefully the health of the Bernese Mountain Dog, who is not thriving in this department.

So which giant dogs are generally not suitable for service dog work, and why? The Irish Wolfhound is a name frequently put forward due to her impressive height and weight. However, the breed is a sighthound and has a high prey drive, liking nothing more than to dash off after cats, rabbits or anything else that is small and furry. I never say never, so she could be a great option for expert handlers who have always lived with and/or just adore the breed, in a similar way someone might buy a working line Belgian Malinois for service dog work.

If your primary goal is to find a service dog for bracing and counterbalance, consider what would happen should your Irish Wolfhound turn out to not be suitable? This breed has a high prey drive. There, I said it again, since I cannot emphasize this enough. The Irish Wolfhound will be rambunctious and playful as an exceptionally large puppy, and at this time she will almost certainly take her handler for an unplanned jog. Or two. Or three. You might end up face down in the mud just before your dog hating, snobby in-laws are due to visit. The afternoon will be spent full of dirty looks, and the whispered phrase, "I told you so."

Another breed that is extremely large is the English Mastiff. Coming in at a similar height as a Great Dane, this breed can weigh considerably more, with some male dogs tipping the scales at as much as 200 lbs. Calm, confident and courageous, with a low prey drive, in some ways it's surprising this breed has not gained more popularity in service dog circles for giant dog connoisseurs who really want to think outside of the box. The breed's rarity is almost certainly a factor, with only one thousand English Mastiffs existing in the UK. Plus, you really need to love slobber. I mean *really* love slobber.

The English Mastiff is considered by many trainers to be hard to train and extremely stubborn, but then so is the Rottweiler that in reality is easy to train if a teamwork-based approach is used, rather than one of master and servant. This dog is massive, however, and if she says "no," it's a battle you'll never win with force. Mazey went through a phase of refusing to get out of the car if she felt short changed by the length of her walk. I was able to simply pick her up as she squawked in protest, but with the English Mastiff, this would not be a possibility after she reached the age of twelve to sixteen weeks. Unless your hobby is bodybuilding or powerlifting, that is.

Due to her sheer mass, the breed is quite lazy, and she loves being with her humans, which could be an advantage depending on your circumstances. Although counterbalance and bracing task-work would be no problem for her, other mobility tasks that involve fetching and carrying objects, opening doors, helping undress her owner, etc., may not be her idea of fun. As may be expected, her totally calm demeanor and outlook on life make her a good candidate as a psychiatric service dog.

With an English Mastiff you would have no problem getting to the front of the queue should there be a shortage of toilet paper: she would simply plow through the hordes of pushing and shoving elbows and knees. Due to her low exercise requirements, she's happy snoozing her days away in a small home. Her sheer bulk could prove intimidating to the general public, and fitting her into a suitable space on public transport could prove difficult. Traveling by air with an English Mastiff would be a challenge to say the least.

Originally a guarding breed, some English Mastiffs can be very suspicious of strangers, which would be less than ideal. Finding a good breeder would be a priority, as would raising your English Mastiff puppy correctly. Her height and weight theoretically make her a contender as a mobility service dog, but in reality, her rarity has me doubting we will see many, if any, English Mastiffs working as service dogs any time soon.

We can't leave a discussion on giant breeds without touching on the magnificent dogs which make up the livestock guardian breeds, which also typically have a huge amount of brute strength and size. These dogs are bred to work independently from humans, making their own decisions and not having to demonstrate a high degree of obedience. This is not ideal for working as a service dog, particularly as guarding flocks from harm requires a somewhat suspicious nature. Livestock guardian breeds would include the Tibetan Mastiff, the Anatolian Shepherd, and the Great Pyrenees.

It may not seem like there is a lot of choice of giant service dog breeds, and that would be correct. These magnificent dogs are not popular as pets, due to some of the negative aspects of their ownership which we have already discussed, primarily their cost of upkeep, health problems, and short life span. However, where you need a counterbalance or a dog to brace against, they are invaluable.

I enjoy math, so at the end of the chapter I've created a quick reference table giving examples of the giant service dogs able to perform counterbalance and bracing mobility task-work, correlated to a variety of disabled people's heights. I've also included a table of the average height and weight of the giant service dog breeds I've discussed, and the maximum height and weight of handler they can work for. Hopefully these tables will help you find the giant service dog of your dreams.

If you don't require a giant breed for bracing and counterbalance, but still want a big, powerful service dog, perhaps to assist in pulling a wheelchair, then there are many *large* breeds to choose from that are overall top picks as service dogs. I'm going to start with the Rottweiler, and cover this breed in the most detail since this is my heart breed, this is my book(!) and also it's the breed I use as my own service dogs. A lot of what I say regarding the Rottweiler will also apply to some of the other high-energy, high-drive breeds, irrespective of height and weight.

The Rottweiler is a sturdy, imposing dog. Not massively tall, bracing and counterbalance would not be her forte, nevertheless her powerful physique means she is quite capable of assisting with mobility tasks that involve pulling. I've taught Mazey the command, "pull pull," which means she pulls into her harness, helping me walk up hills when my joints and muscles are very painful. In terms of mobility task-work, retrieving may not be her favorite task, though she enjoys anything that involves tugging, such as helping me undress.

Extremely confident and self-assured, with a natural guarding instinct, the Rottweiler is often used as a psychiatric service dog. For those suffering with PTSD, she can be trained to conduct a premises search to make sure there are no intruders in a house. For most handlers, though, this is a waste of time, as previously discussed. Unlike many sensitive breeds who can get nervous with an anxious handler, a fearful human creating a fearful dog, the Rottweiler tends to have the strength of character not to do this. However, it's important to look for an open and balanced dog, one that is not naturally defensive and suspicious of strangers.

In terms of personality, the Rottweiler is *extremely* loving and affectionate with her family, which includes any pets. She enjoys sitting or lying on her owner's feet, including leaning her full weight against her owner's legs, glancing lovingly upwards, fluttering her pretty black eyelashes. That is, when she is not actually lying on top of her owner or squeezed up beside him. There are many times I have woken to someone spooning comfortably against my back, tenderly kissing my neck, hoping to wake me so I can prepare breakfast. Alas, it was not some handsome suitor come to sweep me off my feet, but, of course, Mazey or Mina. They're not called Snogweilers for nothing you know.

A Rottweiler is not clingy, in the sense that she doesn't tend to suffer from separation anxiety. She will just curl up and go to sleep when left alone. However, her strong preference is to have her owner close enough so she can smell, hear, see and ideally be in physical contact with him at all times, particularly when in the house. This includes when you're washing the dishes, vacuuming, and bathing in the tub, where she may well try and join you. Please note, a Rottweiler displaces a lot of water, is heavy and has bony elbows! Quite simply, your Rottweiler loves you dearly and is not afraid to show it.

Rottweilers can be aloof with strangers, which more often than not is a good characteristic for a service dog, since she is not distracted by people while out working. She focuses her attention on her owner, which is important for tasks such as medical alert. A confident, tolerant dog, even if not overtly friendly, she will allow strangers to touch her, with no fear, defensiveness or aggression. Other Rottweilers are everyone's best friend, and they have an uncontrollable tail and bottom wiggle should anyone make eye contact with them. Ahem Mazey. I love Mazey's friendliness, but I know it would irritate other service dog handlers.

Most Rottweilers will not bark or alert to noises inside or out of the house, unless it's an unusual noise and there's a very good reason to do so. They tend to be thinking dogs, taking time to consider if there's a genuine threat, rather than reacting first, thinking later. I find the quiet, peaceful nature of the Rottweiler to be very calming and beneficial, as I personally don't like noisy dogs due to my sensory issues.

Rottweilers are sensitive. They do not like feeling that their handler is not happy with them. In general they are easy to train, and this is particularly true in experienced hands, especially with a trainer that will play with them using the types of games Rottweilers enjoy, such as tug, fetch or using a flirt pole. They may adore their owner, but nevertheless they cannot be bullied into complying the way other sensitive working breeds can be. The Rottweiler instead could turn stubborn and resentful. They do need fair boundaries that are consistently and firmly enforced, or they will simply please themselves.

Rottweilers have lots and lots of energy. They have a little internal nuclear reactor providing puppies and adolescents with their copious amounts of power, though they have a better "off switch" while indoors than many other breeds of high energy dogs. As they're not naturally very reactive or buzzy in the house as adults, they're not the best fit as a hearing dog, or for tasks that require constantly getting up and down to retrieve objects and do things at a distance from their owner. A Spaniel or a Retriever breed is a better fit for this type of work.

Rottweilers have very good noses, and are extremely attentive to their owners, making them an ideal choice for a large medical alert dog. The size and imposing appearance of the Rottweiler may deter thieves from trying to steal a purse or bag should their owner be incapacitated when unwell, if having a seizure for example. It's an extremely sad reflection on society that this even occurs or should be a consideration, but it's far more common than you may think.

However, despite her excellent qualities, the Rottweiler is not suitable for many, if not the majority, of service dog handlers. What gives the Rottweiler her greatest of virtues can also be her biggest of downfalls. All energetic, high-drive dogs require experienced handlers, and the Rottweiler is no different. Her innate self-confidence, great intelligence and extremely high regard for her own abilities(!) often leads her to believe that she is the best-placed individual to make any decisions for the service dog team.

This natural independence and tendency to take advantage should the opportunity arise can occur even in very well-trained Rottweiler service dogs, such as when the handler is having a bad day. This is not "dominance" (if you describe it in a negative "I want to hurt you" sort of way) or "being an alpha." The dog is just making decisions she feels are in her best interests, as we all do in life. Mazey, for example, may suggest that the path for the two-hour walk is the best one to take, temporarily becoming deaf as I stare at her fast disappearing black and tan bottom, when all I want to do is sit on my sofa with copious amounts of ice cream.

I adore my Rottweilers, but I'm realistic about the breed. At one time I would have said the average handler can learn to train and work a Rottweiler service dog for most tasks, particularly show lines, but I have seen too many lovely dogs purchased as puppies and later re-homed, or kept as pets, having too much energy, drive, and unchanneled intelligence for their disabled owners to cope with and work reliably in public. I also see this frequently with people who are not disabled and who buy Rottweilers as pets without enough care or consideration.

In conclusion, it takes a lot of skill, time, energy and commitment to get the best out of your Rottweiler service dog. If you're in a position to do this, then you will, in my opinion, end up with the most excellent service dog imaginable. Dare I say it, the Rottweiler makes the very best service dog in the world. In the history of the world most probably. If we're being honest, the Rottweiler is the best breed in the entire multiverse, both forward and backward in time. That's what Mazey says about herself—not that she likes to brag or anything.

Having left the Rottweiler snoring on the most comfortable side of the bed, with her head in our lap, drool spilling onto the keyboard, let us now look at another wonderful large breed: the bold and the beautiful German Shepherd. I'm very conflicted about this breed as it's one of the breeds I grew up with, but the breed has undergone a severe split in terms of working and show lines. The German Shepherd of my childhood has all but disappeared. Many of the show-line dogs I've seen recently display nervous temperaments and an inadequate structure to enable them to stand up to a working life.

There are, of course, fantastic working-line German Shepherd Dogs, but the majority of these would be a massive challenge for the average handler. Not everyone wants to revolve their life around their high-energy dog. However, I will provide the caveat that there are many more well-bred German Shepherds working successfully as service dogs in the U.S. than in the UK. In Europe we have a great gene pool for working-line German Shepherd Dogs for police and military use, whereas the U.S. seems to have many more dogs suitable for service dog life.

Much of what I have said about the Rottweiler applies to the German Shepherd. This dog is for experienced trainers only. Although both breeds have a tendency toward aloofness with strangers, in the German Shepherd this can be heightened to an unacceptable level due to an increased defensive drive in the dog, which manifests as heightened suspicion of strangers. Many people believe that a breed that has the extreme sensitivity toward the handler, as German Shepherds do, are a good choice for psychiatric service dog work. I would tend to disagree.

Psychiatric service dogs that work for an anxious handler must have a robust, confident, absolutely solid temperament. Where sensitivity is combined with too much defensive drive, or worse still, a fearful, nervous temperament (as can often be the case with some of today's German Shepherds), then you have a dog and handler team feeding off each other's fears. Eventually the dog becomes unhappy and scared in her day-to-day service dog work, leaving the handler without a service dog, or battling to retrain a dog with reactivity issues, something which is never easy, particularly if simultaneously fighting personal demons.

The German Shepherd will need plenty of exercise, and as she is extremely loyal, she prefers to be in the company of her owner and his family at all times. Unlike the Rottweiler, a well-trained German Shepherd will take direction from a competent handler who is not her owner, so should he become incapacitated, she can easily be walked by an experienced dog walker.

Obedient and exceptionally focused on her handler, a good German Shepherd is hard to beat, as she can turn her paw to just about every service dog task imaginable. The breed has and does commonly work as guide dogs, mobility service dogs, medical alert dogs and as psychiatric service dogs. Although affectionate with her family, she is not a clingy dog, and is happy to sleep in her crate or on the floor. She does not insist on sharing a bed.

In conclusion, if you have the training and handling skills, and can find a well-bred dog from a reputable breeder, then you may find the German Shepherd is the perfect service dog for you. I have felt a bit guilty when writing negatively about the breed, as they would be my own personal second choice behind the Rottweiler. I have to be true to my own feelings and experiences, though, and it saddens me to see so many nervous German Shepherds with poor physical structure and health here in the UK.

The German Shepherd is now snoozing in her crate, and above the sound of her snores, I can almost hear the stomping of impatient feet here on the Wirral. What about the scrumptious Standard Poodle? One of the fab four (and I'm not talking about the Teenage Mutant Ninja Turtles), Standard Poodles have traditionally been used as service dogs for a long time, initially as guide dogs. An old breed, the Standard Poodle, like all Poodles, is a hardworking, versatile, intelligent breed, and dare I say it, she also has a good sense of humor.

If you're a big, tough bloke with a reputation to keep up, don't be put off a Poodle if everything else about this breed is right. Standard Poodles are not the foo-foo dogs they're often portrayed to be in the media. They don't need lovingly hand-knitted sweaters to venture out of the house, should they otherwise perish with cold, and only show dogs sport a lion cut. For a working service dog, a puppy cut is perfectly adequate, and you can choose to have the hair slightly longer or clipped closer to the skin, whatever style suits you and your Standard Poodle best. Better still, as they do not shed, there's less vacuuming to be done. Yay!

The coat of the Standard Poodle is dense, and there's a *lot* of it, which requires very regular brushing. Even if the coat is cut short, areas typically kept longer such as the ears, face and tail, will still need to be carefully and thoroughly brushed daily, as well as body parts prone to matting, such as under the armpits. Ears will need to be plucked. I have arthritic hands, and would struggle with all of this, finding it a chore instead of a bonding opportunity. Plus, don't forget to add on the cost of professional grooming every six weeks, which is essential, unless you can competently groom to a similar level yourself. YouTube videos and kitchen scissors are not enough—grooming is not as easy as it looks!

Requiring plenty of exercise as all large dogs with a working heritage do, these gorgeous dogs can be walked by anyone, which is a great advantage should you be unwell, either at home or if you're admitted into a hospital. If lots of exercise is unfeasible for you, never fear, the smaller Poodle varieties are well worth consideration. Bear in mind, though, unlike the Standard Poodle, Miniature and Toy Poodles may be more prone to nervous behaviors and yapping.

This is a breed that tends not to take advantage of their disabled handler when feeling unwell, remaining obedient and continuing to look to their handler for direction, rather than taking charge themselves. Standard Poodles are clowns, in the non-creepy sense of the word, and though they have a decent off-switch indoors, they will never fail to raise a smile from you, even on the bleakest of days. In fact, their good off switch means you can easily settle your Standard Poodle while out and about, such as having a meal or a quick coffee with friends.

Some Standard Poodles will have quite a high prey drive; therefore, care must be taken when looking for a reputable breeder. Despite their drive (if present), when properly introduced they are affectionate with small pets in the household, as they are with children. Well, with anyone really: dogs, kids, adults and fellow pets in the home. The Standard Poodle is a lover, not a fighter.

The breed can be slightly aloof with strangers. They are not as gregarious as Labrador Retrievers or Golden Retrievers. This is good for a service dog since their slightly reserved attitude means they aren't easily distracted by random people trying to make eye contact or kissy noises to them while out working. Those kissy noises can be like fingernails down a blackboard. Eek.

Very loving and affectionate with her owner, the Standard Poodle adores a cuddle but does not need to be surgically attached to her owner's hip at all times. She will not constantly sit on feet nor lean on legs, like Mazey, for example. The Standard Poodle combines sensitivity with intelligence, making her suitable as a psychiatric service dog, provided, of course, that the breeder you select produces dogs that are bold and not prone to skittishness. She is a dog that is adaptable and easily trained, so will excel in every service dog task you can think of, including as a guide dog, hearing dog, mobility service dog, psychiatric service dog, and medical alert dog.

Alas, nothing in life is perfect, and like all Poodles, the Standard Poodle does have a large array of potential health issues. I mean a *lot*. The good news is many of these can be screened for, which is why using a reputable breeder is so important. He should be able to prove to you the health of his breeding stock, and that your puppy will not inherit any of the genetic conditions that DNA tests can eliminate. Make sure temperament has also been tested. I have met some really lovely Standard Poodles that are simply too excitable for work as a service dog, in addition to some lines being prone to nervousness.

I've covered quite a few large dogs now, and how can anyone match up to the wonderful Standard Poodle which we've just discussed? Dare I say it, have I left the best for last? Yes, I think I have! How can we discuss large service dogs without admiring the amazing Golden Retriever? After all, when many people think of service dogs, the breed that pops into their head is the Labrador Retriever, with the Golden Retriever nipping (oh so gently) at her heels. A taller, more substantial dog than the Labrador, the Golden Retriever is my top pick for a large service dog, pushing the adorable Standard Poodle into second place.

I'm sure Standard Poodle owners across the nation are slamming shut their books, or stabbing madly at the little black cross on the corner of their screen, depending on how old school they are. Don't be miffed! There really was very little difference between the breeds, and you can put it down to me being from the UK, where Standard Poodles are not as popular as Golden Retrievers. All issues settled, patting our Poodles lovingly on their curly little heads as they gaze at us with adoration, lets now turn our attention to the amazing, the gorgeous, the golden girl of the service dog world. That's right, it's the Golden Retriever.

The Golden Retriever is a breed that has it all. She is bright, friendly, easy to train, and can perform pretty much every service dog task there is, within her height and weight capacity. I would say there *are* better choices for a hearing dog, though, or where you need a mobility service dog that is really buzzy and always on the go, though she does enjoy retrieving. The Golden Retriever is outstanding in her work with autistic children, not being upset by loud noises, and being very tolerant and kind.

The Golden Retriever shines bright wherever she goes, and that's not just her beautiful coat. She's a people dog, friendly with everyone she meets, her feathered tail constantly wagging in good humor. This may be a challenge for some handlers, as the natural inclination of most Golden Retrievers is to live up to the mantra, "no such thing as a stranger." She will make eye contact, wag her tail hopefully, and if her prayers are answered, at least one person will come up and start petting her. This could prove annoying for some people, though personally I love this type of dog.

Although willing to learn and easy to train, the Golden Retriever may seem to take a little longer than some other breeds to learn new tasks. This is due to her calm, sensible temperament. Instead of offering every single behavior she has ever learned in rapid succession, the Golden Retriever will tend to have a think, then often she will offer the correct solution the first time. What can be seen as slowness is *not* indicative of a lack of intelligence. It's simply her learning style. Compared to a buzzy breed, it doesn't take any longer to train the Golden Retriever as once she has learned a new skill, she has it for life and will not forget.

A laid-back breed of dog, the Golden Retriever is gentle and kind with everyone she meets. Hugely sociable, she loves her family deeply and adores strangers too, whether they be young, old, human, dog or any other species, from horses to cats and other small furries. She has a low prey drive, so won't pull her handler over should she spot a leaf blowing in front of her on a windy day. Playful and active, she doesn't tend to have the fastest recall in the world, though she will come directly back instead of heading off in another direction should a more attractive prospect present itself.

When working in public, the confidence and reliability of the Golden Retriever is a massive asset. Not overly sensitive, she won't hang on her handler's every word, but she is obedient and will not take advantage of her handler, instead always striving to be a good girl. She is energetic and needs her walks, but luckily anyone can take her out, and she will be her usual, happy self, which is a bonus in a service dog.

A large dog with a double coat, the outer layer quite long, the Golden Retriever will require daily brushing, which takes time, so bear this in mind. She also sheds. A lot. As a gundog, the Golden Retriever likes water, and consequently mud. She will not hesitate to find a muddy puddle and roll joyously in it, having the most amazing time, which will take a lot of effort to sort out once you return home.

My number one pick of the large service dog breeds—what's not to love about the Golden Retriever? She may not be the absolute best choice for some tasks, but she will be competent at them, able to turn her paw to almost anything, and be worked by anyone, which can be said about very few other breeds. Not requiring to be sat on your lap, we will leave her comfortable on the hearth rug, while I give a few honorable mentions in the large dog category.

If none of the traditional large service dog breeds float your boat, then there are some excellent other contenders. These breeds may not be able to do all tasks, but nevertheless are worthy of consideration. The Rhodesian Ridgeback is a confident breed that can make an excellent mobility service dog, medical alert dog and also psychiatric service dog, along with the Giant Schnauzer. Both these breeds need a very competent handler, but if that is you, then like the Rottweiler, they could be good large breeds to consider.

I'm aware I have not mentioned any of the sled dog breeds, though many would be categorized as medium-sized dogs rather than large ones. I do know of one handler who has trained several Alaskan Malamutes over the years, hence their inclusion here in this part of the chapter covering large dog breeds. His service dogs assisted him by helping pull his wheelchair, plus serving as psychiatric service dogs, though he was successful in teaching them little other than extremely basic task-work in this role.

Alaskan Malamutes and other sled-dogs tend to be very friendly and social dogs. Their bold, confident personalities place them in good stead as service dog prospects in this regard. On the other hand, their independence means they are not necessarily always attentive to their handler, and on top of that, there is no disputing that their recall leaves a lot to be desired. Many owners never let their sled dog off-lead at all, other than in an enclosed area, or if they do it's with a GPS tracker on, "just in case." This is not ideal for service dogs that genuinely need a chance to unwind and relax after work.

Although intelligent, sled dogs are not easy to train as service dogs, since they may not consider typical service dog tasks to be particularly interesting. If used to pull a wheelchair, either alone or in tandem, beware. Sled dogs have, "tons of go but not a lot of whoa." Due to their need for an expert trainer, and the variability of success in task training, in general I do not recommend them, unless they are "your" breed, in which case, go for it! As always, there are exceptions, and some sled dogs (and their crosses) can be awesome in their role as service dogs.

The breeds that are just a big fat no (for me) as large service dogs go are the Wolfdog and also the large fighting dog breeds such as the Japanese Tosa, which still retains dog aggression as part of its basic genetic makeup and personality. Dogs of these breeds may be excellent with people and have many great qualities. Others are suspicious of strange people and every dog they may meet. It's important that your service dog prospect not be dog reactive nor have the genuine desire to rip apart any service dog she may meet in a store.

Wolfdogs, along with many of the fighting dog breeds, are banned in plenty of countries that will not make an exemption for your service dog/Wolfdog should you fly in on holiday. As I understand it, in the U.S., although there may be local state or municipal laws banning the keeping of some breeds as pets, most notably Pitbulls, if the dog is a legitimate service dog, then these laws will not apply to you. That doesn't mean you won't struggle in shops or to obtain housing due to discrimination, so keep your attorney on speed-dial.

Please also note, Wolfdogs are not actually dogs, but a hybrid. As such they have behavioral characteristics in line with wolves, not dogs, making them unsuitable to work as service dogs. Wolves do not look to humans for direction and are *much* more shy, cautious and nervous than are dogs that underwent a long process of domestication to become what they are today. Wolves need to be this way to survive in the wild, and although it's a good trait there, it's not a winning characteristic in a service dog.

Having left our Wolfdog on the sofa bed with her pack, all intent on watching *An American Werewolf in London*, it's time to look at medium-sized breeds, a group that contains not only two of the fab four, but also other popular service dog breeds, including our next candidate. Constantly on the go, this breed is smart, energetic and always in a good mood, ready to tackle, if not leap over, whatever life throws at them. It's the gorgeous, the gregarious, the gentle English Cocker Spaniel. Or American Cocker Spaniel. I'm not going to differentiate based on a fancy hairdo.

The Cocker Spaniel is an energetic, cheerful dog with an absolutely amazing nose. A firm favorite with the police and military for scent-work tasks such as drugs and explosives detection, she is also a fantastic choice as a service dog in any scent-work type task. She excels as a psychiatric service dog due to her fun, confident, extrovert personality that never fails to raise a smile. If you're looking for a small mobility service dog, you'll find her keen to please, and full of energy and smarts, which also helps if her role is working as a hearing dog.

The Cocker Spaniel is good with other dogs and people alike, her beautifully feathered tail a veritable blur. A neat size, she is easily fitted onto public transport and at restaurants when eating out. Quite substantial and strong for her size, she has no problem helping her handler with basic mobility skills, such as helping pull off socks and other items of clothing. She enjoys retrieving and will be happy to fetch any items you need around the home, including your medicine bag if performing medical alert.

However, no dog is perfect, and the Cocker Spaniel can be very high energy, particularly the working-line English Cocker Spaniels. This means that as with all high-energy dogs, you will need to make arrangements for a dog walker if you are unwell, unless you own a farm where she can rocket round at 100 kph. If you hear a boom, don't worry; she has simply broken the sound barrier.

Not all of the working-line Cocker Spaniels are capable of working in public easily as a service dog, since they can struggle to concentrate around the many different smells that are typically found in an urban environment. Loving people as they do they can be easily distracted, with some dogs struggling to control their bladder, such is their excitement. In addition, some Cocker Spaniels do suffer from rage syndrome which is obviously a big no-no as a service dog. Again, it's a matter of choosing a reputable breeder to buy from.

Your Cocker Spaniel will need plenty of brushing, though she won't need to be constantly at the grooming salon, unless you want to show her. Her love of life and energy mean she is a good choice if you want to participate in agility classes or scent-work. She's a dog that loves people, so a service dog role where she is always with her handler is one she will excel in. She has a long life, with many Spaniels living into their early to mid-teens, which is also a bonus in service dog selection.

Before I move on from the Cocker Spaniel, I should give an honorable mention to the Springer Spaniel that shares pretty much every single wonderful characteristic with the Cocker Spaniel. I see them as very similar, and though there are fewer Springer Spaniels used as service dogs, there is no good reason for this that I can see. If I'm honest, my heart more goes to the Springer Spaniel, as a friend of my mom had two gorgeous Welsh Springer Spaniels, Zoe and Cally, and I spent much of my childhood helping to walk them.

There are lots of great medium-sized service dogs, so we leave the Cocker Spaniel and move onto perhaps the most famous service dog of them all. This breed needs no introduction—best described as the service dog extraordinaire, she is the Labrador Retriever. I have put her in the medium-sized breed category, though she is in the upper end of the size and weight scale. Apart from counterbalance and bracing work, she is suitable for every type of service dog role, as a guide dog, a hearing dog, as a mobility service dog, as a medical alert dog and also as a psychiatric service dog.

The Labrador Retriever has many similar attributes as the Cocker Spaniel. Good with people, good with other dogs, confident, kind and easy to train, the Labrador is smart and confident. What's not to like about this lovable dog? The Cocker Spaniel is buzzier overall, including the show lines, and a show-line Cocker Spaniel may be more suitable as a hearing dog and for medical alert service dog tasks than a show-line Labrador. However, a working-line Labrador will have no problem with these tasks.

If I were looking for a Labrador Retriever to train as a guide dog, I would more lean toward either a show-line, or a working-line Labrador that has been specifically bred as a service dog and so has sufficient drive for the task, but that will not be too high energy. There are many breeders out there now that breed Labradors specifically as service dogs, and these can be an excellent choice. They should be able to choose for you a puppy that will be suitable for the tasks you will require.

Although Labradors require plenty of exercise, other than super high-energy working lines, they should be able to cope with temporarily being in the house for a few days if you're too unwell to be able to take her out. Her wonderful temperament and confidence mean she'll be happy to go for a walk with anyone, and will be generally very obedient, even off-lead. The Labrador Retriever has a great, easy-care coat, which for me is another big bonus of the breed.

Like all young dogs, adolescent Labradors of working lines can be challenging, so if you do require a working-line Labrador to help mitigate your disabilities, make sure you have sufficient help with her training and her exercise. By contrast, we have all seen older Labradors in the park who are under-exercised and have turned to, well, flab. Mazey is saying something about stones and glass houses. I wonder what she could possibly mean?

In conclusion, the Labrador Retriever is now squished beside me on the sofa with the Cocker Spaniel. They appear to be pointing out my spelling and grammar mistakes, conferring with each other, as it seems they don't seem to want to hurt my feelings. Is there anything these dogs cannot do? Before we leave them to write this book for me, I should point out that both Labrador Retrievers and Cocker Spaniels are commonly crossed with Poodles (of various sizes) to produce Doodles and Cockapoos, which can also make good service dogs.

Doodles and Poos, particularly F1 crosses, being a direct cross between a Poodle of whatever size, and either a Cocker Spaniel or a Labrador Retriever, will more often than not be a little bit of a lottery. With an F1 cross we never know which characteristics we are going to get, so you may end up with a very high-energy dog that can be more skittish and excitable than you would ideally want for a service dog. Or you could get the most perfect characteristics from each breed. I would tend to go for a full pedigree dog of either breed, unless you are dealing with a reputable Doodle or Poo breeder who run health and temperament tests for their breeding stock.

I have seen ginormous Doodles working as service dogs, the dogs in question being Standard Poodles crossed with a Labrador Retriever, and when I say ginormous, think liger size. These Doodles always seemed to be taller than their Standard Poodle parent, in addition to having the same substance of their Labrador Retriever parent. This makes her a very strong, powerful dog indeed, one that could potentially be tall and substantial enough for counterbalance and bracing work. It can be difficult to ascertain how a puppy will turn out, so if mobility work of this type is what you are relying on with your Doodle service dog prospect, buy a young, green dog that has already attained the height and weight you require.

Funnily enough, the Golden Doodles/Groodles I have seen—Poodles crossed with Golden Retrievers—have not had the height and substance of a Standard Poodle crossed with a Labrador Retriever. I'm not sure why this is, though as with mules/hinnys and liger/tigons, genetics is a funny thing. If you don't believe me YouTube is your friend for the day.

I also want to emphasize that with Doodles and Poos, no matter what the "other" parent is, as an F1 cross with a Poodle they will almost certainly require professional grooming. Many Doodle owners buy them not understanding this, then wait until they are six months or older to drag them along to the groomers for a trim where they come out scalped, the poor groomer being unable to do anything else with their matted coats.

Mats are painful! Don't let them happen. Keep your Doodle groomed. An F2 puppy may tend toward not having such a curly Poodle-type coat, but then they may. Puppy characteristics may be different from those of adult dogs, particularly if you do not buy through a reputable cross-bred breeder who knows his lines inside and out. Bit of an oxymoron, but some do exist. If daily grooming and the cost of groomer appointments every six weeks aren't good for your wallet or fingers, perhaps pick a dog with a lower-maintenance coat.

Having flirted with the Golden Retriever, the Labrador Retriever, the Poodle and the beautiful Doodles and Poos, the last breed on the list is the Collie. I'm going to examine the Border Collie as it seems to be the most popular service dog breed of Collie these days, and it's simply not possible to cover all of the Collie breeds.

This is not going to be popular with Border Collie owners, but I suspect the reason that people place Border Collies into the "fab four" category is a historical one with their early use as guide dogs. Truthfully, I'd edge the Border Collie out of the fab four and replace her with the Cocker Spaniel because Spaniels aren't as nervous as Collies. Careful throwing those stones now, they could hit the Labrador Retriever and Cocker Spaniel who are currently writing this book for me.

I know, I know, Border Collies are incredibly intelligent and quick to learn, excelling as working sheepdogs and bearing an unparalleled reputation as competition obedience dogs and agility dogs. However, sheepdogs tend to work in rural areas, and obedience dogs and agility dogs are not working calmly for long periods of time in busy public places. Rather, they are working for short periods, concentrating intently on their handler in the controlled environment of the competition ring. As such, these Border Collies do not have lots of strange people coming up close and personal to them as service dogs do. Extraordinary intelligence does not equal easy to train, particularly if exercise needs cannot be met.

All that being said, the right Border Collie in the right environment will offer you a super high-energy, incredibly obedient, easily trainable service dog, provided of course you are the right trainer to cope with her exuberance. If her temperament is not a nervous one, and she is not skittish around people and other dogs, then you could just have the perfect service dog for you, particularly if you also want to compete in obedience and agility competitions with her.

The Border Collie excels at jobs that require brains and energy, so she makes an excellent hearing dog, medical alert dog, psychiatric service dog, and as a mobility service dog. In the past, yes, she has been used as a guide dog, but she would not be my first choice as a guide dog these days, where the speed of life is so much faster than one hundred and fifty years ago.

Your Border Collie service dog will require a lot of exercise come rain, hail, sun or shine. If you don't think you can generally manage this, along with the brain games and intellectual stimulation she needs for her well-being, then she is not really for you, particularly as she won't tend to want to be walked by a stranger. She has a pretty easy coat to care for, needing a bit of brushing to look its best so it doesn't tangle, but she won't need professional grooming. Once you know a Border Collie, she's your obedient, willing friend for life. But as with many herding dogs, they are super sensitive and many have an innately suspicious personality, often making them nervous and snappy with strangers.

As the Border Collie rushes off to prepare me a Martini (shaken, not stirred), I quickly want to discuss a UK breed that proliferates in shelters and shares some characteristics with the American Pitbull Terrier. We will discuss both together even if there is a quite considerable size and power differential. Yes, you've got it in one, it's the Staffordshire Bull Terrier and the American Pitbull Terrier.

Staffies and Pitties, as they are affectionately known respectively, when they are well-bred, well-balanced dogs, tend to be exceptional with people. They are friendly, loving, loyal and affectionate with adults and children alike. However, and it's a *big however*, traditionally many have been bred by backyard breeders and do have a reputation of not being good with other dogs, which sadly can be true. Not all are, don't get me wrong, but the reputation comes from somewhere, which is their genetic heritage. We can't get away from it. Many Staffies and Pitties are aggressive with other dogs. A service dog needs to be dog neutral at the very least, so a major concern with either of these breeds in the context of service dog work is dog aggression.

Staffies and Pitties are smart dogs and easy to train. They are confident and happy, with a typical bully smile. Being Terriers, they do have high energy levels, and where their needs are not being met in terms of exercise and intellectual stimulation, they can become destructive. Sadly, this is one of the reasons why so many Staffies and Pitties end up in dog shelters. Other reasons for surrendering the dog commonly include dog aggression (as mentioned) and overall behavior problems.

A well-balanced, dog-friendly Staffie or Pittie makes a good hearing dog, or an enthusiastic partner as a mobility service dog. Her loving, confident nature means she also excels as a psychiatric service dog. Both breeds have a surprisingly good nose, and can be used for medical alert. In fact, some police forces in both the UK[5] and U.S.[6] have taken rescue dogs and successfully retrained them for police work. However, most police officers are experienced dog handlers.

Unless this is "your" breed in the same way the Rottweiler is for me, one you see with rose-tinted glasses, I would not go for either a Staffie or a Pittie as a service dog. Yes, the best of them are outstanding, but you will suffer a great deal of prejudice and make life difficult for yourself in a great many respects.

So many medium-sized service dogs, so little time. I'm having one half of my face thoroughly washed by the Staffie, with the Pittie washing the other half, and so what better time to look at small service dog breeds, which will include toy breeds. Many toy dogs actually do make amazing service dogs, even though this is not in line with their original purpose, unlike Terriers who do have a working background.

Don't let the stature of small dogs fool you. Many are extremely intelligent and may be an ideal choice where the service dog needs to have low exercise requirements (for some breeds), and well, just doesn't need to be big. In general, small dogs are very easy for an inexperienced owner to train themselves, having a sparkling, friendly personality. Depending on breed, though, they can be a little shy, usually not wanting to wander too far from their handler when outside. Terriers are usually high-drive, but unlike a high-drive large dog, small dogs can be picked up if the need arises.

We're first going to look at the awesome Yorkshire Terrier, mainly as the first dog I ever owned was a Dorkie, a Yorkshire Terrier crossed with a Standard Longhair Dachshund. "Puppy" (yes, original, I know) had inherited the soft blonde hair of her Yorkshire Terrier mother, and although she had the long back of her father, she had quite long legs and was surprisingly athletic, able to jump onto a round bale with a bit of a scramble. I didn't know it at the time, but I inadvertently trained Puppy to perform quite a few service dog tasks for me, such as blocking people from getting too close. Rest in peace, beautiful, until we meet again.

The Yorkshire Terrier was originally bred as a ratter. Although she has morphed into an excellent lapdog, her working heritage still shines through, making her

My first ever dog: Puppy. Puppy was a Dorki (Dachshund × Yorkie) and was the best dog ever. Photo by the author (1989).

a good choice as a small service dog. She is energetic and brave, and has an incredibly sweet nature. Many small dogs can lack confidence and be dog-reactive, a disadvantage when working them in public, but the majority of Yorkshire Terriers take public access in stride. However, she will bark and yap at loud noises around the home, and, if allowed, may enjoy sitting on a window ledge barking at passersby. This can be very irritating for both you and your neighbors if the dog is not properly trained to be quiet on command.

Clearly a dog of this size cannot perform any mobility tasks that require strength, but she is able to help with other mobility tasks, such as helping to take off clothes. They may be small, but Yorkshire Terriers have a determination about them that makes games like pulling off socks lots of fun. She is a little small for tasks that involve more physical strength, including opening doors using a rope, unloading the washing machine or picking up large objects. However, small items such as retrieving phones or a (very) small medicine bag should pose no problem for her, as the breed enjoys retrieving objects and learning games and tricks. Their active nature makes them good hearing dogs, medical alert service dogs and psychiatric service dogs.

Her calm temperament (for a Terrier) means that the Yorkshire Terrier is quite content with minimal exercise, and where her owner may be incapacitated or bad weather has made pavements slippery, she can be kept content for several days just with environmental enrichment around the home. In general, though, she should have a couple of short outside walks round the block to do "dog things," including checking her canine e-mails by sniffing scent marks other dogs have left.

There have been many times tramping around the woods at midnight in the snow and dark that I have wished to be snuggled up in front of the fire with a Yorkshire Terrier. Some Yorkshire Terriers are trained to use a cat litter box or pee pad—a great advantage if you're temporarily bed-bound and cannot take them out for toilet breaks.

Her slightly standoffish demeanor is an advantage for a service dog, and the Yorkshire Terrier will keep her focus on the handler while working. As she is small, care should be taken in very busy environments where people may simply not see her and accidentally kick or stand on her. Some wheelchair users allow their dog to sit on their lap while out shopping, and I have seen people put their small Yorkshire Terrier in the child seat of their shopping carts which can (rightfully) be problematic in many stores. If going to work as a service dog, then all dogs, including small ones, should be capable of walking on their own four feet without being nervous or getting underfoot.

In general, the Yorkshire Terrier is good with older children. All dogs should be properly supervised with children and this includes small dogs, who may have a lower pain threshold and snap if treated unfairly by young children pulling hard on ears and tails. Bigger dogs can have a higher pain threshold and be more tolerant, but if they do snap, then they do more damage by virtue of their larger teeth. Train your children, people!

One of the advantages of the Yorkshire Terrier as a service dog is her long life. Many can work into their early teens and can live on into their mid-teens. The Yorkshire Terrier is not a brachycephalic breed and will cope better working outside in hot weather than other more popular pint-sized dogs. They are prone to dental problems though, and their teeth should be frequently brushed. Their coat will also need regular care. It has been said their coat is "human like" and relatively hypoallergenic due to producing less dander, though I would not rely on this if you have an allergy to dogs.

In short, if you want a very small service dog with a big heart, then the Yorkshire Terrier should be at the top of your list. Leaving the Yorkshire Terrier snuggled beside the cat on a delicately embroidered footstool, we ask the question: what about other small breeds? We have covered Poodles already, and if you want a small service dog, a Toy Poodle may fit the bill very nicely indeed. I won't cover the breed as a whole again, so if you need any reminders, please see the Poodle section earlier in this chapter. If you want a small service dog, but not a Yorkie or a Poodle, then which one? The other Terrier breeds, of course.

Terriers on the whole have the advantage of courage and feistiness over other small breeds of comparable size and weight. However, some Terriers can be hard to live with, since their quick-thinking minds must be kept occupied, though this can be an advantage for service dog work where the dog appreciates having a real job to do. As I consider the category of a dog that likes a job, my two top picks of Terrier are the Jack Russell Terrier and the Patterdale Terrier.

Both of these Terriers have a lot of energy, and they are not the best service dog breed for someone who has restricted mobility and cannot take the dog for adequate daily walks. However, for the person looking for a hard-working small service dog with a genuine work ethic, then the Jack Russell Terrier and the Patterdale Terrier could be ideal.

They do require several long daily walks, including sufficient off-lead time, and can suffer from small dog syndrome, where they think rude large dogs need to be taught a lesson. Or two. By them. This is not a good choice when faced with a dog whose head is bigger than your small dog's entire body, a fact that would not deter them one bit.

These Terriers, therefore, require a confident handler who has owned and trained a dog before. They are not terribly forgiving if they think they can do their own thing in the park for several hours, then once hungry and requiring their tea, return back to the car in order to be chauffeured home in the manner to which they are accustomed.

As with other small breeds, both the Jack Russell Terrier and the Patterdale Terrier excel as medical alert dogs, as hearing dogs, as small mobility service dogs and as psychiatric service dogs. Being buzzy and easily trick trained, they will enjoy a game of tug or removing socks and clothing, in addition to retrieving phones and other items around the home. Their confidence in public means they do not easily scare in crowded, busy environments and will in general be delighted to greet anyone who wants to say hello to them.

Jack Russells in particular can be real barkers, and though the Patterdale Terrier tends to be quieter, don't count on it. Both enjoy digging and will happily dig under the fence line to escape if given the chance, so if you're going to leave them alone in the garden, even for a trip to the loo, make sure it's secure. They can jump surprisingly high, so don't imagine a three-foot fence will contain them. They are not the best breed if you have children who also want rabbits, mice, guinea pigs, etc. They may look at the cages adoringly, but don't be fooled. They have murder in mind.

Some Jack Russell Terriers can be neurotic, hyperactive and nippy. You've surely heard the phrase "the shorter the dog, the closer to hell?" Take three guesses about the dog to whom this applies. In general, if these dogs are not having their intellectual or exercise needs adequately met, they will rebel, and it is not the dog's fault.

Both of these Terriers are great choices as small service dogs but the owner *must* be committed to their training and exercise. They each have low-maintenance coats and have long working lives. They will mellow with age and become less inclined to start a local fight club chapter at the dog park, but their intelligence and exercise requirements should never be underestimated.

Most of the Terrier group has similar characteristics in that they are a lot of dog in a small package. But some, such as the amazing West Highland White Terrier, and the feisty but cute Scottish Terrier, may need less exercise. Leaving our Terriers to perch on the back of the sofa, looking out the window in order to protect us from incoming foes (such as the neighbor's cat), we shall move on.

Those of you with small breeds I have not included, for example the adorable

Chihuahua, or the gorgeous French Bulldog or wonderful Pug, please do not misunderstand me. I love these breeds as pets, but this is a book about service dogs. Yes, there are some of these breeds that excel as service dogs, but very rarely have they been specifically bought and trained to be service dogs. Rather, they've picked up the role as they went along.

Unless you want to carry your Chihuahua with you, they are in real danger of being stepped on in the average supermarket or shop. Plus, their cute looks will attract unauthorized patting. Yes, even if strapped to your chest in a baby carrier. Brachycephalic breeds, unless purpose bred by a breeder who is striving to deviate from breed standard, simply have limited health and longevity. The average lifespan for a French Bulldog in the UK is now said to be four and a half years, which is absolutely tragic.[7]

This short lifespan of the French Bulldog conflicts with the ten to twelve years quoted by most websites on this breed. There are some factors that may have skewed the data, such as the high proportion of young French Bulldogs in the UK dog population (given how adorable and popular they are as a breed). Nevertheless, if you are considering a brachycephalic breed, and have not owned them before but are an avid fan, speak to your veterinarian to get an opinion on life expectancy and health.

Before we end our journey through service dog breeds, I want to look at some up-and-coming breeds. The first one is a breed that is greatly overlooked but that can make an excellent service dog in the right circumstances. Meet the elegant Greyhound. Most sighthounds do not generally show up on service dog radars, as they are not the most obedient dogs in the universe. They have quite independent personalities along with a love of killing small furries. The Greyhound is no different and so her tasks as a service dog are a little restricted. She is suitable as a psychiatric service dog.

In the UK there are always former racing Greyhounds up for adoption. For a person firmly determined to have a rescue dog as his service dog, the Greyhound could be worth considering, depending on the tasks required. In the U.S., at the time of writing, there are only three Greyhound racing tracks left,[8] with one soon due to close, so rescuing an ex-racer may not be that easy. Of course, shelters are full of dogs, but as we are looking at specific breeds, the Greyhound is worth considering.

Clean and quiet in the home, Greyhounds can make themselves surprisingly small for such tall dogs. They do feel the cold and can often be found languishing beside the radiator. Due to their racing background (where applicable), the Greyhound's former living arrangements mean they generally get along well with other dogs their own size, and will have been trained to walk nicely on the lead. Unobtrusive but confident, they will happily and patiently accompany their owner wherever they go. Greyhounds require less exercise than may be first thought and after a quick blast, during which they are mesmerizing in their beauty, they tend to be quite lazy.

Greyhounds are not the best with complex obedience tasks or small furries, including cats, rabbits, squirrels and, sadly, small dogs. Their heritage as a sighthound should not be discounted, and off-lead exercise needs to be very carefully monitored. A reliable recall is essential. Your Greyhound needs to be set up for success, so don't take chances with small dogs running about unless you are sure they will not be a target for her to chase and kill. Put simply, she is not welcome to mix and mingle at the Weiner Dog World Convention.

The next contender for up-and-coming service dog breeds is an astounding athlete. She's the Belgian Malinois. Much of what has been said about the Rottweiler applies to the Malinois, with just as much caution and expert help required from a good trainer who knows the breed. A balanced, working-line Malinois is a wondrous thing to behold. But beware. Many just want to bite, bite and bite again. Like other herding dogs, they have more sensitivity and nerves than the average Rottweiler. And more energy. So much energy.

Be very aware that working-line Mallis are *not* for the faint of heart. This includes well-bred ones that look amazing in films, or performing dog sports such as IGP, or police work with an expert handler. Such a dog should be extremely confident and not demonstrate any nerves or shyness, though they will, of course, be sensitive. Most will also be aloof. Unless you also want to compete in IGP, protection sports or obedience/agility, go for a steady, brave show-line/multipurpose dog as your service dog prospect.

A well-bred Malinois means a dog from a reputable breeder, who runs health and temperament tests on their dogs, and who provides their puppies complete with KC/AKC papers—not cheap, unregistered puppies that may well have the A22/A22 genotype. The A22/A22 genotype has been associated with dog behaviors such as biting and viciousness.

The A22/A22 genotype is important because it's associated with out of control, neurotic behavior in the Belgian Malinois. An out-of-control dog should never be trained as a service dog. It won't end well. You do not have the dog training skills (nor looks) of John Wick. If, however, you are single and tick these boxes, and appreciate the more mature woman, then hit me up. What are you waiting for????

Don't believe the excuses for the lack of papers on a cheap puppy on Craigslist, such as that it's just a "reputable" breeder out-crossing to a slightly different Belgian breed, such as the Tervuren, the Laekenois, or the Groenendael. Or that it's an "oops" litter. Or that because the parents are working dogs, they don't need papers. Or that the cross is with a German Shepherd for this, that, or the other reason. You get the idea by now. Do. Not. Touch.

A Mali thrives on plenty of exercise, and again, like other high energy breeds, you need to have in place suitable people who can take your dog out should you not be able to. A dog slat treadmill can be a very useful tool for keeping your Mali well-exercised, both for when you are unwell and just generally, as they love to run and burn off their energy, even if indoors. They are canine gym rats.

A well-bred, well-balanced Belgian Malinois should be able to do pretty much every task, apart from counterbalance and bracing work, with some bitches being a touch too small for guide dog work. Even with a show-line dog, this breed is not for first-time dog owners. Don't think you're ready for a Mali because you have trained a small Terrier that may be a bit feisty but that can be picked up or dragged off in the event of a behavior problem. A large, feisty dog who actively scares people is a very different prospect from a small yappy Terrier.

I have recently seen too many Belgian Malinois, including show-line dogs, purchased as service dog prospects. Only one has worked out, and this was a dog owned by an experienced IGP trainer. The rest failed miserably, often as destroyers of houses, bored, under-exercised, out-of-control dogs whose owners increasingly stopped public access as the dog grew out of cute, controllable puppyhood and into adolescence.

One ex-service dog I know bit someone in a shop. One dog was just out of control, though it's fair to say the dog was hammered with too much obedience at too early an age, and she turned out resentful and sour. One Mali even attacked Mazey in a shop. The dog was escorted out, and I saw her a week later with a different family. She was muzzled and on-lead, presumably with her service dog career behind her.

I really hoped the poor woman who had the (now) muzzled Mali was not conned into buying this adult dog as a trained service dog. She was in a mobility scooter, and had the dog not been tethered to the scooter, it would have been game on as far as a fight goes. Luckily Mazey trusts me to sort stuff out and is not at all reactive to other dogs that may start kicking off at her. She just kept attention on me when I asked her to, and she ignored it. However, had the dog reached her and bit her, it would have been a different story.

And so, we are at the end of the chapter. I do hope you made sure to carefully read my short, yet fascinating account of how wonderful a breed the Rottweiler is. Seriously, though, there really is no breed of perfect service dog out there. What may be the best dog in the world for me may be a nightmare for you. We must all be led by our individual needs to find the dog that is right for us, both as a breed and as an individual within that breed.

Breed Suggestions for Mobility Task-Work

These tables will help you determine which breed of dog is suitable as a mobility service dog. The tables take into account your height, the minimum height of dog you will require, the maximum weight of handler each breed has the ability to cope with, and the dogs' own weight. I have used average breed statistics in creating the tables and have rounded up the numbers to give you a rough guide.

Human Height	Minimum Dog Height	Breeds
5 ft. 4 inches	26 inches	Irish Wolfhound male or female Great Dane male or female English Mastiff male or female Newfoundland male or female
5 ft. 6 inches	27 inches	Irish Wolfhound male or female Great Dane male or female English Mastiff male or female Newfoundland male
5 ft. 8 inches	28 inches	Irish Wolfhound male or female Great Dane male or female English Mastiff male or female Newfoundland male
5 ft. 10 inches	28 inches	Irish Wolfhound male or female Great Dane male or female English Mastiff male or female Newfoundland male

Human Height	Minimum Dog Height	Breeds
6 ft. 0 inches	29 inches	Irish Wolfhound male or female Great Dane male or female English Mastiff male or female
6 ft. 2 inches	30 inches	Irish Wolfhound male or female Great Dane male or female English Mastiff male or female

Dog Breed	Average Dog Height	Average Dog Weight	Average Bitch Height	Average Bitch Weight
Irish Wolfhound	*34 inches*. Max human height: 7 ft	*160 lb*. Max human weight: 266 lb	*33 inches*. Max human height: 6'9"	*130 lb*. Max human weight: 216 lb
Great Dane	*32 inches*. Max human height: 6'8"	*175 lb*. Max human weight: 290 lb	*30 inches*. max human height: 6'2"	*140 lb*. max human weight: 233 lb
English Mastiff	*32 inches*. Max human height: 6'8"	*175 lb*. Max human weight: 290 lb	*30 inches*. Max human height: 6'2"	*140 lb*. Max human weight: 233 lb
Newfoundland	*28 inches*. Max human height: 5'10"	*140 lb*. Max human weight: 233 lb	*26 inches*. Max human height: 5'4"	*110 lb*. Max human weight: 183 lb

Table of Breed Suitability: Giant Breeds

Breed	Size	Tasks	Handler Ability	Recommended?
Great Dane	Giant	Mobility Psychiatric	Good	Yes
Newfoundland	Giant	Mobility Psychiatric	All handlers	Yes
Leonberger	Giant	Mobility Psychiatric	Good	Yes
Bernese Mountain Dog	Giant	Mobility Psychiatric	All handlers	Yes
English Mastiff	Giant	Mobility Psychiatric	Very good	Possibly
Irish Wolfhound	Giant	Mobility Psychiatric	Excellent	Generally, no
Livestock Guardian Breeds	Giant	N/A	N/A	No, just no

Table of Breed Suitability: Large Breeds

Breed	*Size*	*Tasks*	*Handler Ability*	*Recommended?*
Golden Retriever	Large	Mobility Psychiatric Medical Alert Guide Dog Hearing Dog	All	100% Yes
Standard Poodle	Large	Mobility Psychiatric Medical Alert Guide Dog Hearing Dog	Good	Yes
Greyhound	Large	Psychiatric	All	Yes
German Shepherd	Large	Mobility Psychiatric Medical Alert Guide Dog	Very good	Yes, with care
Rhodesian Ridgeback	Large	Mobility Psychiatric Medical Alert	Very good	Yes, with care
Giant Schnauzer	Large	Mobility Psychiatric Medical Alert	Very good	Yes, with care
Rottweiler	Large	Mobility Psychiatric Medical Alert	Excellent	Yes, with care
Sled-dog breeds	Large/Medium	Mobility Psychiatric	Excellent	Generally, no
Fighting Dog Breeds	Large/Medium	N/A	N/A	No, just no
Wolfdog	Large	N/A	N/A	No, just no

Table of Breed Suitability: Medium Breeds

Breed	*Size*	*Tasks*	*Handler Ability*	*Recommended?*
Labrador Retriever	Medium	Mobility Psychiatric Medical Alert Hearing Dog Guide Dog	All	100% Yes
Cocker Spaniel	Medium	Mobility Psychiatric Medical Alert Hearing Dog	All	Yes

Breed	Size	Tasks	Handler Ability	Recommended?
Springer Spaniel	Medium	Mobility Psychiatric Medical Alert Hearing Dog	All	Yes
Doodles & Poos	Large Medium Small	Mobility Psychiatric Medical Alert Hearing Dog	All	Yes
Border Collie	Medium	Mobility Psychiatric Medical Alert Hearing Dog	Good	Yes, with care
Pitbull Terrier & Staffordshire Bull Terrier	Medium	Mobility Psychiatric Medical Alert Hearing Dog	Good	Yes, with great care
Belgian Malinois	Large Medium	Mobility Psychiatric Medical Alert Hearing Dog Guide Dog	Excellent	Yes, with care

Table of Breed Suitability: Small Breeds

Breed	Size	Tasks	Handler Ability	Recommended?
Yorkshire Terrier	Small	Psychiatric Medical Alert Hearing Dog	All	Yes
West Highland White Terrier	Small	Psychiatric Hearing Dog	All	Yes
Scottish Terrier	Small	Psychiatric Hearing Dog	All	Yes
French Bulldog	Small	Psychiatric	All	Yes, with care
Pug	Small	Psychiatric	All	Yes, with care
Patterdale Terrier	Small	Psychiatric Medical Alert Hearing Dog	Good	Yes
Jack Russell Terrier	Small	Psychiatric Medical Alert Hearing Dog	Good	Yes

Chapter Six

How to Get Your Grubby Mitts
on a Service Dog

This chapter deals with obtaining a service dog the good old-fashioned way. In other words, not stealing or otherwise appropriating one by nefarious means. You meet all sorts when you own a service dog, you know. Anyway, we have three main options: getting a dog from (a) a service dog charity/organization or (b) a private service dog provider/trainer—remembering (a) and (b) can be virtually identical in practice—or (c) training your own service dog.

I'm going to use the term "charities/organizations" instead of separating them out, as they can be virtually identical, though legal structure will vary depending on the country you live in. A private seller, on the other hand, can charge what they like and do not have to comply with the strict rules that charities/organizations do regarding fundraising, charitable donations and who runs the business. However, a private service provider will receive no public funding or help should they fall on hard times, meaning if you buy a dog from a private seller and they go bust, you may not have any recourse to have your money refunded, which may sometimes be the case when a government body bails out a charity/organization.

Having determined what a charity/organization is, we are going to first examine obtaining a service dog from the type of charity/organization that trains the dog for you, providing you with a fully-trained service dog, usually after a period at a training center. There are pros and cons of obtaining a service dog trained entirely by a charity/organization and since we are optimistic little puppies, we are going to look at the benefits first.

One of the great benefits is cost. Most charities do not charge for the service dogs they provide to disabled clients, with organizations charging a substantial percentage below the cost to breed or source and then train a dog. Given how expensive it is to breed/source and then train a service dog, though, you may have to go with a service dog trained by a charity as even the sums charged by an organization could be too much. Some privately trained service dogs may be comparable in price to those trained by an organization, but you have to be very careful about the standard of training and task-work of the dog provided.

Different types of service dogs will cost different amounts, since the training period can be anywhere between six weeks to two years. Guide dogs are very commonly charity trained, and are more often than not bred in long-standing breeding programs. From cradle to grave, Guide Dogs of America estimates that it takes two years to train a dog, and costs $48,000 to support one throughout her life.[1] That's quite a sum! However, other charities/organizations source healthy green dogs from local and national shelters, sometimes for free, and the dogs undergo only six to eight weeks of training before they are placed.

Times are hard, and charities/organizations have recently been diversifying greatly, including selling failed service dogs that are healthy and may have many good years of work left in them. Such dogs may be sold to the police to be trained as explosives- or drug-detection dogs, or to hospitals and schools as ESA or therapy dogs. Depending on the dog's problem, a minority of dogs can work for an individual with a different disability, though charities/organizations will tend to pass dogs among themselves rather than sell to the general public. No harm in asking, though!

Charity/organization-trained service dogs tend to be extremely well trained, or at least they used to be. The force-free/purely positive ideology many charities/organizations now adopt has resulted in a significant drop in the standard of obedience of charity/organization-trained service dogs. However, it must be said: in the past too much force was used in the training of some service dogs. It was common to see sad, shut down dogs that were dead behind the eyes, trudging around stores as if they had descended into one of the nine circles of hell.

A good charity/organization will produce well-behaved service dogs, trained kindly with plenty of rewards, but also with boundaries firmly put in place. The dog receives an excellent standard of training, which is a *huge* advantage. The charity/organization may have been operating for many years, and may be expert in the training of service dogs for this type of task-work. Over the years it will have developed sophisticated training programs for both the service dogs and their new disabled handlers, often involving a complex handover in bespoke facilities.

Big charity/organization programs will have many dogs graduating at one time, and therefore have a bigger pool of dogs to choose from when matching you with a suitable dog. In general, best efforts will be made to match you with a dog that suits your personality, living conditions and lifestyle, including whether you work, if you live in the town or countryside, etc., etc. Smaller programs may not have this luxury, and if you and your assigned dog do not click with one another, it could be quite a wait to be assigned another dog, even if you remain at the top rung of the waiting list ladder and don't plummet to the bottom of the snake's tail.

However, we can't discuss charity/organization-trained dogs without mentioning the word "conformity." This is a word I'm not fond of, but when it comes to service dogs, this word can be a good thing. Pinky promise! Service dogs coming from a charity/organization should all be trained to a certain minimum standard, and a disabled person receiving a dog from such a charity/organization should be confident in the obedience and the skills of the dog they are going to get.

This is not just a matter of the actual standard of basic training, but also with respect to the tasks the dog will be trained to perform, and how the dog will perform them. Humans are creatures of habit. When an old service dog retires, it must be disconcerting to have to work with a new service dog, never mind that the service dog is working in a totally different way, responding to different commands, etc. In these circumstances, conformity can be great.

Access rights are another big advantage with charity/organization-trained service dogs. Service dogs that come from nationally recognized charities/organizations tend to have an easier time accessing facilities and services, including international air travel. It should not be this way, but it is. Unfortunately, some service dog charities/organizations have grouped together to form national/international bodies and have been known to promote to individuals and businesses the idea that owner-trained dogs are inferior to their dogs, or even illegal, and must not be given access rights. This is simply not the case.

Price, excellent standard of training, conformity and easy public access rights are very big pluses. Very big indeed. So what are the negatives? Well, many of the negatives relate to the positives! The price of obtaining a dog from a charity/organization may be far too high for ordinary people, including the most profoundly disabled who are unable to work. Oh, the irony. This can be especially true for charities/organizations that train service dogs for children, including autistic children.

After all, people will do anything for their kids. They'll remortgage their house if they have to in order to obtain an expensive service dog. Sadly, some charities/organizations will take advantage of this, particularly the ones that have a captive market with little to no competition. If I'm honest, I have real anger as regards some of the charities/organizations that deal with autistic children. Some charities/organizations cut off help to autistic children when they reach a certain age, and others demand kids undergo ABA (torture, for want of a better word) to receive a dog.

As I have briefly mentioned, some service dogs from charities/organizations are no longer very well trained. It is what it is, though it has to be said: if I was paying a lot of money for a service dog, I would not be pleased if the dog settled herself onto the sofa and started telling me what to do. In a parallel universe I can imagine a newly arrived Mazey demanding I hotfoot it down to the butcher (alone) for some bones while she had a snooze. To settle her in, you understand.

This leads into the topic of conformity. I, for one, do not like being told what I can and cannot do—for example, being forced to put a head-collar on my service dog, particularly if it's clear the dog doesn't like wearing it. No. Just no. I'm also not a fan of my service dog having to wear a vest or cape which advertises which charity/organization my dog has been trained by, and hence what my disabilities are, to everyone. My actual disabilities are a private matter. If I choose to tell a person what they are, then it's all well and good, but I should not be forced into being a walking advertisement for a charity/organization. This may seem a bit hypocritical having written a book all about me, but there you go. I'm a woman of a certain age and being contrary is my prerogative.

If you own the service dog provided by the charity/organization, and if you refuse to use a head-collar or want to switch to a balanced method of training, then you may be asked to leave the program and return any vests, capes and identification that were furnished. As you can then work the dog as an owner-trained dog, this may not be a big deal.

However, many charities/organizations can be spiteful and will inform third parties such as a housing provider that the dog is no longer affiliated with the charity/organization and is therefore no longer a qualified service dog. This is, of course, false. The service dog is still a service dog and separation from a charity/organization does not change the dog's legal status. But you can see how such actions by a charity/organization could be problematic.

This might sound bad, but this is not the half of it! Even though you may have paid a lot of money to a charity/organization for a service dog, the dog could in fact only be leased to you—that is, the dog is not legally yours at all. In such an instance you will have to conform and comply exactly with the charities/organizations' requirements, or they may take the dog back. This can relate to all manner of things, from the way you train your dog, to the equipment your dog wears, to where you live. If you move into a care home or are going to be in a hospital for several months, your dog may be removed from you and placed with another person, never to be seen again. In such circumstances, don't expect a refund on the price you paid to lease the dog.

Some charities/organizations will require you to hand a dog back when the dog retires. They may not give you the option to keep your service dog, whether you get another service dog from them or not. Having to return a service dog you have relied on for your well-being and independence would be absolutely heartbreaking. I would advise where possible to make sure you are the legal owner of your charity/organization-provided service dog so that she cannot be forcibly removed from you.

Of course, some people are not in a position to own two dogs and may have to give up their service dog on retirement, no matter how much they love their dog. If you have to do this, it's not for anyone else to judge you. In such an instance it would be preferable that a charity/organization own your dog and thus be responsible for finding a good retirement home and any specialist veterinary treatment she may need in her old age.

When getting a dog from charities/organizations, another issue is that they will generally take all responsibility for assessing your needs and partnering you with a dog. They won't always listen to your opinion, or if they do, won't necessarily act on such information. I can fully understand that giving the power and decision making to an expert in the field may be a great comfort to many people when looking for a service dog. For others like me, it would be like being forced into an arranged marriage to my nemesis. I simply can't imagine being told what my needs are, and which dog I have to accept. Heaven forbid, I may be assigned any breed but a super duper Rottweiler. Blasphemy of the highest order!

Many charities/organizations are experts in only one area of disability. If you have complex needs as I do, you may not find a charity/organization that can help you. Mazey does light guiding work, mobility work, medical alert tasks and psychiatric work. Whew! Talk about a Jack of all trades but master of none. Were you about to nip my bum, Mazey? I said you were a master of *all* trades. Ahem, are my pants really on fire? Anyway, a great many service dogs are the same as Mazey, spanning many areas of task-work, though this is more common with privately purchased or owner-trained service dogs.

With a charity/organization-trained service dog, you may not be given much choice in the tasks the dog will perform. The tasks will not necessarily be decided based on your needs but rather on a descriptor of your disability. Some tasks may be obsolete for you, whereas the dog hasn't been trained to perform others that you do need. Most charity/organization trainers are not disabled themselves, and as such may not fully understand the disabilities they are working with. If the charity/organization will let you train the dog for these additional tasks on your own or in conjunction with another trainer, then happy days.

In my mind, perhaps the biggest disadvantage of obtaining a service dog from a charity/organization is the time it takes to receive a dog. This tends to be particularly applicable to charities that provide dogs for free or at a very low price. The number of dogs trained simply cannot keep up with the number of applicants, and it can take two or three years to be provided with a service dog after your application is approved, which can take six months or more.

Even those whose current service dog is retiring can suffer a long wait for a replacement. In such situations, including the unexpected retirement of young dogs, you would imagine an immediate replacement is provided. Not so. Generally you will wait for a dog along with everyone else, irrespective that it's not your fault you no longer have a service dog. Having depended on a service dog for your independence and health, this must be very hard. It's a big reason why many people switch from a charity/organization-provided service dog to training their own dog.

If you're looking at getting a dog from a charity/organization, please don't let me put you off. As an autistic person, I do have quite unusual needs, not to mention black-and-white thinking. Being given misleading information and being told that I was not disabled enough to be eligible for a service dog from a charity/organization were very off-putting for me. On top of that, there's the issue of how UK charities have behaved toward the owner-trained service dog community, which is nothing short of disgraceful.

For many people who do not share my circumstances, a charity/organization-provided dog can be an outstanding choice. It really can. I'm not saying this with gritted teeth and a revolver to my head. Much will depend on the urgency of getting a service dog, the individual's financial situation and type of disability, the range of tasks/type of dog required, and the matter of owning the service dog outright versus simply leasing the dog, bearing in mind this may be a plus for some people and a minus for others.

The next way of sourcing a service dog is to buy a fully trained dog privately. There are not that many vendors who sell service dogs in this way, mainly due to the complexity and length of time it can take to properly train a dog to work in public, never mind adding task-work, particularly given the low profit margin most sellers would realize.

A private seller who will receive no charitable donations or government funding has to rely solely on selling dogs for their income, which is a risky business. Once a dog is sold and has been handed over, the new purchaser may very well ignore the seller's advice and mess up the dog's training. He may want to return the dog several months later for a full refund, with no fault on the part of the dog or her trainer. If you only train and sell several dogs per year, one or two returns could destroy your entire business. For most dog trainers, given the amount of profit compared to the stress and risk, training service dogs is simply not worth it.

Several years ago in the UK, there were some sellers who suddenly appeared offering service dogs. Unfortunately, it was little more than a scam. The dogs being sold were affordable(ish), but had a very poor level of public access training and were neither obedient nor confident in public places. Their task-work was either nonexistent or poorly executed. The company shut down after multiple complaints, but there are still dogs who occasionally pop up that have been inadequately privately trained and then cheaply sold. However, there are still a small minority of people who do privately sell very nice service dogs, often in a specific area as they are experts in training for that specialized area of task-work.

Sometimes private service dogs are sold before they even start task-work. They are very green dogs that have been trained to behave well in public and are now ready to learn task-work, often with another trainer. Some trainers will sell a green dog, and then for an extra fee will train for the task-work a specific owner requires. This can be great if you have very specific needs and require maximum flexibility.

One last thing that has put off many trainers from selling privately trained service dogs is the attitude of some of the aforementioned international service dog organizations. More often than not they will only accept members that are charities/organizations, which can make it hard for a private seller to maintain credibility, especially when the organization is providing false information regarding owner-trained dogs, which in their view includes service dogs that have been privately trained and then sold.

Whichever service dog you go for, whether buying a green or fully task-trained service dog, make sure the dog is healthy. Ideally the dog will have a minimum of scored hip and elbow x-rays that can be confirmed via microchip or ear/lip tattoo. A full clinical health examination, including blood tests and urine samples, should be done by your own veterinarian on arrival, or an independent veterinarian in the area before the dog is transported. Do not take the word of the seller's veterinarian.

We like to think veterinarians are all honest, and for the most part they are. However, as with any profession, there are people good at their jobs and people not so good, plus the odd bad apple. For such an important and expensive purchase as a service dog, make sure a trusted veterinarian of your own choice is involved in the vetting process. Blindly trusting the word of other people is never a good move. You should carefully check the credentials both of the dog's trainer and the attending veterinarian, where an independent veterinarian is used.

In conclusion, buying privately can work well if you do your research and find a reputable private seller who has an excellent reputation as a trainer and who has put sufficient work, time and effort into the service dog they are selling. Such a dog will not be cheap, even if the dog has no task-work, and has only undergone solid public access training. The flexibility that a good, privately sourced dog can offer may be far and away the best option for those who can afford to pay for such a service dog that is a rare and exotic flower indeed. The dog, not the seller.

However, don't despair if a charity/organization dog is not an option and you can't find a privately trained dog for sale. Owner training is taking off and can be a fantastic choice for many people, myself included. Hence, we have kept the best for last. There are lots of options with owner training, from doing everything yourself to working with a local trainer weekly, to buying a dog and then sending her away for a board and train. Those who take such a route receive a fully trained service dog that performs all the tasks they need to mitigate their disabilities.

A sort of hybrid between owner training and buying a fully trained private service dog for sale, then, is to buy a dog that you own and to then send her away for training at a certain stage(s) of her life, perhaps once, perhaps several times. This means you can select the breed you want or pay the trainer to source a puppy or young green dog for you, whichever suits your time, experience and wallet.

A puppy would ideally stay with you for bonding and go away for task-training when approximately one year old, or for public access training as and when required. Or you may feel unable to cope with a puppy and want the trainer to source and train a nice green dog for you. This is a solution which offers maximum flexibility in terms of the dog, the trainer, training ideology, the speed of training the dog, and the tasks the dog is trained to do. The downside is this could prove expensive, depending on how much or how little of the process you carry out yourself.

In addition to hiring a private trainer to help you, or going to bog-standard dog training classes, there are more and more charities/organizations that specifically help people who are owner training their own service dogs. This route is becoming increasingly popular, as it can give you many of the benefits of a charity/organization, including experienced trainers, identification and legal backup, but also provide you with flexibility.

Such charities/organizations will range from those employing full-time administrative staff and dog trainers to those that are little more than one man living in his parents' basement selling you overpriced gear and an identity card, so thoroughly research which charity/organization you join (if any). Easier said than done, I know, as there can be a lot of conflicting advice out there. And often you can't know if a charity/organization is good or not until you are actually a member and have paid membership fees.

Owner training, then, can cover a wide range of scenarios. I would say the biggest advantage to owner training is the flexibility. You can choose your own breed, your own trainer and your own ideology, or a mix of ideologies. Maybe you have private task-work training sessions with one trainer who is force-free/purely positive and also go to a weekly group class given by a balanced trainer. You're not stuck with doing things any one way. All dogs are different, and there's no one-size-fits-all in dog training. You may set out to take a balanced approach and find your dog never puts a paw wrong so 99.99 percent of your training can be force-free/purely positive, the only force being a collar and lead.

Owner training may seem like the most attractive option for many people, and indeed it was for me. I have no regrets going down this route. However, training a service dog by yourself can go wrong, particularly if you buy the wrong dog and use the wrong trainer or training ideologies. This is why I have spent so much time on these issues in this book, to try and give you the real skinny. The transition from pet owner and trainer to service dog owner and trainer is not necessarily the easiest one. Behaviors we may accept or think of as cute at home, such as jumping up asking for a kiss, is not acceptable when the service dog needs to do tasks in public.

So where do you find information if you decide the owner training route is best? Well, you're reading this book, which is a good start. It demonstrates your exquisite discernment and incredibly good taste, even if I do say so myself. Service dog charities/organizations that help people train their own service dogs often have some fantastic resources on owner training, including access rights, housing, etc. I would check out some of these sites as one of your first steps, particularly where the information relates to legal issues and the law in your own state.

As regards actual training, you can take a lot of what is said on these websites with a grain of salt. In the UK, at any rate, all service dog charities/organizations are piously mounted on space hoppers, bouncing about on the force-free/purely positive bandwagon. This is great if you intend to go down the force-free/purely positive route, but if not, it can get old and be a bit patronizing.

Some of the self-train charities/organizations are a bit like the service dog

Mazey says training is fun, particularly when on the beach. Photo by the author (2020).

equivalent of Judge Dredd, proclaiming, "I am the law," even where their information is blatantly incorrect or just made up on the spot, such as "legally all service dog bitches must be spayed before starting public access training." That's a hard no from me on that one. Pediatric spays are not in a dog's best interests, and provided she is not in heat while working around other dogs in public, spaying her is neither here nor there and is a matter of personal choice. It's certainly not the law of the land, though it may be a requirement of a specific charity/organization for membership. Just watch out for incorrect and misleading information that may be provided.

The best, most reliable sources of information for the self-train newbie are the websites of state and government bodies, at least to start with. If you use other sources of information and there's a conflict, you can at least cross reference back to the actual law. The Equality and Human Rights Commission in the UK has a great PDF for businesses (and aspiring service dog owners), and the Department of Justice in the USA also has a fantastic page on their website, full of valuable information.[2]

There are a lot of online service dog groups on Facebook and other social media platforms, and my advice is to run and never look back. Ok, I get that there may be some friendly groups with nice people out there, and indeed I met one of my best friends in such a group, but only because he was the sole person to defend me when I would not conform to their proclaimed absolute rule that Rottweilers and Malinois should *never ever* be service dogs, as they are vicious, and they eat babies for lunch! Skinned alive!! Raw!!! Oh, also everyone should have a mixed-breed rescue for your service dog or you'll burn in hell for eternity. So, I'm a bad, bad person then. Sigh.

My own experience is that most online service dog groups are akin to cults. Like some of the more militant charities/organizations, they require complete conformity. If you don't agree with everything their supreme leader says, the members will attack you with a ferocity that would intimidate Attila the Hun. Yes, of course, there can be some wonderful, kind, helpful members, but for me personally the drama was not worth it. I'm happy to scroll past things I don't agree with online. You can't fight stupid, after all. However, I can't easily bring myself to leave in the lurch a person being attacked for not kowtowing to the supreme leader and his agenda.

There does always tend to be an agenda with these groups, and with that agenda will come a lot of misinformation, and the ramming of "advice" down your throat. Usually by a "qualified service dog trainer" and his cohorts. He will invariably be aged seventeen, if he's a day, and is training his first-ever dog, a one-year-old rescue of indeterminate breed, to be a service dog. His qualifications will have been obtained from an online academy, and he'll spend more time flexing his parents' credit card in order to attend expensive seminars and courses than actually getting down and dirty training dogs. Everyone has to start somewhere, but paper learning and all the letters of the alphabet after your name does not make you an expert dog trainer in real life.

So if you do join any of these social media service dog groups, go prepared with a bag of popcorn and a bottle (or two) of wine. Or vodka. Whiskey perhaps? Who knows, it could be fun! I'm assuming it's legal for you to drink.

When it goes well, owner training can't be beat, particularly if you have complex needs. However, I would suggest that you don't jump into owner training without having a good look at all of your options. Weigh every variable to make an informed decision. Practically, the sad truth is that you may suffer discrimination and access

This photograph was taken at midnight in winter, with a full moon. I would not feel as confident going out at night with a Spaniel as I do with a Rottweiler. Breed choice is one of the great advantages of training your own service dog. Photo by the author (2020).

issues for not having a service dog trained by one of the major charities/organizations. Plus, if you're the unlucky type, you could buy the wrong dog (that can't be returned) and never achieve the high standard of obedience you need to work your service dog in public. It happens.

On the other hand, if you elect to train your dog yourself, you will have incredible flexibility in terms of the dog you buy, the way you train her, the trainers you use, and the tasks you prioritize. I'm sure you've formed a picture of me in your mind. Can you imagine me with a Chihuahua, forced to wear a tiny cape promoting a certain charity/organization, trudging past the friendly neighborhood drug dealers in the dark park of an evening? Hoots mon! Okay, so the Chihuahua may be more protective and fiercer than my Rottweilers, but I would not want to put the size of her teeth to the test!

CHAPTER SEVEN

The Down and Dirty
on Service Dog Selection

Okay, so you know you want a service dog, you know the breed and you know you want to self-train. Now is the big moment to try and select your actual dog. The selection of your service dog is vitally important. This is the dog who is going to be your working partner, who will stand by your side through thick and thin, from divorce(s) to lottery wins. The dog who will no doubt receive lavish Christmas presents from the staff at your local supermarket. At this point, it should be noted that telling them, "Mazey would like a box of chocolates and a bottle of wine this year," does not work. It will fall on deaf ears, and you will get a squeaky ball regardless. Most importantly, this is the dog who will be your best friend and who may very well save your life.

Chapter Five dealt with dog breeds and their own unique characteristics, and hopefully by now you have a shortlist of breeds that will suit your lifestyle and the tasks you would like your service dog to perform. Although puppy temperament assessments are available,[1] in general these tests are not terribly useful for determining suitability to be a service dog. Rather, breed characteristics and the dog's individual personality are better determinants. For example, banging two metal pans together while singing death metal will not go down well with a toy breed puppy. Or any breed of puppy with taste. Good taste, just so we are on the same page. Apologies, death metal fans.

But before you can go to view dogs, you must know where and where not to buy your service dog prospect. This is not as easy as it sounds. There are some unusual options, such as from the police, and the more common options that spring to mind, such as reputable dog breeders. Much will depend on your budget, the breed you want, the tasks you want your service dog to perform, and the dog's age. This chapter deals with puppies: types to avoid and reputable sources for sales.

Service dogs are a special purchase, in that if the dog is unhealthy or unsuited for the task at hand, it can be literally life or death for a disabled owner. Even with a lot of knowledge about dogs, my autism meant I struggled to know practically what to ask breeders when buying a puppy, and I sometimes overlooked things I shouldn't have. I was tricked by a back yard breeder ("BYB") once, which left me suicidal as I had a sick dog, very little money to look after her and a less than helpful insurance company. Therefore, this chapter is from the heart. I want to try and make sure you find the dog of your dreams, whether that be a service dog or much-loved pet.

Most people who have a little knowledge of dogs know the term BYB. If you don't, please don't worry. You are certainly not alone. I will explain why you should

never buy your puppy from a BYB. If you already have, that's no reflection on you or your wonderful dog. I have made the same mistake myself. Although I loved my dog with all my heart, she unfortunately did have some serious health issues.

Before I start my rant on BYB in earnest, the first point I want to make is that buying from a BYB has ethical implications, in that it enables the BYB to enjoy a lavish lifestyle while abusing animals. Mazey says they deserve a good, hard nip on the arse. By her. Old though I am, I still have my own hair and teeth, but as you can imagine, Mazey's Rottweiler teeth are far sharper than mine. Even though I suspect menopausal rage would be of help. But I digress. Please, please, please remember, no matter how convincing they may sound, how well designed their website, how charming they are or the size of their social media clout, BYB always put profit before puppies. And that means you too.

When you buy from a BYB, you have a high chance of buying an unhealthy puppy, or one with a poor temperament, both unsuited for service dog work. Now many of us will know a friend of a friend that went to a BYB and got a nice, balanced puppy. One that is a well-adjusted member of their family, saved Auntie Marjorie from a fire, learned medical alert on her own, detected Uncle Bill's prostate cancer and is the best service dog **ever**. All achieved at ten weeks old. But then I'm sure we also know of a person (you now know me) who was not so lucky, ending up with massive veterinarian bills and even larger heartache as their puppy was unwell. My puppy's ill health almost tipped me into suicide, and I spent many nights crying into the fluffy baby hair of her ears.

BYB are easy to identify: they have frequent litters, they advertise on dodgy online pet sale pages, they place puppies for sale in pet shops, and they offer a wide range of breeds. They may offer to deliver your chosen puppy to your door quicker than your local pizza delivery. The list goes on. One thing they all have in common is that their dogs have inadequate health checks, meaning you stand a chance of buying a sick, unhealthy—and if you're especially unlucky—dying puppy. But don't worry, you will be a BYB expert shortly.

So what should you look for? All puppies should come with a basic certificate of health from a veterinarian, dated within three days prior to purchase or collection of your puppy. This is just one point in time, but at least you know on that day the puppy was healthy. This is not to say the puppy cannot fall ill with a health problem such as parvovirus after they visit the vet, or that they won't have a genetic defect that takes time to show, but at least on that particular day, the veterinarian will have confirmed the puppy is healthy. This helps protect buyer and seller.

The veterinarian will have performed a basic clinical examination, checking for ear mites, worms, fleas, coughs, sneezes and any other signs of ill health. He will have listened to the puppy's heart and lungs, and made sure the puppy does not have a hernia. He will also look for signs of congenital defects, such as an overbite, underbite or retained testicle(s). He will put the puppy's legs through a full range of motion, and make sure there are no early signs of joint problems. The puppy should be identified by a microchip or tattoo at this examination to ensure a BYB cannot swap puppies.

However, not all health conditions can be picked up by a veterinarian. Many conditions are purely genetic and do not show up until a puppy is much older. This is where health screening of the puppy's parents comes in. One example is Progressive Retinal Atrophy ("PRA"), which causes blindness, and which is present in many of the most popular breeds of service dog, including Poodles, Cocker Spaniels and Golden Retrievers. PRA can be prevented by a simple DNA test.

If you're unsure which health conditions apply to your chosen breed, and what issues your puppy's parents should have been screened for, please visit the websites of the Orthopedic Foundation of America ("OFA")[2] and the UK Kennel Club ("UK KC").[3] Please note, each country will have slightly different recommendations. Both sites will allow you to search and see what your puppy's parents *should* have been screened for and what they actually *were* screened for. In order to check the parents' health screening results, you will need their registered pedigree name (with exact spelling for the UK KC) and not just their kennel name.

If a breeder says the parents have been screened, but there's a glitch in the matrix, and that's why the results don't show on the OFA or UK KC websites, ask for written proof. If the dog has been imported, again, ask for written proof. Ask for it in English if you cannot read the language from an overseas veterinarian. Most overseas veterinarians will happily reproduce the test results in English for a small fee, which the breeder should have already arranged.

But I want a Doodle or a Poo! Yes, I know what many of you are thinking, as you gaze lovingly at a breeder's website, filled to the brim with curly-haired super-cute puppies, sat in hand woven willow baskets, accompanied by fluffy yellow chicks. But don't you board my trigger train! I *adore* Doodles, Poos and crossbreed dogs of all shapes and sizes. My first canine love was Puppy the Dorki, after all. That is not the issue.

Health screening of the parents of Doodles, Cockapoos, Golden Doodles, Poos and crossbreeds, in general, applies just as much to them as it does to the parents of pedigree dogs. Don't believe a breeder's patter that the parents of crossbreed puppies don't require health screening: at best it demonstrates inexperience and at worst a BYB. To give one very small example, Cocker Spaniels, Golden Retrievers and all of the varieties of Poodle suffer from PRA. Therefore they *must* be screened for PRA before being bred together to produce a service dog. The Australian Labradoodle Association[4] screens for hip and elbow dysplasia, the PRA-prcd gene and *nine* other inherited conditions. Nine. When you mix breeds, you may have to potentially screen for *more* conditions, not less!

Not all BYB are easy to identify. It's like that super-hot guy your mother warned you about and you thought was different, that you could change. Put him into nice clothes, stop his smoking in the house and sleeping around, and he'd be perfect. Right? He wasn't, you couldn't and the same goes for BYB. Some BYB are skilled at their craft with a silken tongue, selling expensive pedigree puppies with every health test under the sun. Excuse me? I hear you say. Excuse me? How can this be a BYB? Let me explain what to look out for.

Often a crafty BYB will be very self-righteous and proclaim they only breed with fully health tested stock, going way beyond the generally required health tests, looking down on anyone who does not do the same. Which is true. They have done lots of tests. Lots and lots of tests. What they fail to mention is that although countless health tests were performed, not all were passed(!). Usually the most important ones.

Typically such a breeder will hide behind a raft of genetic tests that are extremely rare in the breed. But lurking like an STD in that super-hot guy are bad hips or elbows in your service dog prospect. Remember, your puppy will be too young for a hip or elbow score. All you can go on are the results of close relatives—parents and grandparents, but also aunts, uncles and cousins. The crafty BYB knows most buyers cannot understand the grading systems for hips and elbows. A buyer, seeing 15 "clear" remarks in the genetic testing, may not do further research on how to interpret a hip or elbow score. When looking for a puppy, check the scale for yourself and see what the average score is for the breed in question. Ask your veterinarian for advice if you're unsure whether the result is acceptable or not.

A legitimate looking BYB may also sell dogs that did pass their health tests, but which are very closely related to dogs with serious health issues that did not. Their unhealthy siblings, parents, grandparents, aunts and uncles could be kept out of sight in the back yard—hence the name BYB. Dogs that are crippled and hardly able to walk. Dogs your puppy sends a "Happy Birthday, Uncle Dad" card to every year. Not quite written in your puppy's own fair paw it has to be said, but what are credit cards and online card shops for, if not for this?

So. Would you buy a puppy from this breeder if you knew the facts? I would not. You would not. But the problem is, we just don't know about this BYB's antics. From the outside they look like a fantastic breeder. However, a breed club may very well know what they are up to, and a breed club is often a good way to find a reputable breeder when looking for a puppy destined to be a service dog.

There are also the middlemen, "breeders," who invite you to their suspiciously clean home, providing biscuits without even bothering to sprinkle a smattering of dog hair on top to give that authentic feel. There will be no photographs of dogs plastering every inch of the walls. The downstairs toilet will have no dog wallpaper, and all loo roll, although abundant and soft, will be of a plain pattern and lack embossed paw prints. The doorbell will not chime with a bark, and most importantly, there will be no sign of the puppy's mother. She will conveniently be "at the veterinarian," or "out for a walk."

Run and never look back, as this is not a breeder but the equally dodgy, closely related species: the middleman. The puppies have probably just been delivered from a puppy mill, where the dogs live in horrendous conditions and many are infested with fleas, worms and often with infectious diseases such as parvovirus. Do *not* take a chance on one of these puppies, even if you feel sorry for them. If a "mother" is procured, look at her relationship to the puppies. Does she act like their mother? Does she look like she has recently been producing milk? If you have doubts, leave the tea, slip a few of the biscuits in your pocket for the drive home, and *leave*.

Not all breeders are evil, though, and what looks a little like a BYB can actually be fine with more investigation, and the litter produces some nice service dog prospects. For example, unregistered crossbred puppies who have a pet mother and father (not related!), and whose owners have done all the necessary health and temperament tests, and simply wanted to breed a litter from their lovely dogs. The lack of pedigree papers for such puppies should, of course, be reflected in the price.

Though not as common as health screening, temperament tests are also important, particularly for a service dog. When looking for a puppy, temperament tests can be a good way of making sure the parents have a temperament characteristic of the breed. Often they are carried out at breed shows if the breeder produces show-line dogs, and sometimes they are required for license to breed at all, such as the ZTP for Rottweilers in Germany. Also, you can look to see if the puppy's parents hold any awards such as Kennel Club Bronze, Silver or Gold awards for behavior/obedience, or any working titles.

If you do end up buying from a BYB, or even a legitimate breeder, in some countries you may have legal recourse to get some compensation if you buy a sick puppy, either via a puppy contract as is common in the USA, or via legislation/common law. However, obtaining restitution, even if you should win a court case, may be difficult, as BYB are notoriously slippery. Plus you are still left with the absolute heartache of a sick dog who cannot now be your service dog. Nothing ever makes up for that.

Health testing and screening, including temperament testing, does not guarantee a healthy puppy suitable to work as a service dog. However, it does rule out many serious genetic conditions found in common service dog breeds, putting the odds ever in your favor. And who doesn't like that? Being disabled often means living in poverty if you're unable to work. There's nothing more heartbreaking than to save, literally for years, in order to buy a service dog prospect, only for that dog to have health problems after a year or two and live out her life with you as a much-loved (but expensive) pet, leaving you no closer to obtaining a service dog to help with your own health issues.

We've covered the ugly, so let's next focus on the good. Like a good heart, good

Always buy from a good breeder. Mina is an example of a well-bred Rottweiler puppy, with quality oozing out of every pore. Photo by the author (2021).

breeders can be hard to find. However, if you've decided on your ideal breed and it's a pedigree dog, then a good place to start can be a local breed club or society. Members may have upcoming litters, and if not, the club should have a good idea of breeders to avoid, or breeders who are not members but nevertheless produce very nice dogs. If you have your heart set on a Doodle or other crossbreeds, then there are breed clubs emerging that promote responsible breeding of that cross, including health and temperament testing. Look for them!

In short, a good breeder will be an expert on your chosen breed, carefully breeding dogs of merit. He will health screen and ideally temperament test all of his breeding dogs within OFA/UK KC guidelines. All of his puppies will be registered, with a five-generation pedigree; and he will provide a puppy contract, puppy pack, free insurance, microchip & vaccination(s), plus a lifetime of guidance and support. As with the BYB, take this as guidance. There may be cultural differences according to where you live, but be mindful of the red flags previously discussed. A good breeder is pretty much the opposite of a BYB.

So, you think you've found the perfect breeder. What's next? You'll need to ask some questions regarding the dogs they breed. Don't send the breeder a short text message, such as, "how much for pupz?" This will not go down well and will probably be ignored. Use the method of communication that suits you.

I have autism and am often very uncomfortable with phone calls; I leave them as a last resort. If I have an email address, email would be my chosen method of communication at first, until I get comfortable with the breeder. In the email you should be polite, but quite short and to the point. Be polite and suss the breeder out, getting some basic information.

You could start off by introducing yourself and mentioning your source for the name of the breeder. This could be from a local breed club, a Kennel Club list of assured breeders (as in the UK), a breed directory or even a person you have met at a dog show or supermarket with her own service dog, who has the type of dog you are looking for, and who has pointed you in the right direction.

I would follow up by telling the breeder a little bit about yourself and your experience with the breed. This is important for most breeders who care about their puppies, particularly if they produce large, high-drive dogs that are not for everyone. Remember to tell the breeder that you're looking for a service dog prospect, as it may be their dogs simply do not have the temperament for this type of work.

Just for fun, here is a sample letter.

Dear Count Dracula
Hell-hound Puppies

Ms. Harkness from the Waggy Tails Hell-hound Club referred me to you, since you currently have a litter of quality Hell-hound puppies for sale. I have previously owned two Hell-hounds and have been to hell and back with my disability, so I know the breed well. I am now looking for a suitable puppy to train as a service dog. I can provide a loving, permanent home and would be very grateful if you could contact me should you have a puppy you feel is suitable.

I look forward to ~~killing you with a stake~~ hearing from you.
Best regards,
Dr. Van Helsing

Once you have a positive reply from your breeder of choice—and it may take several days—you can start to ask more detailed questions about the litter of puppies, and expect to be asked questions about yourself in return. If you have owned a dog before, or currently have a pet dog or cat, some breeders like prospective purchasers to provide references, such as a letter from your veterinarian. If you have never owned a dog before, the breeder may want information as regards the trainer you intend to work with. Since he is selling you a service dog, he may ask about potential membership of service dog charities/organizations.

Unlike rescues, in general most breeders will not do a home check, nor ask to see proof a puppy is welcome under your lease/HOA regulations. They will, however, probably want brief details of your family circumstances—for example, if you have young children. They may also request pictures of your home and garden to ensure you have suitable accommodation for a puppy, and so they can give advice as appropriate. If you're lucky, you may be emailed pictures of the litter. This is a sure way to contract puppy fever, which is quite deadly, though it tends to wane at the adolescent stage, occasionally replaced with the "what have I done?" malady. Never fear! This passes quickly to the happily ever after phase.

If you're unlike me, you may be more comfortable with a telephone conversation as a first step, as often pertinent information can be gleaned more quickly, and you can get a feel for whether the breeder is someone you want to buy a puppy from. Always trust your instincts. If you don't like the breeder as a person, then don't buy a puppy from them. One breeder was really rude to me when I called. I didn't listen to my instincts, and though I can't say I lived to regret it as I loved my dog, I got no help from the breeder when things went wrong.

When on the phone, ask questions that are important to you, such as health screening of the parents, any show or working titles they may have won, the number of puppies in the litter, the sexes of the puppies, their color (black and tan, I hope!), when will they be ready to be viewed, how they have been brought up, e.g., in the home. Also ask when they will be old enough to come to your home. Oh, and the price and deposit details.

It's tempting to arrange an appointment to view puppies straight away, but often it's best to calm down and sleep on it overnight. If the breeder wants an immediate deposit, or says the best puppy will be gone if you can't pay in full up front, then walk away. There *will* be other puppies. When arranging an appointment to view the puppies, please discuss any mobility requirements (such as wheelchair access) with the breeder who should do their best to accommodate you.

If the breeder does not consider a service dog home suitable for his puppies, put the voodoo doll, sewing needles, bleach, and matches away. "No" doesn't need to be an insult. When you contact a good breeder about a litter they may be planning, or currently have for sale, the breeder will be assessing you as much as you are assessing them. None of the puppies may be a good fit as a service dog, and better your feelings are a little hurt than you spend twelve years with the wrong dog. Therefore, please do not be offended if a breeder turns you down.

Good breeders often have waiting lists for their puppies, and it's not unusual for these to be several years long. This is too much a wait for most people, including myself. If you can't wait, ask the breeder if he can refer you to another breeder who he knows is reputable, or who is breeding with his lines. Don't despair and don't hesitate to get in touch if a breeder's website states that there is a waiting list, as buyers can pull out and breeders will place puppies with the most suitable home, regardless of waiting lists. That may be your home.

Some breeders of the fab four and other popular service dog breeds do now breed with the intent of producing at least several, if not all, puppies suitable to train as service dogs. Specialized breeding like this comes at a cost. If you can afford it, often it's worth paying a well-deserved premium for such a puppy, whose parents may have been service dogs themselves. They will also have the requisite health and temperament testing you would expect. Not all puppies will make the grade, even from a breeder like this. But again, as with health screening, making good choices means you are biting on the heels of success.

Breed-specific rescues (or general rescues) may have puppies or young dogs available for adoption, which have been temperament tested for different purposes, have been fully health checked and are available for payment of a small fee. Often these dogs have lived in foster homes as part of the family and received an excellent early education. Although most rescuers won't look for service dog potential, they should have a clear idea of the type of home their dogs will suit.

Now, these puppies may not be from health-screened parents, that is true, and I *have* been rabbiting on about the importance of health screening. The difference between buying a puppy here and from a BYB, is (a) a BYB doesn't get rich off the back of suffering; and (b) if something does go wrong with the puppy's health, then the rescue may very well support you emotionally and financially, helping with vet fees, etc., so the puppy can go onto a working life with you, if possible. Don't discount the emotional aspect. Having a sick dog is *hard*.

If you have by now found a suitable puppy, prepare to raid your piggy bank. Good puppies are not cheap. Breeding dogs is done for love, not money. A massive amount of work goes into producing quality puppies, including preparing their parents for the show ring, training and entering working breeds in their own working trials, plus health screening and temperament testing. In general, the breeder works to produce healthy, happy dogs he is proud of.

Many breeders follow their puppies' progress for their lifetime. They want the best for their puppies, and when visiting a good breeder, please respect all of the work that has gone into producing their puppies. A puppy destined to be a service dog is a wondrous thing; a breeder will be incredibly proud to have bred her.

Before you make an appointment to visit a breeder, if you have not already asked, you should have an idea of the market value of your breed of puppy. Don't waste a good breeder's time if you can only afford half of the market value. Don't try to haggle for a discount as the dog will be a service dog. If the breeder feels it is appropriate to give you a discount to help you out, he will offer it in due course. Don't expect it, but it can happen.

I would say most, if not all, disabled people have been totally broke at some point, perhaps coincidentally when looking for a service dog prospect. If you can, it's best to save for as long as possible. Or, if that's not an option, I would recommend making contact with a local or national breed club. Be honest. Explain your situation and budget, and most will do their best to help you find an affordable puppy. It may be there's an emerging breeder who wants to make a name in the service dog world, or a breeder that has one puppy left, a favorite they would like to see do something extraordinary, such as save a life and become a service dog.

Put your feelers out to as many breeders as you can where there's no breed club, or where the breed club is not helpful. Often even the best breeders do have cheaper puppies for sale such as those with a cosmetic problem. Some Rottweiler puppies, for example, may be born with a white patch on their chest. This is a disqualifying factor for the show ring or breeding, but a few white hairs don't matter to most folks wanting a pet or working dog. A massive white patch, though? Oh, hell, no! But such a puppy may otherwise be very nice indeed in structure and temperament and may make an affordable, suitable service dog prospect.

Rescues will be much cheaper than breeders, and as a very last resort, perhaps a breeder would agree to a payment plan. I'm a wimp so would never ask, but as my mum used to say, "if you don't ask, you don't get."

Although it's a bit like going on a date with your crush, it's finally time to visit your prospective puppy. Similar rules apply. Basically, be on your best behavior. Be polite. Be on time. Call if you're running late. Do not arrange more than one date on the same day. Dress in clean, freshly washed clothes that have not been near any other dogs. Smile lovingly at the puppies that will be the breeder's pride and joy. Do not smile lovingly at the breeder, particularly if their spouse is in the same room. That would be creepy.

On entering the breeder's premises, you may be asked to walk through a disinfectant bath and to thoroughly wash your hands, then to remove your shoes and/or put on removable shoe coverings. For this reason, do not wear stilettos. Some breeders may give you clean overalls to wear. All of this is to ensure you won't put the puppies in danger if you are inadvertently carrying any infectious canine diseases. If the breeder requires none of this, it's not necessarily a red flag, just the sign of a very relaxed breeder.

You should already have determined that the puppies are being raised in a home environment, as this is most conducive to a puppy being relaxed about different noises and unusual goings-on. You will therefore be entering the breeder's home, so be polite, even if the kitchen tiles are reminiscent of a bad acid trip from the 1960s. The puppies may be in a separate whelping room, or they may be in a whelping pen in a common room such as a large kitchen or living room.

Depending on age, mum should be with the puppies. If they are older, mum may have had more than enough of them for one day by the time you have arrived, and be resting elsewhere. This is an essential part of weaning them, so don't be alarmed, but make sure you do see her with the puppies at some point, in order to ascertain that she really is the puppies' mother.

Don't rush into the whelping pen/room until invited in by the breeder, particularly if mum is there with her puppies. Bitches with young puppies can be very defensive and may not appreciate strangers, whereas other bitches will stand on them and crush them in her efforts to come over and greet you. Be guided by the breeder. Don't pick up puppies unless the breeder says it's fine or hands one to you.

Everything in the whelping room/pen should be clean and tidy with plenty of environmental enrichment for the puppies, such as puppy toys. The breeder is on his best behavior too, and as such should present to you clean, well-fed, plump, healthy puppies, with no signs of health problems, such as runny eyes, noses or bottoms, coughing, sneezing or lethargy. Unless the litter is very small, the puppies will probably have different colored collars on so that the breeder can tell which puppy is which.

Whereas small breeders may keep all of their dogs in their home, big breeders may have outdoor kennels where they keep most of their adult dogs. Most breeders will offer to let you visit the kennels and meet his other dogs. If a working breed, and if it's important to you, he may offer to demonstrate the puppies' father or other dogs of his going through their paces. This can be very informative. If the breeder does not want you to see the kennels or say hello to his other dogs, this should raise red flags. What is he hiding back there? As with the whelping room, the kennels should be clean and tidy, and the dogs well-groomed and in good health.

If the puppies' father is not there, this is not a cause for concern. Good breeders will use the sire that best complements their bitch, and therefore the sire will often belong to another breeder. If you do meet him, he, depending on breed, should either be neutral, or friendly and keen for you to say hello and stroke him. There may be a reason for a new mother to be a bit defensive, but the same does not apply to the father. Yes, different breeds have different characteristics, and every dog has his own personality, but a defensive or nervous father that does not want to be touched by you does not bode well for any of the puppies having a suitable temperament to make a service dog.

It may sound counterintuitive, but it's worth considering letting the breeder choose your puppy for you. Mazey, my service dog, was "Miss Yellow," and I first saw her at three weeks old. Even at that age, she was the breeder's pick for me as a service dog, mainly as she had initially been hand-reared and was one of the breeder's favorites. I still have the first couple of little yellow paw-print collars she wore while with her breeder. One, two, three: "aww." Mina, on the other hand, was also picked by the breeder for me (a different one) and was one of only three puppies, so there was no need for a collar. The breeder was far away, and I didn't know which puppy would be mine until the day before she arrived, delivered at eight weeks old by a pet courier.

Personally, I would at least consider letting the breeder choose the puppy or puppies he feels would best suit your requirements as a service dog. You may not like it, but it can be for the best if the breeder is a good one—and I'm assuming he is! The breeder sees the puppies all day every day, and knows the individual puppies, as well as the personalities and working abilities of the puppies' parents, grandparents and so forth.

I have never chosen a service dog puppy for myself, by myself; rather, I have relied on my chosen breeder to pick the puppy he felt would be right for me given my lifestyle and the tasks I require. However, the breeder may say they would all suit, and you have a choice. Or you may feel you would rather perform a temperament test than rely on the breeder, or maybe you simply want to choose your own puppy as you've fallen in love with one specific puppy from the pictures the breeder sent to you. These are all perfectly valid choices.

When looking for a service dog prospect, I prefer to keep it simple. I want a puppy that turns into a confident and self-assured dog, has a good work ethic and is open and friendly. If not friendly, then open and tolerant. I also want a trainable dog. Intelligence helps, but it's not the be all and end all. A "slow" dog may take longer to train, but once she "gets it," she will be a solid, reliable dog. Some of the most intelligent dogs that are quick to learn are the hardest to train, manage and to live with.

What I do not want is a puppy that turns into a dog scared of her own shadow, and that tries to escape and hide when unsure or afraid. I don't like a puppy that reacts negatively to noise, lights, or moving objects. Aggression is a big no-no, whether toward people or other dogs. It's also important that a service dog is not over excitable, is too sensitive, or lacks concentration to work in public. These attributes, both good and bad, apply to green young dogs ready for task-work training and also to adult dogs.

Unfortunately, many personality characteristics on these lists are very hard if not impossible to determine in young puppies, and to a great extent you must be led by their breed and breeder in terms of what to expect when your puppy grows up. I will discuss puppy temperament tests further below, but first I will tell you practically why I look for these attributes in a grown dog who is working day in, day out, as a service dog.

The positive attributes I list above are self-explanatory. A dog with a bold, confident personality will suit most handlers and be able to perform the majority of tasks that may be required. A confident, self-assured service dog will give a nervous handler confidence. I have autism and PTSD. On days I feel scared of the world and, in particular, people, Mazey boosts my low mood and makes me feel that by her side, everything will be okay. Heartbeat by heartbeat by heartbeat.

Remember, puppies are still growing physically and mentally, and are reliant on their handler who is molding them. If you want a very sensitive breed, which is highly intelligent but prone to being slightly nervous and fearful, it may be possible if your heart is totally set on it. However, don't get a puppy or a young dog. Get an older dog with a fixed and stable personality that has been fully trained and has demonstrated that she has the nerve, confidence and bravery to be in a position to give you the full support you need.

I want to see a service dog that is not aggressive or scared of people or other dogs. They don't need to be friendly with people and/or dogs—just have the capacity to be neutral and ignore them, not reacting or acting out. I don't like everyone I meet, and I'm sure you don't either. The same goes for dogs. My dogs Mazey and Mina love everyone and everything (their love of squirrels is from a gastronomical viewpoint, you understand) and that's great for me. But a dog that ignores everyone, is aloof and focuses on you, the handler, may be a top pick for many people, tasks and medical conditions. A fearful dog is very different from an aloof dog. This is important to remember.

Fear of people can often be seen in puppies when they first come home, and can be quite normal, particularly puppies brought up in a very quiet environment with no kids in the house, no visitors—just peace and Classic FM. Puppies also have fear periods, one of which starts at about eight weeks, just when they are due to come home. However, if I visit puppies in their own home environment at the breeder, it's a red flag if they're scared of me and won't engage in a game or be gently handled.

For example, a friend's eight-week-old Cocker Spaniel was "petrified" of her children when he came home and spent the first week cowering under her legs (which was unfair to him—he should have been given a safe space such as a crate). He turned into a lovely, confident service dog as an adult. He was only scared for the first week or so in his new home, in part, no doubt, due to entering a fear period while also getting used to an entirely new family and home life.

Fear of other dogs is similar. It's hard to judge in a puppy, other than one who shows an immediate, intense fear and is of a breed that is frightened of life in general. Many smaller dog breeds, particularly from the toy group, are quite rightly scared of big dogs and always will be. That's who they are. And it's common sense when you're the same size and weight as a hungry Rottweiler's head. However, if such a dog is to work as a service dog in public spaces, then she must learn to trust her handler and control her fear of other, larger service dogs. It should be noted that puppies from most breeds in the Terrier group fear nothing and no one.

When fear turns into reactivity towards other service dogs, then this is a problem, one I have seen time and time again. It's no fun being in a shop, rounding a corner, and coming face-to-face with a reactive service dog that suddenly lunges and attacks your service dog that is standing patiently by your side. Often with small dogs, the owner thinks reactivity to other service dogs is acceptable, since the dog meets very few other service dogs. This may be true; however, dogs are dogs, and two reactive service dogs can start a fight. Even if they can be dragged in different directions, passing shoppers may quite rightly be alarmed and complain, resulting in the handlers permanently banned from that shop.

While out and about in the wild, I have seen many small, fearful breeds of dog, ostensibly service dogs, strapped into the child seats of shopping carts, secured in handbags, etc. If they were put on the ground, they would be pulling on their leads and trying to run away since busy, loud environments clearly scare them. These dogs display tense, unhappy body language: the hair on the backs is raised, their whale eyes are bulging. The poor little things are constantly licking their lips, only pausing to leave a lip curled up over a tooth as they emit a low, warning growl.

This has made me incredibly sad to see. In part for the owner, who often is oblivious to his dog's discomfort, but mostly for the dog that had no choice in the matter of being dragged into an environment that scares her. In every case, these small dogs have displayed fear aggression toward Mazey as we have been walking past. The small dogs yap and try to lunge at her from the relative safety of their cart. Mazey's body language has always been relaxed, and she has always simply ignored the tiny aggressor, but not all service dogs would. I have also seen larger dogs, including Labrador Retrievers, similarly scared and reactive in shops, which is unusual for the breed.

Sometimes these reactive small dogs, most often featured in "Dogs of Walmart" memes, are fake service dogs. But more often than not, they are genuine service dogs who do a wonderful job of tasks such as medical alert or psychiatric assistance. I have seen small dogs who are sensitive and smart, who have learned how to detect an oncoming epileptic seizure entirely on their own, with no formal training. However, they were bred and purchased as pets, and temperamentally are not cut out to work in public places where it is busy, where there are loud noises, and where they are regularly in danger of being stepped on and squashed if not put in a shopping cart.

Over-excitability is another factor that can make a dog hard to work, including reactivity through frustration, not aggression, toward other dogs. Once again it's hard to assess in puppies. Instead, look to the reactions of the parents and also the breed as a whole. A service dog that urinates with excitement if she spots your best friend in the supermarket is not going to be appreciated by the staff, and will not make a good working partner until she calms down. If ever. I have met a couple of Standard Poodles that fell into the "I love everyone but can't control my bladder" category. They were wonderful dogs but were not good service dog prospects.

As I said earlier in the chapter, I don't particularly like puppy temperament tests, mainly as they're generally one point in time, on one day, and they're not designed for service dog selection. These tests lean toward what is preferable in a small pet dog that's easy for a first-time dog owner to live with and train. Some of these puppy temperament tests are free; some are not. In addition, many people feel they are simply not accurate at all. I admit I'm not always right, so if you must have a temperament test, the American Kennel Club (at the time of writing) points to the following tests on its website: the Volhard Puppy Aptitude Test, the Avidog Puppy Aptitude Test, and the Dognition Assessment.

For me, aggression and fearfulness toward people are always disqualifying factors for a service dog prospect. Although a tolerance of adults that may ignore them may be achieved in a fearful dog, the dog will rarely be happy in crowds, and who has not run out of toilet paper with the family due to visit on Christmas Eve? Children are also a massive worry with a fearful dog. Even though a dog may be used to children who live in her home, strange children who may run over and stroke or even hug her in public without asking for permission cannot be accounted for. No one wants to see a child, or adult, get bitten.

I personally would be hyper-vigilant, stressed and unable to relax while out with my service dog if I felt she was not reliable with everyone we may meet. Once a 6'5" bloke built like a quarterback ran over, got on his knees, and hugged Mazey tightly in the supermarket. Mazey, being Mazey, loved it and tried for a cheeky snog. With full Rottweiler tongue. The majority of service dogs would quite rightly have been scared in this situation, and an already fearful dog would almost certainly have panicked and bitten this lovely gentleman.

The 6'5" bloke, Alan, has Down Syndrome and no one had ever mentioned to him not to hug service dogs without asking. He saw a friendly dog with a waggy tail and they shared a really special moment together. It was actually beautiful to see. I had a nice chat with him and his mum, and whenever we meet in the supermarket, Alan is always polite and asks to hug Mazey. She very happily obliges. However, you can imagine what would have happened if a fearful service dog had bitten Alan. I don't think I would ever have forgiven myself or had the courage to work such a dog in public again, irrespective of what is reasonable to expect from a service dog. If I no longer had a dog I could rely on, I would lose my independence, as it is my only way of leaving my home without a care worker.

With my autism, I love that Mazey is super friendly. She introduces me to so many people, like Alan and his mum, and I feel included within my local community. Before I got her, I was lonely and isolated, with no family at all, and only online friends. I had no face-to-face conversations with any other humans for months at a time. Mazey changed all of that for me. However, it can be scary to be approached by strangers, and not everyone wants a super friendly service dog like Mazey that wags her tail, bottom, and body at everyone who makes eye contact with her.

Some people may select a service dog breed that is typically aloof, as, unlike me, they do not like being disturbed. This is totally understandable, and I can see why typically aloof breeds that are very handler focused are popular as service dogs.

Breeds in this category would include the German Shepherd and the Border Collie. Truth be told, Mazey should be a lot more aloof being a Rottweiler, but even within a breed, every dog is an individual.

It's okay for a dog to be aloof for service dog work. She may simply not be interested in being friendly to people, which is fine if at the same time she will be neutral and not react negatively if she is patted. This is very different than a dog that darts out of reach, growling under her breath if a person reaches out their hand for her to sniff, or that curls a lip if someone dares to look at her the wrong way, let alone touch her. Because I guarantee one day someone will touch her, most probably a child. Such a dog is a liability, and it's not fair to the general public, or the dog, to work her in public places.

Everyone loves a puppy, and you should by now have a good idea for what to look for in one in terms of basic personality. However, if you need a dog to help you with your disabilities sooner rather than later, then buying a young, green dog between six and eighteen months may be an excellent option for you. This may be preferable to a puppy that will spend a long period of time doing nothing but growing and eating you out of house and home.

A big advantage to a young dog over a puppy is the ability to make sure you are purchasing a healthy dog. Many orthopedic conditions such as hip and/or elbow dysplasia may have already reared their ugly head in an adolescent dog, and with a bit of luck can be picked up in a basic clinical examination of the dog by a veterinarian. For an expensive green dog of a breed that tends to have orthopedic issues, it may be preferable to have a basic set of x-rays performed, just to give you peace of mind.

In addition, the dog's basic temperament and suitability for service dog work can now be ascertained with far more accuracy. Calmness in public, reactivity or aggression to dogs/people, boldness, trainability and talent for certain tasks (such as medical alert), can all be tested for, irrespective of adolescence. If the young dog has received a good standard of basic education, she may be ready to start task training shortly after coming home, cutting down on years of waiting in some cases.

However, there may be disadvantages of buying a green dog, the main one being the cost. The seller will have fed, insured, paid vet bills, and trained the dog for far longer than a puppy, and so will seek a return on his investment. This is only reasonable. The prices for good young dogs have absolutely soared, and even for a dog with little to no training, expect to pay double if not triple what you would for a puppy.

An older dog will be toilet trained (a bonus) but may take time to settle into your home, and indeed introducing an adult dog into many homes simply will not work out well, or at least there will be a massive amount of stress involved. In my own circumstances, as I have two cats, I won't risk introducing into my home a young, green breed with a high prey drive such as the Rottweiler. It's too dangerous. Time and again I've seen cats killed in such circumstances. It's far easier to raise a high-drive puppy among cats or other small furries than to bring in an older dog and expect the dog to respect the resident cat. On the flip side, an older, curious small breed of dog that has not been raised with cats but thinks it may be fun to chase them may lose an eye to an angry cat that is cornered. It goes both ways.

If a green dog is for you, and your piggy bank is overflowing, then there are a number of places to find them. Often a breeder will keep a puppy or two back from each litter, to work, show or to breed from. If the puppy is not going to be suitable for whatever reason, then the breeder may sell her as a green dog. There are also shelters and breed-specific rescues to try. As with puppies, these can be excellent sources of nice, green dogs.

Depending on where you live, your local police force may have a breeding program and sell green dogs unsuitable for their purposes, but nevertheless may make a very nice service dog. For example, a Spaniel that would rather be reclining on a sofa watching *CSI* than looking for criminals may make an outstanding service dog for you (if you enjoy murder mystery programs, that is). These dogs tend to be expensive, but will have a good standard of basic training and character evaluation, and should come with x-rays and a comprehensive veterinary examination.

Also check how much your potential service dog has seen of life outside of her home. Although public access may not have figured in a green dog's life up to this point, if she's of a suitable breed and her personality is right for the job, provided she's had positive environmental exposure, then public access in and of itself should not be too problematic. If she has led a very sheltered life, and has a personality which is either over excitable or not very courageous, although with training such a dog may eventually "get there," it could be a struggle.

I met one service dog prospect that on paper was ideal, but was not a good choice for my friend who was considering him. Let's call him Harvey. A one-year-old show-line Labrador Retriever, Harvey was a very friendly, sweet boy, with a gorgeous fox red coat. However, he had led an extremely sheltered life with his breeder. At home he was a bit hyperactive but extremely willing to please, and the breeder admitted he had not put as much time into Harvey's training and education as he should

Choose your green dog wisely. Mina, it appears, would rather star in a reboot of *The Omen*. Photo by the author (2021).

have done, but he felt that with plenty of exercise and attention Harvey would make a great service dog.

In public, Harvey was a different dog, struggling with the most basic of commands, and unable to concentrate, shaking with a combination of fear and excitement. Harvey found it confusing and distracting to have lots of strange people pass by and ignore him. At home he was always the center of attention! Harvey was scared of metal under his feet, and for a service dog there's a lot of metal flooring about, such as escalators and elevator floors. Don't laugh, but poor Harvey had no idea how to go up or down stairs(!), having lived in a totally flat environment in his breeder's house and garden.

Harvey was reactive to strange dogs, not from fear, just excitement. He had only known his mother and father after his siblings left at eight weeks, and as he had never been taken for walks, he had not known such a thing as a strange dog existed. Trucks were to be hidden from and bikes to be chased. In short, he was a gorgeous dog, but far too strong for my arthritic friend, and with too many issues to overcome. Harvey was returned home shortly after he arrived, having enjoyed a wonderful day out!

Therefore, when selecting a green dog as a service dog prospect, in addition to considering the usual factors (breed, parents' health screening, health exam, and behavior in the home environment), I would ask to take the dog into a public place to see just how she reacts.

Okay, so we have found a nice, green dog that we have observed in her breeder's home. She seems calm, balanced and obedient. She has shown no aggression, reactivity or fearfulness towards people or other dogs. Just what we want to see. She may have a varying level of training, but she should know a few basic commands and be able to walk nicely on her lead at home. Depending on breed, she may be aloof with strangers, but should not be reactive, defensive or fearful if you try to handle her or stroke her. As we can determine more about her than we could a puppy, let's do a green dog suitability test for service dog work.

Don't worry if it all seems a bit much. It really is mainly common sense. You can do some of the tests, all of them or none of them. Play it by ear and the dog's reactions on the day. You'll want to bring with you basic supplies, including food treats and her favorite toy, plus a long line. You don't want her going AWOL. A lead sleeve and/or cape/harness that states she's a service dog in training is optional, but recommended if going into a non-pet friendly shop. You'll also want an experienced, objective person with you if you can, who may want to record the sessions. Ask the breeder permission to do this first, though.

The breeder should be coming with you, and the dog should be insured for public liability. This is his responsibility. Depending on how litigious a country you live in, should anything happen, you may want to make sure insurance **is** in place and you cannot be held liable for anything bad that occurs. Not that we will be doing anything dangerous. This is not a tryout for the SAS. Let the breeder handle the dog first, and if you like what you see, have a go yourself. That's what you are there for, after all.

Once the breeder has arrived, observe the dog's basic demeanor, both in the breeder's car and immediately on getting out of it. Did she become defensive and start to bark as you approached the car with her in it? Is she calm? Excited? Scared? What gear is she wearing? A prong collar, front pull harness or head-collar may indicate the breeder has had problems with reactivity, pulling or simply keeping her under control. Start with a quiet environment with no distractions, then work your way up to more exciting places if you're happy with the dog's initial responses.

I like to see a calm but alert dog, happy, interested in her surroundings, and attentive to her handler. However, there is nothing wrong with enthusiasm and some excitement in a young dog. I do not want to see a dog that is nervous or hiding behind the handler as you approach to say hello. For a handler with physical limitations, a dog levitating three feet directly upwards through excitement is not a match made in heaven. Watch to see if her demeanor changes over time and if she calms down/gains confidence.

Firstly, how are the dog's manners? Let the handler do a little basic obedience before you take the lead. Does she try and jump up to greet you? What does she understand? Are her reactions sharp or slow and uncertain? Can she concentrate in this strange place, or is she all over the shop? Is the dog happy to leave her handler and go a short distance away with you, or is she immediately worried, ignoring your offerings of verbal reassurance, treats and/or a toy?

In terms of her education, does she understand lead pressure? Does she pull? What about "sit, down" and other basic commands? Will she let you examine her gently all over with your hands? Very importantly, can you attract her attention and engage her verbally using a fun, excited voice? Will she engage when you're offering food, or does she prefer it when you show her a favorite toy and indicate you should play a game together? Do none of these things work and she's off in her own little world? Is she sniffing about oblivious to you and her owner, or is she visually scanning the environment around her, slightly concerned about who or what may appear?

Although this young, green dog does not know you, depending on her breed characteristics plus her own personality, a service dog prospect *should* want to engage with you if you're sufficiently enthusiastic and interesting, offering her something you know she likes, the owner having advised you on her preferences. Some breeds however will just not want to engage and work with a stranger, in which case her owner can be asked to do the tests. You can observe how she reacts with him, and how she may be expected to work with you once she gets to know you.

A dog that is too independent and that would much rather do her own thing than engage with you/her handler is not what we want to see in a service dog prospect, though if this is her first time away from her home, she may quite justifiably be overwhelmed. Again, this is not ideal, and although she may come around with work, it's much easier to start with a dog that has had a good basic upbringing and really wants to engage, play and make friends with you.

Put a few pieces of low-value food down on the ground. If she's not too excited, she should be happy to eat some. Have someone put down another few pieces, letting her observe the person doing this. Can you call her to follow you away from this distraction of food, either using a toy or great verbal enthusiasm on your part? Or does she totally ignore you, fixated on the food and pulling like Thomas the Tank Engine toward it, dragging you face down in the dirt to do so?

A love of food can be handy when training(!), but I like to see a dog more keen to work and engage with me as a person than she is to just snarf down a little bit of low-value grub. The best reaction of all is if she is bouncy and keen to come to you/ with you when called or when offered a game with you and her favorite toy. Some dogs prefer toys as a reward, some food, and some want to engage with and love on the handler more than anything. Everyone has their own preferences as regards their service dog's personality, but I like a dog that wants to be with me, including playing with me. This dog does not know you, but nevertheless, this test should give you a little insight into her personality.

If all has went well with the food, do the same exercise with a toy. It does not have to be her favorite one—you can keep that if need be. Can you still easily engage her? This comes partly down to obedience, but some dogs have more determination than others, and this can be a good or a bad thing depending on the tasks you want and what you are capable of coping with. A toy should be considered more arousing to her than low-value food, and if she would rather come with you and play with you as a team rather than picking up the other toy to play with on her own, so much the better.

There is no right or wrong answer in these tests. They are just there to give you a feel for the dog and whether you feel you could form a partnership with her. It's good to know how easily she's distracted and how obedient she is. It's good to know whether a toy sends her excitement levels through the roof, or if she's a calmer, more composed dog that still enjoys playing, but is more docile. Knowing whether she prefers food or toys, and which she would rather work for, is always handy, as is knowing whether she's a confident dog that is really focused on people, keen on doing new things and playing with a complete stranger. Or she may be more reserved and cool toward you, but very responsive to her owner, and the tests may tell you how she would react when settled with you in her new home.

Let's move on. Is she interested in lots of scents? A dog that is really into scents and using her nose can often make a good prospect for medical alert tasks *if* she will concentrate on you, and not just the scents around her. Some breeds such as the Cocker Spaniel will happily engage with you when asked. A bloodhound, not so much. You don't want to spend hours looking for your dog every night as on their evening walk they have smelled a fox and are off to investigate, recall be damned.

What does she do when a person she doesn't know well passes by from a distance? Then closer? Then closer still. What if they circle the dog and handler? Does she walk with a loose lead and ignore the person? Does she lunge to try and say hello? Does she hide? Does she vocalize? Is she defensive? Can the handler get her attention back when someone passes close by in this way? Much of this is training, but it will also tell you a lot about her personality, tendency towards fear, aggression, excitability and/or friendliness.

In addition to reactivity to people, you must also look for dog reactivity. In order to test her dog reactivity, you can also do the above test with a suitable stooge dog—a dog she does not know and that will retain a neutral body language and not engage her, or otherwise react to her behavior should she kick off. If you don't have a suitable dog, then don't try. The last thing you want is a dog fight. If in a park, other dogs will invariably pass by, so watch how much distance her owner is confident in keeping, and see what happens. Her owner is also worth watching. Does he tense up on seeing a dog on the horizon?

If you have a long line or can use a retractable lead properly, see how easily you can recall her. Will she come just by calling her name? Will she come if you offer a game with no toy? Will she come for food? Will she come for a toy, and what games does she like? Does she like a ball? A tug? Does she try and engage you in games, such as bringing a thrown ball back to you, or trying to put her tug rope in your hands, or does she take it and leave you behind? I want a dog that wants to be with me and initiate games we can play together.

If the opportunity presents itself, I always find it interesting to test the dog's reaction to a mild verbal correction. This may not be for you if you go down a force-free training route, or don't feel confident handling a strange dog, though I'm only suggesting something as simple as redirection such as "**ah ah**," or the word "**no**" for example if she is sniffing the ground and you would like her to stop sniffing and follow you on a loose lead. If she ignores you verbally asking her to come with you, what happens when you use a small amount of leash pressure? I'm interested to see the dog's reaction to an extremely mild correction, and hence her sensitivity. That is all. The aim is not to hurt, scare or upset the dog in any way.

With a green dog that is an adolescent or already an adult, a very mild correction is not going to hurt or emotionally traumatize her. So, if the opportunity arises, what is her reaction to a mild correction? Does she totally ignore the correction and carry on in her own little world? If so, why? Is she overexcited, so much so that anything you say will not get through to her? Or does she just prefer doing her own thing, and does not care if she is corrected? If this is the case, what is her threshold? Do you think she will have enough sensitivity to be a service dog that is right for you, or will she have more of a strong personality where there may be a frequent battle of wills? In some breeds, this may be the norm.

Ideally I would like to see the dog stop what she is doing on hearing the verbal correction, and look at you for direction in a neutral, inquiring way with no fear, at which point I would give lavish praise and encouragement. Then perhaps I would ask for a very basic command such as to come with me if that was what was originally asked, or to come to me and then "sit" whereupon I can again shower her with praise. I like a dog who is sensitive enough that she immediately wants to try to please her handler, but I do not want a dog that reacts in a resentful or a fearful way to a mild correction or looks like her world collapsed from something as simple as "no." I would worry such a dog would be too sensitive for the rough and tumble world of public access.

A service dog should tend toward listening to the handler, and want to work with him, enthusiastic about the adventures you are about to go on together. She should not be too independent, and she should certainly not be scared or nervous. If she is scared, then I would also be asking: why? You are looking for a service dog prospect, not a dog that does not want to work with you and may need behavioral modification work if she has been roughly handled in the past and is either shut down, nervous or defensive on being corrected.

If you can, test the dog's reaction to a surprise. What happens if someone suddenly steps out from behind a bush, or a parked car, for example? Or a loud, unusual noise. Being scared momentarily is fine, but what's her immediate reaction afterwards? Is she so scared she tries to run away? Does she bark and become defensive? Does she collect herself and think about what happened, staying still? Does she advance, and if so in what way? Is she friendly, excited? If this happened in a shop while she was working as a service dog, would you be happy with that reaction and able to keep this dog under control?

The tests set out above are generic, and there are many more tests you could use.

These are in my mind most important for a service dog. There is no one best or worst answer or reaction, apart from reactivity to dogs/people, defensive aggression, and also fearfulness that can't be quickly recovered from. I don't want to see any of these in a service dog prospect, green or not. But a lot will depend on the breed, the tasks, the handler and their disabilities. Look at what *you* feel you can work with.

I personally like a super confident, friendly dog, with plenty of energy and can easily get engaged with me. A dog that will want to play with me, with a strong work ethic. A lovebug that will be loyal and affectionate. Hence, I have a Snogweiler, a breed that is perfect for me, but "too much dog" for the majority of people who may well live their best lives with a Cockapoo. Or a Great Dane. We are all different.

This is all reality. Are some of the tests fair? No, not really, not on a dog that doesn't get out much and may not know you. But life isn't fair. Many people may say all testing should be done in a controlled environment, with an expert trainer. But life is messy. You are looking for a service dog that will stand by you come what may, one that suits your personality and needs. You need to do the testing, and don't be afraid to use your intuition in determining if this dog may be the one for you.

Similar tests can be used in more crowded, urban spaces, not just in quiet environments. If you're happy the dog is not reactive to people in an open, secluded space, then a little more pressure can be put on her in a more crowded street with a variety of pedestrians. See how she reacts. Will she walk on a loose lead? Will she pay attention to you when you try to engage her, bearing in mind you don't know her particularly well?

In this setting you should be able to see her reaction to a variety of people, including children. Do *not* take any risks getting close to adults or children if you have any doubts whatsoever about this dog's temperament, particularly if you are currently the one holding the lead. Look at the dog's owner as closely as the dog. If he looks on the point of cardiac arrest and takes a stranglehold of the lead when a yelling child or a jogger gets ever closer, take note. Try and find some traffic. What's the dog's prey drive like? Does she want to chase bicycles or cars? Is she scared of traffic, including buses and trucks? Again, use your intuition and if all seems good, perhaps try her in a shop.

When training young puppies and giving them environmental exposure, I don't like pet supermarkets, or other places where lots of dogs are brought into. However, with a green prospect, it's an ideal place to test her. If the dog is a he and not a she (the pronoun I have been using), is he tempted to lift a leg and scent mark inside, simply because lots of other dogs have been allowed to do this?

Again, we look at his behavior around people, any other dogs, and also new and intriguing smells of pet food, rabbits and other small furries that may be for sale in the store. If he catches sight of the aforementioned small furries, what does he do? His reaction may tell you a bit more about his prey drive and his impulse control.

I suspect that is probably enough testing for everyone concerned. You don't have to do all of this in one episode. You can do whatever you and the dog feel up to. Some sellers may not want you to take the dog out and just treat him as a totally untouched project picked up from his home. The price should reflect this, as this is a service dog prospect you are looking to purchase, not a pet. If you're fine with that scenario, be aware she may become a different dog when arriving in your home.

Some breeds you would expect to remain confident, to remain boisterous and to bond with you immediately. Others may have a bit of a hiccup, becoming shy or maybe a bit aloof. Give her time to settle.

Always see what the contractual terms are, and if you can return her if she proves unsuitable. The bond and the love are immense when you become a working team, and my dogs are pets first and foremost. But when trailing dogs, don't get stuck with a dog that turns into a pet because you feel a bit sorry for her and suspect she may well be unsuitable as a service dog. Not unless you can afford an extra mouth to feed, and to insure and train an extra dog. There is nothing worse than a dog you love but that breaks your heart time and time again as you try to overcome training issues.

Chapter Eight

Before Puppy Comes Home

Ok, so this chapter, despite the name designed to thrill and excite, looks quite a bit at insurance (boring). Stop! Before you flick past in disgust, we will also look at *bringing home a new puppy.* Pics!!! Puppy pics!!! Oh be still my beating heart! Although many of the most important things when preparing a home relate to puppies, they often apply to older dogs too. So all dogs in essence. I could have said that in much fewer words, couldn't I? Without further ado, let's talk about puppies. Squeee! I'm now quite overcome giggling with delight.

Sooooo...... I don't need to encourage you to give your credit card a workout when puppy fever strikes. Before getting a puppy all bets are off—for you, me, and everyone else in the multiverse. The Gods of Spending get free rein over my wallet, and suddenly I declutter. All of those old yet serviceable puppy-sized collars, harnesses, leads, etc., etc. neatly hanging up beside the door? Well, they disappear into a cupboard, out of sight and out of mind, and so *of course* I need to splash out on new things for puppy. I'm sure you are the same.

Chapter Twelve on equipment deals with the main items you will require for a service dog prospect, such as collars, leads, training sleeves, "in training" vests, etc. However, in addition to equipment for working outside the home, your house, garden and car will need to be puppy proofed and you will also need to consider insurance. Very briefly: unless you are seriously poor (or seriously rich) and plan to pay out of pocket for veterinarian fees, it's always best if you can obtain some sort of pet insurance policy, plus public liability insurance. More on that later.

Toys are one item you will buy plenty of, and I tend to have a toy box of articles the puppy can take and play with at any time. I also have toys that are reserved just for play with me. These are the best toys, which I keep special and separate so she gets excited about them. I use them for interactive play involving me, the toy being used to create engagement and a quicker, stronger bond with me. Care needs to be taken regarding access to cat toys that may prove a choke hazard, and also bear in mind any possible jealousy and squabbling about toys if you have other dogs.

I admit, I'm one of the crazy people that rearranges my life for my dogs, including my home and garden. Of course, a lot is going to depend on the puppy you purchase, your lifestyle, home layout and if this is a service dog prospect or not. There are some discomforts you might endure while your puppy is growing and learning to be good around the home, **but it will be** worth it in the long run.

Before bringing your puppy home, first of all be sure to puppy proof the room(s) you will spend the most time in with your new puppy, particularly should you need to leave her alone for very short periods without crating her, such as bathroom visits.

For you, not her! It's surprising how much damage those needle-sharp teeth can do in only a few seconds, particularly to cables, which could end up electrocuting her. I tend to put a coating of a non-chew substance on cables that are unavoidably exposed, so they are unattractive from day one.

Watch out for not-so-obvious cables and do a thorough room sweep. Pretend you're the FBI, just looking less for bugs and more for things attractive to puppies. Not so long ago Mina noticed a very nice box protruding from the wall under my bed (that I had not realized was there), and I was then without internet for two weeks. It happens to the best of us. She also once tried to jump off the sofa to grab a lampshade lightly swinging in the breeze from the window, but that's a story for another day.

Your puppy's first evening in her new home is important, so consider where she is going to sleep before she arrives. Dogs are social sleepers, adapting their sleeping pattern to match that of their owners and, if allowed, enjoying close contact with them. I see no need to banish a new puppy to sleep in another room like a nineteenth-century orphan sent to boarding school, unless you just can't stand having a dog in the bedroom with you. I have autism and noise sensitivities, and there's nothing worse than hearing that lick lick lick noise at 2 a.m. (and I don't need to point out where they are licking) so I can understand this is not for everyone long-term.

My adult dogs sleep on my bed with me, and I have a large crate in my bedroom for puppies, on top of which the cats Izzy and Levi have their beds. The crate is right beside my bed, so I can reach down and stroke and comfort a puppy during the night. My dogs don't get to sleep on the bed until they are over a year old, as Rottweilers do not mature skeletally until quite late, and I want to preserve their joints.

Until they have the privilege of sleeping with me on the bed, my young dogs can choose their bed in the crate, or a bed beside the radiator on the other side of the room. Whatever you do, don't just go to sleep with your brand spanking new eight-week-old puppy cuddled in beside you as I see so many people do.

Your puppy has no sense at this age, nor are they toilet trained. They can and will poo and pee on the bed, and can and will jump off the bed, and can and will be injured. You don't need to be the one contributing to your veterinarian's Bahamas retirement fund, even if you hope to be invited there on holiday. If you have put a mattress on the floor so you can co-sleep with your puppy for the first few weeks, fair enough, but if she's very small and you are a heavy sleeper and a heavier person, as with human infants, be careful not to squash her.

I much prefer to have a crate beside the bed where my puppy can easily see me, smell me (though she can smell me throughout the entire house anyway) and where I can reach down and touch her. Touch is very important for puppies, particularly the first week or so in a new home. I have had many a crick in my neck where I have slept with my hand dangling over the bed, reaching through the bars so my puppy can snuggle against my fingers. This touch really seems to calm a puppy, as opposed to just being able to see your slumbering shape.

You'll get a lot of different views on how to care for a new puppy on the first night. There's no right or wrong. This is just how I like to do it. The crate helps with toileting and keeps my puppy (and my stuff) safe. Sleeping beside me, touching me, helps comfort a sad, confused, lonely puppy. Do not let them "cry it out." This is your service dog, who needs to have an absolute bond of trust with you. First impressions count! She will settle far more quickly into a new home where she feels safe and secure than one where she is unnecessarily stressed and upset.

I get up several times a night with a young puppy and would do so even if just to take her to puppy pads if I didn't have a garden. I don't want the puppy going to the toilet in her crate. For a large breed puppy in a massive adult-sized crate, use a partition to temporarily create a smaller space where she will not want to toilet then lie in it. After a few nights you will be able to gauge how long your puppy can sleep without waking to need to go to the toilet. Alternatively, many puppies very quickly learn to wake you when they need to go out. All puppies are different. I have had some that are able to hold themselves all night from eight weeks on, others may be twelve weeks or more before they are comfortable to sleep for eight hours overnight.

Personally, I would not leave a new puppy alone without human company at nights, particularly for the first few weeks or even months, but that's just me. I'm sure many people are horrified that I share my bed with two large Rottweilers and two Bengal cats, though the window cleaner seemed rather amused the other week. I'm not sure he expected a lady of a certain age to live with such a menagerie, or at the very least he expected cats to outnumber dogs, or for me to have little foo foo breeds.

On the subject of company, I definitely would not leave a new puppy alone with other dogs, either at night or during the day. No matter how trustworthy and kind that other dog or dogs may be. Puppies are annoying, and your current dog is not the puppy's mother, nor sibling, nor unpaid babysitter. Mazey was so invested in mothering Mina she started regurgitating her food for her, but even still, they were never left alone together when Mina was young.

One of my top knicker-hiking moments is when I see lovingly shot social media posts showing new puppies slipping and sliding about on polished wooden floors, as if competing for an Olympic ice dance title. Sure, it's great videography in a pretty location instead of a muddy garden that looks like you keep ponies (and llamas) in it. Even dog trainers show such videos. But is slipping and sliding good for a puppy, adolescent dog or older dog? Not so much. Actually not at all for any dog, yet do we commonly consider flooring when bringing home our new pride and joy? No, hence the paragraphs below were born.

As my home came with tiles which are slippery, dry or wet, and since I can't afford to re-floor the entire house with new, non-slip permanent floor coverings, I put down some off-cut carpets in the living room, hall and bedroom using carpet glue, just before Mina came home. This was to make sure she was not in danger of slipping and sliding all over the slippery floor, damaging her joints. Once I'm a millionaire (I have been not so patiently waiting a great many years now) I will put down permanent non-slip flooring, but when I got Mina, fancy was not an option. So off-cut carpets it was, which are very cheap and easily replaceable. Admittedly I did just. Well. Put it down myself, meaning I … errrr … carpeted around the furniture, as I could not move it alone.

I have few visitors so some oddly colored, erratically laid down carpet works for me. It's not the 1980s and it's a dog, not a horse, so everything doesn't have to be matchy-matchy. I can appreciate a crazy colored home may not be for more normal souls, but at the very least make sure the room your puppy will spend the most time in has a non-slip surface for playing, enrichment activities, and any indoor training. This may involve the removal of rugs.

Non-slip surfaces can be carpet, non-slip linoleum or whatever convenient material can be removed in six months or so when your puppy is sensible and not breaking the sound barrier when she has the zoomies. It also means you can enjoy your puppy and don't need to be so worried about the removal of stains should your puppy have an inevitable accident, knowing the temporary floor covering is soon headed for the big skip in the sky.

Having puppy proofed one room, including having tastefully laid down bubblegum pink off-cuts, interspersed with purple swirls, consider how to keep her contained in such a paragon of modern design. My house is small to put it mildly, so there is no room for multiple crates. I have a large crate in the bedroom, then I partition my home with baby gates. When I had stairs, the bottom was blocked with a baby gate, and the puppy was carried upstairs by me every evening to go into her crate at bedtime. Many people also have crates in the living space, which is great if you have room, but otherwise a baby gate at the doorway can suffice.

Baby gates are invaluable for sectioning your home, even if you do also use crates. They stop your house and things being trashed, and start your puppy getting used to being temporarily alone from you: the best way to avoid separation anxiety. I don't want my puppies underfoot constantly, so I tend to make the living room a safe space as far as I can, and from the beginning my new puppy gets used to being left alone without me for very short periods of time, such as when I use the toilet. This can literally just be thirty seconds at a time, multiple times during the day (and night) as I'm at that age, don't you know.

As I have cats, I use baby gates with cat flaps in them. But unless you intend to use baby gates when your (larger) breed of dog is an adult, then they're a bit of a waste of time. Puppies, even large breeds, fit through baby gate cat flaps for a *long time*. It took both Mazey and Mina until they were six months old before they could not fit through the baby gate cat flap, and during that time I had to put steps on either side so my elderly cat Holly Bengal could easily get over the baby gate.

Cats always need to have a safe means of escape from a puppy. This includes a way to get out of the room entirely, in addition to high places they can climb, such as cat trees. The number one reason for eye injuries in puppies under six months is being scratched by a cat, so do not *ever* let your cat be chased or bullied by your new puppy, no matter how placid the cat. It's not fair for the cat nor the puppy.

Both cat and puppy need to see each other as friends, and the number one rule in my home is that no one gets bullied. Ever. By other dogs, by cats, by humans. No bullying! If my puppy chases the cat, she will be told this is *not* acceptable behavior. This does not involve scaring or hurting her, as the most important thing for her to learn being in her new home is that she is safe and loved. However, she does need to understand the cat is off limits for her own safety, which generally involves redirecting her and quickly getting to her and picking her up/restraining her. You would not let a toddler touch a hotplate just to demonstrate it hurts, similarly do not let your puppy learn the hard way that cats have claws. Older puppies can wear leads in the house for this purpose, but not very young puppies.

Anyway, before we detoured to cats... When using a baby gate, very quickly get the puppy used to the fact the living room is a fun, safe place to be. I let them know I will pop in and out of the room, which is of no concern. Remember, most service dog prospects will be of highly confident breeds, which right from the start have enough resilience to be left alone for very short periods of time. I mean thirty seconds, not thirty minutes. If you have a pet puppy, you may not find this.

A puppy that is scared and unsure should not be left alone until they are happy and confident in their new environment. If I had a nervous puppy, then they would accompany me to the toilet, enjoy a refreshing shower in the morning (joke, I'm a late riser) and be put in a safe playpen or crate alongside me while I was cooking in the kitchen. Not until the puppy is safe and secure in her environment would I start to leave her alone for very short periods, such as to go to the toilet and later to make myself beautiful, which has to be said could take an eternity. Mazey just wuffed, "beauty is in the eye of the beholder." Bless her cotton socks.

If possible, try and take two weeks off work when getting a new puppy, whether pet or service dog. These two weeks are devoted to making the puppy feel safe, secure and happy in her new home. I ensure my larder is fully stocked and meals are cooked and frozen, so I don't need to spend lots of time apart from my puppy in the kitchen, or have to go out shopping, leaving her in the car (if appropriate) or in her crate home alone. I don't have a spouse, roommate or kids, which means I have to be my puppy's everything. The first couple of weeks must be fully planned before my puppy arrives home.

In addition to the inside of your home, your garden also needs to be puppy safe, with a suitable fence she cannot escape over or under, plus no spaces large enough for a small puppy to slip through. Make sure you have a secure, locked gate and do not leave her unattended. Puppies are very attractive to thieves. I won't rattle on, but use common sense, so no access to ponds, fish, poisonous plants, nice plants you want to preserve, and anything else you don't want her to lay her sharp teeth on.

If you have room in your garden, it can be great to make an enrichment area for your dogs, with different surfaces and articles to explore, sniff and areas to dig in. This can be particularly good for a puppy who has not done a lot of environmental acclimatization activities with her breeder. If this is the case, take it slow and don't scare her with anything too out-there. A Worzel Gummidge scarecrow that removes his head will traumatize her for life, never mind any passing kids. And to think this was considered children's entertainment in the 1980s.

Cars must also be a safe space, and I do try to get my puppies used to the car as soon as possible. As with babies, there's an added bonus that the motion of the car often lulls them to sleep, though be prepared for some travel sickness initially. Once a service dog puppy has completed their vaccinations, you can start public access training in agreeable stores, hence getting my puppies quickly used to cars, so we can get out and about.

Everyone is different when it comes to public access and puppies. Like some of the biggest service dog charities and organizations, I start them early, but only when they trust me and are confident little bundles of fluff. Remember, this is *training*. As such, training a young puppy in public access takes your entire attention, and is not the same as a shopping trip.

I cover public access training and the introduction of it at more length in Chapter Eleven. If you have to, you can take an older puppy into a store, at say six months or more, to grab one or two items of shopping as part of their training, but even so, they really need to have your full attention at all times, which can be hard while packing goods, paying, etc.

Having mentioned vaccinations above, bear in mind when bringing home a new puppy that vaccine protocols are going to vary greatly depending on what you are vaccinating against, the vaccine brand used, any outbreaks of disease in your area and even your breed of puppy. Some puppies have finished their vaccinations on coming home, others have had none and need you to start the process from the beginning. Still others are halfway through a course, the breeder having given one or two vaccinations, with a further vaccine being required to finish the program.

Not all vaccine brands can be overlapped with another brand if your puppy has an unfinished course, so check with your own veterinarian and your breeder regarding vaccinations before having any administered. There's nothing worse than having to potentially restart. Some veterinarians will bring in a vaccine just for your puppy if they don't carry the brand, others may ask you to go to another veterinarian to complete the course. This can be a nightmare with your insurance forms. What fun!

It might sound surprising, but breed does influence which vaccines are necessary. My beloved Rottweilers, like other breeds that have black and tan coloring, are susceptible to parvovirus. Therefore, should your service dog prospect be a big strong Rottweiler or a tiny, cute Manchester Terrier, your puppy may have a slightly different vaccination schedule, including potentially a third/fourth vaccination at five/six months old before moving onto an annual/three yearly vaccination program.

Even before a vaccination program is complete, some veterinarians may be happy for you to take a service dog puppy out and about in your arms, allowing your puppy to gain important environmental socialization/acclimatization. Others will advise you to wait, particularly if there have been a lot of cases of a particular virus in your area. More often than not it's parvovirus, which could be on the hands of any passerby that wants to say hello to your puppy. Please note, parvovirus can be, and indeed often is, fatal.

I have seen an entire litter of fully vaccinated puppies die of parvovirus shortly after going to their new homes. The owner suspected that another dog owner at the veterinarians, one whose dog had undiagnosed parvovirus, had said hello to one of the puppies through the bars of her carry crate, infecting her and the rest of the litter. Puppies are *not* fully protected immediately after the last vaccine is administered; it takes time for the full immune response to occur. Your veterinarian is in the best position to advise whether there is an outbreak of parvo in your area, or whether you need to take special precautions. They can also let you know when your puppy is safe to freely leave your home.

This is a short chapter, so the last thing to think about is insurance, both for veterinarian's fees and also for third-party liability. If you have a dog from a service dog charity/organization, you may get free or discounted insurance through the organization, but always double-check. Not all will provide insurance, particularly if you own the dog outright and she is not leased or otherwise borrowed by you.

If you're buying a puppy from a reputable breeder, your puppy may come with six weeks of health insurance and public liability insurance. This means if there are any health problems, it cannot be counted as preexisting, which is often the case when acquiring health insurance from scratch for a puppy. In general there is a two week period where no claims can be made other than accidents.

Your puppy should always be taken to see your own veterinarian for an independent health check within days of arriving in your home. Do this irrespective of any certificate of health a breeder may have given you. This subsequent health check may pick up problems, remembering that veterinarians do differ in opinion on some issues, and if you have arranged your own insurance, any investigations and subsequent treatment will not be covered.

I had this issue with Chanel, my Shetland Sheepdog puppy who was the successor of the irrepressible Dorki. My veterinarian was worried about a heart murmur that the seller's veterinarian had failed to mention, thinking it a puppy murmur which would resolve on its own. Luckily Chanel did come with insurance, and all her echocardiograms were covered. Thankfully it *was* an innocent puppy murmur that was gone several months later, but if this had not been the case, I really don't know what would have happened. Except I know it would have been bad. Very bad.

Whether taking out health insurance for veterinarian fees or only third-party liability, check whether service dogs are covered, and disclose this information when getting the policy. These days most good policies should state whether service dogs are or are not covered, mainly in the small print, though occasionally it is on a case-by-case basis.

I know of one UK company that, according to their underwriter, only insures Labrador Retriever service dogs if they are being owner trained. This seems odd, but there you go. Sadly, many policies won't cover service dogs at all, and if they do, the premium can be much higher than for an equivalent pet. I'm sure people imagine that disabled service dog users get a break, but no, quite the opposite when it comes to insurance companies. They charge us more! If it's not specified in the small print, get the insurer to confirm in writing that your service dog is indeed covered. Don't leave it to chance.

This is the reason it's a good idea to have pet health insurance: sometimes dogs require medical care. Mina needed to wear a cone after stifle surgery. Photo by the author (2021).

Not everyone can afford top-dollar insurance forever, though I would recommend a high-limit policy for the first two years of your puppy's life, when more often than not any long term and/or serious ailments will rear their ugly head. Not always, but often. This particularly applies to orthopedic problems such as hip dysplasia, which plague many service dog breeds. Unless you have a lot of money to pay for veterinarian fees privately, a good policy can be the difference between life and death for your dog, never mind her career as your service dog.

Thereafter, once your dog has reached the age of two and if you're really struggling financially, at that point you can consider a cheaper policy with lower veterinarian fee coverage. The policy could be enough for a one-off unexpected injury or illness perhaps, but would not be sufficient for something like a double hip replacement. Or if you must, you can leave your dog uninsured though this is a last resort and a very scary prospect.

Always beware and be careful when it comes to taking out pet insurance. Read the small print as if it were as interesting as, well, this book, of course. Cheaper policies, even from good companies, sometimes exclude a massive array of medical conditions—for example, only covering one cruciate ligament repair surgery even though two surgeries are almost always needed. This applies irrespective of whether you still have sufficient unclaimed money for the year under the policy. Or they may have a very low maximum that you can claim per condition, even though it looks like you have a lot of coverage overall. Acquiring such a policy is almost useless.

Your veterinarian is often the best person with which to discuss insurance since they deal with claims day in day out, and know which insurance companies will pay out and which are problematic and try to contest claims. Don't believe the marketing of the companies themselves. Insurers that have only good reviews online or have won prizes for insurer of the year are not good if the policy is cheap, no matter what they say. Good insurance is expensive.

Another consideration is that some veterinarians will only do direct claims with certain companies. A direct claim occurs where the insurance company pays the veterinarian directly and you don't have to pay the veterinarian at time of treatment. If you don't have lots of savings then this may be ideal for you. It's worthwhile to check with your veterinarian which companies they are happy with and which will treat your dog immediately, even if you cannot offer them an upfront cash payment.

In addition to health insurance, I would recommend taking out third-party liability insurance that covers bodily injury to third parties as well as damage to their possessions. We live in an increasingly litigious society, and even though our service dogs may be well behaved 99.99 percent of the time, accidents can happen. They are dogs, and no dog is without fault. In addition, your dog could be blamed for something that is not her fault.

On the cheery note of insurance and veterinarians, I would like to thank the wonderful veterinarians who have cared for all of my horses, dogs and cats over my lifetime. I'd like to thank in particular my local practice in Merseyside that treats all of my animals, my veterinarian in Wales who carried out Mazey's stem cell therapy, as well as Mina's orthopedic surgeon in Wigan who did a wonderful job when she got into a pickle. Long may his Bahamas retirement fund flourish, courtesy of my pet insurance.

CHAPTER NINE

Finding a Dog Trainer

Whether you own a pet or a service dog prospect, are a first-time dog owner or an experienced dog trainer yourself, it's always helpful to have another pair of eyes watch your training. However, finding a dog trainer may not be as easy as it sounds, particularly for those of us who are endeavoring to train our own service dogs. If you're not training with a service dog charity/organization, including those who help people self-train, then you can totally go it alone, or you can enlist the help of a dog trainer when and if you need a bit of extra help and support.

I've already written a lot on dog training ideologies, so hopefully by now you have a good idea of the type of trainer you do want to work with, and those that you don't. Remember, this decision is not written in stone. You can mix and match training techniques and trainers as it suits you, at different stages of your dog's development. Just make sure you have consistent and fair boundaries and commands for your dog. A good dog trainer should be able to adapt to accommodate the way you want to train your dog and be honest about the type of training and potential results they can and cannot offer you.

Many trainers are not experienced in training dogs for service dog work, and certain fields such as guiding task-work and medical detection task-work require a trainer with expertise in this specific field. Otherwise you may be paying a trainer your hard-earned cash to make mistakes and learn themselves as they go along. Not ideal, particularly with task-work, where the stakes are high. You could end up flattened under a bus if your guide dog crosses a road by mistake without checking first whether you want to cross.

When buying a service dog prospect, it's quite common to start off with a local trainer for puppy classes, then work through some obedience levels while introducing public access work. This could culminate in teaching task-work in earnest after your dog is about one or one and a half years old. This depends on breed, the tasks required and your dog's physical and mental maturity. Most good trainers with a sound grounding in behavioral theory and practice can teach your dog the majority of what they need in terms of puppy socialization/acclimatization, though they may not understand the trials and tribulations of working a service dog in public. But neither do some service dog trainers. Go figure.

I would say that no matter how sympathetic a service dog trainer is, unless they are disabled themselves, it's hard if not downright impossible for them to understand what it's like to live with and work a service dog day in and day out. I find it difficult to relate to disabled people with disabilities different from mine, even though we might share many of the same problems with public access. I know many service dog trainers don't even remotely understand the reasons why I teach certain things to my own service dogs as a matter of routine. Some of these things have not occurred at all to other service dog trainers, as they're used to training their dogs in ideal conditions, such as shops and restaurants that are well-designed and have given permission for service dogs to be trained there. This is not real life.

Service dog trainers do not deal with badly designed shops, with checkouts that are too narrow for a person in a wheelchair to pass through together with their service dog. Nor do they understand how a service dog must learn to wait outside a normal toilet cubicle alone for ten minutes or more while we sit straining and glancing at our twitching feet as we frantically try to hurry up. This because the toilet for disabled individuals is either out of order or once you get there and desperately faff around trying to get in, you discover you need to go to the other end of the mall for a special key. By which time you've kacked your knickers. (I do just want to say a bit about knickers). These are, well, to put it briefly, briefs. But as a proud Brit, they need to be called knickers. We love our knickers over here. I draw the line at Union Jack Knickers, or even knickers with a Scottish Saltire (a blue flag with a white cross), but I am quite partial to most other designs of knickers. So if you hear me reference knickers again (you will), then you know there's nothing to get your knickers in a twist over, as they are just briefs.

Unfortunately most service dog trainers have never tried to negotiate long, narrow corridors that go on and on, complete with twists and turns worthy of a Stephen King novel, eventually leading to an ATM. With such a corridor your dog may need to go in front or behind you for quite a distance. These trainers do not understand what it is to work a small dog in a busy shop where people are pushing, shoving and standing on her, nor have their long-tailed dog almost docked by a supermarket cart.

So although it's nice to find a trainer who specializes in service dogs, in truth their experience of public access may not be as extensive as you might hope. They should have a thorough understanding of teaching task-work provided they're experienced in training dogs for your specific disability and the type of tasks you may require. Always double-check.

The more specialized the task, the more specialized the trainer. But if you cannot find a trainer with ideal experience, don't despair. Many of us have trained our own service dogs with no specialist help at all, and it's worked out just fine. The main thing when working with a trainer or working alone is having a basic understanding of how dogs learn, and how to link different skills until you can put them together into one complete task. It's not a race. If it takes a while to fully train your dog, don't sweat it. In truth, no dog is ever fully trained, and service dog partnerships are always evolving. We grow together as a team.

Even complex task-work such as medical alert, which may seem daunting, is at the end of the day basic scent-work. Any decent scent-work trainer who has trained dogs for narcotics, explosive detection, etc., would be able to teach you and your dog medical alert together, provided they expand their knowledge to include how to collect and store biological samples. This may necessitate a chat with your medical practitioner and possibly a dog trainer skilled in teaching medical alert.

I always prefer to train face-to-face with a trainer whenever possible, and I would rather have a long drive to meet with a trainer in person than train via Zoom, Skype or other types of video conferencing. This is not possible for everyone, though. And provided you have a sound understanding of theory, then online video links can be a great way to learn and have an experienced trainer check over all your hard work without a long, arduous journey.

Trainers who specialize in service dog work are not that common where I live, though some of the service dog charities/organizations sometimes use freelance trainers. Even if you're not going to be training with one of these charities or getting a dog provided by them, they can still be helpful in referring you to a trainer who can assist you. As I've said before, find a trainer who is flexible, experienced with your breed of dog, and one who likes said breed (!).

If a trainer has not specifically trained service dogs before, a "can do" attitude can make up for a lot of inexperience if their overall ability as a trainer is excellent. Being able to read a dog, to understand how dogs learn, and to link behaviors together is half the battle. Good, general purpose dog trainers will have a vast repertoire of skills.

If going down the general dog trainer route, look for a trainer who has a skillset that matches as closely as possible to the task-work you require. A dog trainer who does a lot of trick training will be more comfortable helping you train your service dog to perform tasks such as unloading the washing machine or undressing you, than a trainer who mainly trains dogs in agility competitions. That's not to say an agility competitor can't train a service dog, just that they tend to train quite repetitive skills with one or two breeds. At great speed!

Some dog trainers are members of professional organizations that certify people whose training methods align with their own. Bear in mind that in both the U.S. and UK there is no formal accredited system of certification for dog trainers. Pretty much anyone can set themselves up as a dog trainer, no matter how much or how little experience they may have. Nevertheless, many of these professional organizations will have varying degrees of membership such as junior trainer, associate trainer, master trainer, etc. They often have nifty websites with search engines to enable you to find the trainer closest to your location.

Other good methods of finding a trainer are word of mouth and personal recommendation. If you hang about the park in a non–stalker-like fashion, it may be possible to

Having cast a pentagram—cunningly disguised as dog hair—on the carpet, Mazey now prepares to hex any trainers who do not like Rottweilers. Photo by the author (2021).

ask owners of well-behaved dogs where they went for training. When Mazey is out and about in shops, she's so well behaved that people often approach me to ask if I know of any trainers.

I'd like to ask, however, that you please not disturb any service dog handlers. They might give you the evils as if you're the devil in disguise when you try and catch their eye. A lot of handlers hate to be disturbed by a strangers' approach while out with their service dog. You may have good intentions. You are not asking for their firstborn, or even a pat (of the service dog, I'm rather hoping). You're just asking for information, but please be sensitive to people's needs. If the handler looks like a bull-dog who swallowed a wasp on your approach, just keep walking.

Your puppy's breeder may be able to put you in touch with some decent local trainers, even though you may have traveled a long way to buy your puppy. This par-ticularly applies if you have chosen one of the fab four, even if your puppy has not been specifically bred as a service dog. Most reputable breeders know each other and will almost certainly have friends or frenemies in the area where you live. They can recommend a decent trainer who understands your breed. A puppy or green dog from a local dog shelter should come with details of trainers who can assist. If in doubt, don't be afraid to ask. They will be thrilled the dog is going on to a service dog career and should be only too happy to help.

Your veterinarian is another worthwhile port of call. The nurses or the veter-inarians will tend to have good personal contacts themselves. If for whatever rea-son they don't feel they can recommend someone for service dog training, they may have a noticeboard with advertisements for dog trainers on it. Other places that tend to have noticeboards or local trainer contacts are your local pet shop(s) or raw food shop(s), or even local boarding kennels. Some may have in-house trainers who use their facilities, especially if they have well-fenced dog exercise yards, agility courses or even dog swimming pools.

Search engines are an easy way to find a trainer from the comfort of your own home, as more and more trainers now have their own website. You can run a hot bath, pour some wine and take your time perusing their qualifications and the ethos they use when training dogs, all while boiling yourself alive. Their services may be reviewed on local business pages, though often these can be manipulated. Bad reviews can be deleted, or good ones added, so don't believe everything you read.

Similar to search engines, social media is a double-edged sword, which you must handle with care. Online personas are just that: what they want you to see. Even though Facebook service dog training groups are where dreams come to die, if you must find a trainer online, it's worth joining a few. You can ask for trainer recommen-dations if you want to watch fur fly, the different factions typically proclaiming their truth is the only truth. Or simply have a lurk and see how various trainers conduct themselves. You may be pleasantly surprised. Or not, as the case may be.

On a similar note, don't be fooled by viral TikTok videos and trainers with large social media followings. Some of the best trainers are old school and do not advertise online or have formal qualifications, as they have been around for donkey's years and simply don't need to. Not everyone likes the bullying and hatred that abounds online these days.

Remember, it's easy to create impressive before and after clickbait videos of one miracle training session that totally turns around a problem dog, the poor sod usually labeled as the most vicious, uncontrollable dog *ever*. In strolls a poor, fearful little Pomeranian who is turning somersaults at her own reflection, so reactive and terrified of other dogs is she. Two minutes later she's strutting her stuff, too sexy for her collar, confident as can be despite twenty large Pitbulls nearby, snarling and eyeing her up as brunch.

These videos are all fake, with the Pom almost certainly the boss of the Pitties, who are all owned by the same person and hence not strange dogs. Unless you see the entire training session from start to finish, don't believe a word of it. In real life behavioral rehabilitation takes much longer than one session, and in any case, you're training a service dog, not rehabilitating dogs in need. Yes, sometimes service dogs do need behavioral modification, particularly if attacked by another dog, for example, but this is not within the scope of this book. They need expert, hands-on help.

When you have a shortlist whittled down and before contacting a trainer, make sure you have a list of questions. Thoroughly check out their credentials: how many dogs they have trained over how many years, and what competitions or titles they have earned with their dogs.

A certified service dog trainer who lists a whole lot of courses, seminars attended and qualifications achieved on his website may have only started training dogs after buying his first service dog. Age eighteen. He is now aged nineteen and has trained exactly two dogs in his life, one of which was his own (for one year), the other belonging to his granny (for two months). Appreciate the honesty but consider whether such a junior trainer is your best choice compared to a bloke who did thirty years in the police force as a scent dog handler and is half the price of the tweenie look alike, simply because being an old bloke he has no paper qualifications.

If you have medical conditions which may make learning or working with a trainer difficult, or if you have a preferred style of learning, do have a chat with your potential trainer before booking to see if they are someone you feel you could work with. Younger trainers with degrees in animal training and behavior should have had extensive training in human learning styles, as after all, 90 percent of dog training is teaching the dumb end of the lead. Just to clarify, that's you, not the dog.

Depending on your circumstances and needs, sometimes junior trainers can be your best bet. I may seem like I'm knocking them, but as long as they have a few years of solid, practical training experience and not just theoretical knowledge, or if they have supervision and/or a mentor, a junior trainer may be your best bet. Often their enthusiasm more than makes up for lack of dogs trained, though this inexperience should be reflected in the price.

To give an example, I have autism. I'm not going to make eye contact with anyone, no matter how loudly I'm shouted at, along the lines of, "look at me when I'm talking to you." Yes, this really did happen with a certified service dog trainer of many years' experience. She was also a high school teacher. She knew I was autistic but disputed it since "people with learning difficulties can't have degrees." I would not know where to start with this, so I won't. I wasn't being rude or disrespectful to that trainer when I was looking at the floor. It's just how I am. She could not understand me in the way many more junior trainers can.

Sadly, I've been bullied out of not just service dog training classes, but also sports dog training clubs too, including obedience classes, scent-work classes and an IGP club, all due to my autism and other disabilities. I don't fit in, and people don't like those of us who are, "odd." It's made me more self-sufficient and a better dog trainer overall, as I've had to work things out for myself and trust my intuition when it comes to training dogs. But it shouldn't be this way.

If you're reading this book and are disabled, or have a child, partner or relative who is disabled, you will no doubt have been there many times yourself. The dog world seems to attract people who are evil incarnate, or to be politically correct, people who are "interesting." Perhaps they imagine that being a dog trainer involves just training dogs, whereas most of the job is actually training people. Liking people. Being tolerant.

So, what I'm saying is, sometimes it's more important to find a trainer on the same wavelength as you. One who you can speak to on an equal footing. Find someone who makes you comfortable. That may be an internationally renowned trainer or it may be someone who's not flashy, but who trains the occasional dog for the love of the dogs themselves. I think you know what I mean.

So you've found your perfect trainer. What's next? Training can either be in group classes or in one-to-one training sessions. There are pros and cons with each. I like to take my puppies to suitable puppy classes, as this normalizes my puppy working around other dogs and learning to gradually concentrate on playing and interacting with me, not making play bows across the room at all and sundry.

If you're organizing going to either classes or one-to-one training sessions, before your first class or session, mention if you have any mobility issues that may affect where or how you can train your dog. This is important for your trainer to know, since a wheelchair and a field entrance of ankle-deep mud are not a match made in heaven.

For me at least, puppy classes are a good thing, though it's important to find and pick the right puppy class. Some classes are primarily training focused and are open to puppies of up to six months of age. The classes will concentrate on teaching your puppy the basics of obedience that she will need as a well-mannered adult dog. She will learn basic commands in a relaxed, informal setting, such as sit, down, stay, etc.

The trainer may have participants swap puppies so your puppy gets used to being gently handed and trained by other people who she does not know. Your puppy may also get exposed to unusual people, noises and objects such as a lady with a high viz jacket pushing a wailing cat in a stroller. What a world, eh? This is all done under the supervision of an experienced instructor, so should anything go wrong, help is on hand to make sure the class is a positive experience for your puppy.

However, there are other puppy classes which are pretty much a free-for-all puppy party, where puppies do no training, and instead snort puppy coke, play together and run riot. I'm not so keen on these types of puppy classes, as it's all too easy for a puppy to get bullied by a bigger, stronger, older puppy and subsequently become frightened and defensive before an instructor/you/the other puppy's owner has time to step in to stop the bullying. Unless the group is very small and the puppies extremely well-matched, there is too much potential for psychological and also physical harm, particularly if conducted inside on a slippery floor.

Such a rough puppy party can scare your sensitive puppy. Or it can go far too well, with your puppy learning that you are most certainly *not* the most important being in the universe as she previously thought. Instead she learned she would far rather play with other dogs wherever possible. This can destroy the recall you have laboriously and carefully nurtured, your young dog merrily heading off to rough-house with the other puppies both in class and out of it. Your puppy needs to learn to be neutral around other dogs, not immensely interested in them.

Though most puppy parties do their utmost to make sure there is no bullying or extra rough play, I prefer classes that are more based around basic life skills. People always assume dogs need dog friends in order to be happy and content in their lives. They do not. Dogs were domesticated to live with humans, and as a service dog, your puppy's first loyalty must be to you. Rather, she must be neutral and not reactive when passing other dogs, and a general training class will help to achieve this. Most puppy parties will simply encourage puppies to become overexcited at the thought of play with other dogs, which renders them deaf to off-lead recall. Should the dog be on lead and see other dogs, she might become reactive and frustrated she's not allowed to go off leash and play as she is accustomed to.

Other people will argue the opposite, that dogs need playmates of their own species and, ideally, age. Even if you have other dogs in the home, puppies need variety in meeting new dogs in a social setting order to be content and satisfy their natural urges as dogs. Without such an outlet for normal dog behavior, they can become overexcited when seeing other dogs. Should another off-lead dog run up to them, they have no idea of dog body language and therefore react poorly with overexcitement, fear or aggression.

I buy this in part. Yes, if you have an only dog and know a couple of friends, perhaps from puppy class, who have well-matched puppies, then it can be possible to meet up once in a while in order for them to play together and let off steam. Just watch that your puppy does not want to disappear and play with dogs she does not know, further afield at the other end of the park. Being a service dog is a very demanding job, therefore the dogs really do need opportunities to play and unwind after work. In some cases, yes, carefully selected dog friends can be a good thing.

With Mina and Mazey, I don't let them play with any other dogs in the park at all, and I would *never* entertain the idea of visiting a dog park where people take their dogs specifically to run loose and play with each other. Dog parks are rife with diseases of all sorts, and you have no idea how friendly dogs in the park that day will be. Your service dog has a very important job, and although it's vitally important for her to have down time, she will not pine for the company of other dogs if you take adequate time out of your own day to provide her with enrichment activities, and to play and bond with her. Dog parks equal disease ridden fight club for dogs. Stay away.

I have two dogs so they do play well with each other, but even when Mazey was an only dog, I never let her run about and play with strange dogs. Occasionally I might let her play with a suitable dog we frequently bumped into on walks if the dogs knew each other well. But these days there's simply too much risk of running into an untrained and/or aggressive dog. Your service dog is more than your pet—she is your independence and lifeline. It's bad enough when a pet is injured while playing with another dog that gets too rough. However, when your service dog is the only way you can leave your home to go shopping, get to work, get dressed, do things about the house and live independently and safely, then her health and well-being take on a far greater importance given they are so intrinsically linked to your own.

Your service dog really will not miss having doggy friends, particularly if you are her world from the start, satisfying her needs for stimulation and fun via play and

Mazey does not get to visit dog parks, but is an avid fan of spelunking instead, which is much safer. Photo by the author (2022).

activities with you. Some people do let their service dog play with other random or known dogs, as I mentioned previously. Others may also take her to doggy day care. We are all different, with different dogs, and therefore our choices in life will be different. Do what suits you and your dog, whether that is keeping yourself to yourself or playing with all newcomers. Just don't say I didn't warn you regarding the dangers of dog parks.

On the subject of doggy day care, most doggy day care facilities will not take intact dogs. They prefer their clients to have had a pediatric neuter/spay, which if performed before one year of age for larger breeds will lead to a lot of physical and psychological changes in your dog. These changes are most frequently seen in large and giant breed male dogs, who might grow extra tall and leggy, and be of a leaner, less muscular build that looks odd and not of breed type if a pedigree.

In addition to jumping through the spay/neuter hoops, there will also be regular worming/flea and tick prevention requirements, which can be onerous. I don't especially like excessive, monthly use of chemicals on my dogs, and would be loath to do so just so my dog could have friends. If you have a large, boisterous breed, you may be asked to leave doggy day care with very little notice, as most people these days own smaller, more refined dogs, who quite understandably do not appreciate being bowled over by exuberant breeds such as Labradors or even Spaniels, never mind louts like Rottweilers or even gentle giants such as Great Danes.

Mazey did not go to dog parks, nor doggy daycare, though she did attend puppy training class. She also went to obedience classes through to Kennel Club Gold level, plus she sat her public access test with an owner-trainer service dog charity. Mina, however, was a Covid puppy, so there were no available training classes, and I do feel that she missed out. I would love to have taken her to a quality puppy class, where she became accustomed to working around other dogs and puppies, maintaining her concentration on me, and adopting a more neutral attitude with other dogs and puppies when they're close to her.

Once you get past the puppy stage and your dog is more mature, there are a wide variety of group classes most dog trainers offer, encompassing every type of dog sport and activity you can imagine, from agility and obedience, to flyball and ringcraft. There are also some training clubs where the dogs are worked on a more individual basis rather than in a class setting. Some examples are scent-work classes and search and rescue, and there are also those classes that are geared toward the working abilities of specific breeds.

Your last, and most expensive, option is to pay for private one-to-one lessons with a trainer. Unless you have a specific problem you want to work on with your puppy, or with a young dog starting her public access journey, one-to-ones are perhaps best put off until your dog is starting task-work. At that point you may feel you would benefit from intense sessions with a trainer. Dogs struggle to concentrate for long periods of time, so it can be helpful when working a dog to let them rest and digest what they have learned before having another short training session, perhaps ending in a walk or some play.

So we end there our adventure into the wondrous world of dog trainers and dog training classes. So mote it be.

Chapter Ten

Basic Service Dog Training

I'm going to start this chapter on the assumption that you have a new puppy or a young green service dog prospect with whom you are beginning basic service dog training. The things you want to establish in this case are much the same in the first six months or so of owning any dog, though you can progress faster with an older dog who is more physically and mentally mature.

The first thing we need to do with any dog, of whatever age, whether from a breeder, a private seller or a rescue, is to make friends with her. In her own time, your new puppy needs to conclude that she has come to the best home ever, and that life with you is going to be safe, as well as full of fun, happiness and adventure. Arriving in a new place is scary, even for confident breeds, and most particularly for dogs who have had not such a good start in life or young puppies who have been given a sheltered upbringing by their breeder.

Your dog's individual personality is very much going to determine what you do and the speed at which you do it. There will always be massive debates over nature versus nurture. It's true that a bad upbringing can destroy a dog, no matter how sound her genetics are. However, the same cannot be said for a genetically unsound dog, even if she is given the very best of training. Chapter Five covered service dog breeds thoroughly. You should by now have a reasonable idea of the character traits your puppy will tend to possess, though individuals within a breed or even a breeder's bloodline can be very different.

During the first weeks of having a puppy home with me, I like to develop a rough personality profile of my puppy's main character traits. This helps me think about how I can develop a training plan which will enhance her strong points and minimize her weak ones. There's no particular science to this: I just look at the traits I personally like in a service dog. The more scientific, standardized tests tend to subtract marks on puppies with traits I actually find helpful in service dogs, for example confidence, a trait I really do appreciate.

All trainers are different, and although we may like different types of breeds and basic personalities, there are character traits which I think universally make for a good service dog. I personally like puppies who are extremely confident, and who are very keen to come forward and explore anything that has temporarily scared them. I like a gentle curiosity—not as much curiosity as a cat(!)—and a dog that is sensitive to my commands and looks to me for instruction. I don't want a dog that's too excitable or one who is extremely reactive to the environment around her.

You may or may not want to try and put together a personality profile for your puppy. I don't know many people who do it: I just find it fun, as well as useful. In any event, the first week at home should be as stress free as possible, so don't go poking her, prodding her and sticking her in the freezer to see how she copes with an unexpected turn of events.

However, there are some essentials she will have to go through that will be potentially upsetting, but which should not be put off. This would include an appointment with your veterinarian for a health check and possible vaccinations. The veterinarian's waiting room can be very scary for puppies, not least due to things we as humans are not aware of, such as the smell of fear and possibly even death.

Speak to your veterinarian about the quietest time for an appointment and explain it's for a young puppy. Many veterinarians will give you a double appointment at no extra cost, so they can take as much time as is required to play with and make friends with your puppy, demonstrating to her that a veterinarian visit is something to be looked forward to and not feared. When you are in the waiting room, carry your puppy or have her in a travel crate. Do *not* put your puppy on the floor, let her greet other dogs, or say hello to people who may ask to pet her. This is especially important if she has not yet completed her vaccinations or is less than two weeks post final vaccination. Veterinarian offices are places for sick dogs, and young puppies are extremely vulnerable to picking up infections from the floor and the hands of other dog owners.

After your veterinarian visit, depending on your puppy's age and vaccination protocol, you may have several weeks' quarantine before she can go out into public places. Environmental socialization/acclimatization is important to your puppy's development, and some veterinarians may give you checklists of what she should be doing, such as meeting people with beards, people wearing hats, folk with umbrellas, older people with walking sticks or walkers, people in wheelchairs or on crutches, people pushing prams, children of various ages, cars, buses, semi-trucks, people on bicycles, joggers, horse riders, dogs of all sizes and ages, and so on and so forth.[1]

These are all excellent things to be introducing your service dog prospect to, but there is no hurry at this stage. Even if you do have to keep her at home for two weeks or more before venturing out into the world, it's not a disaster. It could even be a good thing. She needs to feel safe with you, and how long this takes will vary with each puppy. Don't stress that your puppy is somehow missing out.

In the first couple of weeks your puppy needs to be concentrating on security, settling into her new home, and forming a strong bond with you. Once she trusts you at home, anything she may encounter that scares her when out and about will not be so big a deal for her. However, if you neglect to work on bonding and trust and take her out before she is ready, she may become scared and have no one she trusts to turn to. This can cement the bad experience in her mind and create problems further down the line, problems which she may not otherwise have had.

Your puppy's first fear period is between about eight to twelve weeks old,[2] just when she is coming into your home and starting her new life. A fear period is just what it says on the tin—a period of time when puppies become scared of remarkably innocent things, including inanimate objects, people and noises. Once home, it may be best to restrict your puppy's access to only a couple of quiet rooms until she is settled and confident in her surroundings, rather than overwhelming her by constantly forcing her to encounter new places and people.

Apart from her veterinarian visit, which is essential, take it very easy with your new puppy. Start as you mean to go on by gently house training and crate training her, keeping everything calm and matter of fact. Young puppies spend a lot of time asleep, something you will most certainly be grateful for. Like with a human baby, you only get this time once, so do not allow your new puppy to get worked up and extremely distressed, for example by leaving her alone to cry it out. She is a baby who is not trying to be annoying or defiant. Comfort her, love her and even if in the long run she must sleep in a separate part of the house, you'll get where you want to be quicker by alleviating her fears early rather than placing her into a state of learned helplessness.

Your home will be full of wonderful new things. Don't be alarmed if your puppy is scared of unusual objects. That castor oil plant may be Uncle Horatio in disguise you know. Some breeders do a lot with their puppies before they leave for their new homes, building them veritable assault courses with slides, ball pits, and a variety of different footing, plus getting them used to household noises such as washing machines, vacuum cleaners and even lawnmowers.

Other breeders keep their puppies in outside kennels in a whelping room, with four whitewashed walls and very little noise. If this is all they have experienced, it's not a disaster; it just means you need to take your time a bit more, particularly with breeds that are not so bold. In the short term it's a massive advantage for a puppy to have been raised by a proactive breeder, but with good genetics, a puppy raised in more genteel surroundings will also thrive.

Do not ever force your new puppy into situations which make her extremely scared and uncomfortable. If you have a noisy young family and she's been brought up by a breeder in an adult-only household, don't be surprised if she's frightened and wants to hide behind you or the sofa when your kids let rip. Living in fear is not healthy for anyone, so let your puppy become used to the kids in her own time. Ideally give the kids some quiet activities while the puppy is around, so she feels confident enough to be in their presence.

The worst thing you can do with a terrified puppy in this situation is to make her forcibly confront the things she is scared of. Never lift her up and restrain her in your arms to let kids or other strangers pat her if she's frightened. It will confirm to her that she was right to be scared, and these new, noisy people are trouble. A restrained, frightened dog with no way to escape may well growl and if that is ignored, she may bite, which is the last thing you want.

Your puppy cannot be allowed to learn the lesson that growling and biting will get her what she wants—which is to be immediately and permanently removed from the situation that is scaring her. If she does learn this, then it will become her lifelong go-to behavior whenever she is scared or unsure of something, as she knows it's a tactic which works and results in the removal of the scary stimulus. Your puppy needs to be set up for success, and not placed in scary situations in the first place. Behavioral modification is a book in and of itself, so just be very aware of your puppy's own personal triggers and how much she can handle. Don't move too quickly.

Remember, when she arrives home, your puppy is away from her mother and litter mates for the first time in her life. She will be looking for someone who can step into those roles, giving her protection, security, sustenance, guidance and also someone to have fun with. That person is you, in all of those roles. At the age of eight weeks or so, your puppy is just a baby. Puppies love to play, and you can use this natural instinct to play in order to build a bond of love and trust between you. You can also subtly introduce some training via your games, and not as formal obedience exercises.

As dog trainers (yes, as the owner of a pet dog or a service dog prospect, we are all dog trainers) almost all of us will have all pushed young puppies too hard at one point. We have a new puppy, and armed with new and improved knowledge in dog training, we begin to flex our training skills. The puppy is only with us for a couple of weeks and already she will sit, down, stay, give paw, roll over, wait at doors, walk to heel, go to her place and do all manner of other obedience exercises. Yes, this may all be done with food lures and almost entirely via rewards and positive reinforcement, the puppy looking like she is enjoying herself, so it's all good, isn't it? Well, yes and no.

As I say, we've all been there. It's satisfying when our friends ohh and ahh at how much our puppy can do at such a young age, particularly in these new days of social media when we can film our little angel, well, being a little angel. However, in my experience, these sorts of obedience exercises are unnecessary. They are no more than tricks and are incredibly easy to train quickly at a later date once you and your dog know each other well.

These days when I get a new puppy, I prefer to spend the first six months or so on building a bond via play, plus the essential life skills all dogs need like the setting of important boundaries, and environmental acclimatization. That's all. No more. For a very young puppy, particularly one with not the best of genetics, her socialization period and those initial months bonding with me is a time I can never get back, whereas tricks can be taught to her at any age.

Gentle games, sometimes with food, sometimes with toys, sometimes just with me, can encourage a shy puppy out of her shell. As she gains confidence in herself and in me, accompanying me wherever I go, she can start to overcome her fears and develop resilience and courage. She will not do this if kept in a quiet environment and drilled in obedience and heelwork. A more confident puppy also benefits from forming a strong bond, and understanding that there are boundaries in life, just as there was with her mum and siblings.

The basic obedience most important to me in a young dog, then, is the ability to play with me, to recall and really want to be with me. Gradually through play and bonding, my puppy learns to trust me, develop boundaries, and understands that nothing in life is more fun than me. Not other dogs, not cats, not rabbits, not a ball thrown over her head by someone else. Me. My puppy will never wander too far from me on walks, as any moment she knows I may recall her for a game. Her recall will be fast and reliable. These things are super important for me, much more so than the ability to sit or down or have a perfect heelwork position.

So, when my puppy comes home, I immediately want to put in place kind, consistent rules. An essential is to start toilet training. I will gradually and gently crate train her, including placing her behind a baby gate so I can cook, shower, etc., in peace, knowing she is safe. I will teach her not to bite me during play. She will gently learn chasing the cats is a big *NO*. She will be introduced to a collar and harness and lured into happily walking beside me (on both sides) for very short periods.

My puppy will get used to being handled all over, including close handling. She will learn to enjoy being held and gently restrained, as well as being brushed and having her nails attended to. I will teach her to make eye contact with me and look up into my face when asked to do so. Most of all, I will play and have fun with my puppy, building up her confidence, discovering the games we enjoy playing together—which can very well change as she gets older. Through games she will learn one vital skill in every dog: to have an amazing recall.

These few weeks under house arrest, then, before she is fully vaccinated and ready to go out into the world, are far from wasted. The time spent falling in love with each other allows you to fully prepare her to make the most of being in the outside world during her socialization period, which usually takes place between five and sixteen weeks of age. At that age, she is much more likely to be accepting of new and unusual experiences, and if scared, to quickly pluck up courage to investigate. I find genetically bold puppies will be brave in any event, but for a more fearful puppy, this can be a critical time. It's not make or break, but using her socialization period to your full advantage can make your life easier.

A puppy's first fear period and her socialization period will overlap somewhat, which is why it's ideal if her breeder can get her off to a good start and introduce her to as many varied experiences as is possible before she comes home to you, just when her first fear period typically begins. With a bit of luck, your puppy's fear period should end at about eleven weeks, giving you several weeks to spend her remaining socialization period out in the big bad world.

There is a lot of debate between behaviorists as regards the exact timing of both fear periods and socialization periods. All puppies are different. Large and giant breed puppies who mature slower both physically and mentally may have a slightly extended socialization period of up to about fifteen weeks of age, which should be well past when their vaccinations are complete. With smaller breeds, their fear period may be over by ten weeks of age, with socialization periods finishing at approximately twelve weeks, possibly before she has completed her vaccinations, which poses a dilemma.

With a smaller breed of service dog, particularly if she is of a breed that is prone to fearfulness, if you have observed a fear period and feel she has now passed it but has not completed her vaccinations yet and she still has a lot to learn about the world, then provided you are physically strong enough and she trusts you totally, I would take her into the great outdoors either via carrying her or putting her in a pram or papoose. There are many things she can safely experience with you at this time, such as loud traffic passing, going on public transport or walking through crowds in a shopping area.

You need to be able to read your puppy's reactions to tell whether this type of environmental exposure is benefiting her, if she is indeed learning and taking it all in or if it is having a negative effect. Your puppy will get scared of things occasionally—that's fine and to be expected. The important thing is that during her socialization period, she has a greater ability to be accepting and bounce back from any small scares she may have. If your puppy is quiet and doing nothing, taking little interest in what is happening around her, then she may be extremely scared and going into a state of learned helplessness, in which case you are doing *much* more harm than good.

If you are going to introduce your puppy to the world before she is fully vaccinated, she should not be put on the ground or allowed to meet other dogs, though some veterinarians will be happy with a puppy that has almost completed her vaccinations meeting fully vaccinated dogs in a safe place, such as your own garden. Always check first, though, and heed any precautions your veterinarian advises such as wiping paw pads before entering your home.

If you are taking your puppy out, I would resist letting anyone stroke her, since you have no idea what is on their hands. Even if they say they have not been near any other dogs, people do lie. Friends who you trust are a different matter. Dogs do not generalize well, so even though she has maybe met your friends in your home, it's still a good idea for them to greet her in public. In disguise, even. Just think, you could have a public fancy dress party just for your puppy!

There are no hard and fast rules with puppies, and it's important to do what's right for your individual puppy. Rely on your own intuition. The hardest puppies to deal with can be those very sensitive, extremely intelligent breeds, such as show line German Shepherds or Border Collies, both of whom may be too heavy to carry, but who would benefit from as much correctly timed environmental socialization as possible.

I've already spoken about puppy training classes and puppy parties in Chapter Nine, so if you can find a good puppy training class once your puppy has finished her vaccinations, so much the better. There are some things I would work on from the very start, specifically for a service dog puppy, that you will not find in most puppy training classes. This relates to handling. I've said it many times in this book: one of the main things you will encounter when working a service dog is unauthorized wandering hands. Not all dogs like being touched by someone they don't know, including being patted on the top of the head or even cuddled. Unfortunately, at least once, if not more during your service dog's career, she will have a child or even an adult grab her and hug her in a painful way.

As you can imagine, being grabbed and hugged tightly by a stranger is a frightening experience for the vast majority of adult dogs, never mind a young puppy. Some dogs may never enjoy being patted or hugged, but for your own peace of mind, they must be neutral and able to tolerate it, even if only briefly until you can get the person peeled off of your dog. I suppose in some ways I'm quite a pessimistic person, so for my own service dogs, I prefer a very brave, confident, friendly dog who will not be scared by this type of manhandling even in puppyhood.

If you have a nervous puppy, or one that does not particularly like people, then I would gradually work with her to acclimatize her to being gently patted, at a minimum, before you start public access training in earnest. Not all dogs will tolerate much attention from strangers in the beginning, but some types of brief introductions may be fine.

If that is the case with your puppy, try and gently find a baseline regarding how much she will tolerate. You will need to work her in a slightly different way than a confident, friendly puppy. In particular, you should be vigilant of kids running loose in public, though if you're unsure and nervous yourself, this will rub off on your puppy. Again, it's about setting you and your puppy up for success, perhaps taking her into public only when it's quiet, after kids are typically in bed. Then as she becomes more tolerant of handling, you can expand where and at what times you train her in public.

Adults can also be problematic as regards unauthorized patting, and you just have to be firm. You are your puppy's advocate, and if you have to be rude to people, then you have to do it, even if you are an introvert by nature. A shy puppy can get frightened, a confident one overexcited, whereas the ideal is a puppy who learns to be neutral around strangers.

On the subject of public access training, once again, this is one of these topics where you will get a massively different range of opinions from different trainers. Some service dog charities/organizations place their puppies into foster homes, or puppy walkers as they are more commonly known. The puppy will live there until she is about twelve to fourteen months old, at which point she will return to the charity/organization with basic training, including experience of public access, firmly in place.

Many of these service dog charities/organizations have their puppies going into shops and other public places as soon as their vaccinations are finished, at about ten or twelve weeks. Some other trainers, particularly those helping handlers self-training, don't advise starting public access training at all until the dog is over one year in age and ready to start task-training.

Personally, I like to get puppies out in public early. I go as soon as they can walk beside me with a lure, either food or a toy, and they know the "toilet" command so I can be pretty sure we will not have an accident in a shop. I always ask puppies to toilet before we go into any indoor space.

I want being in public places to be a normal part of everyday life for my puppy. Mazey started her public access training at twelve weeks old, once she had completed her vaccinations. To start with, we literally drove to the local shops, then walked in and out of the entrance, then back home. We did that several times per week, and that was it. She got used to the whooshing electric doors, the strange surfaces underfoot and the in-store music. We even had a trip on a canal boat.

Five minutes may not sound like much, but on top of getting used to a car journey, it was more than enough for Mazey at this very young age. She also had short daily car journeys to the local park for enrichment activities, where she got to play off-lead and occasionally meet friendly dogs. Going to a strange shop or public place should be as much fun for your puppy as a trip to the park, and the training exercise is done with the enthusiasm of a teenage girl given a backstage pass at a Justin Bieber concert. If you want to train a service dog, you must not be scared of making a fool of yourself!

When performing public access activities your puppy should be waggy tailed, bright eyed and full of bounce, showing a keen interest in what is going on about her. She shouldn't be held in an obedience position with a lure when walking, rather given the chance to walk beside you in a natural manner while looking around her. Lures can be used to encourage her to walk with you, but she needs to take in her surroundings.

You may want to stop for a minute or two after entering a shop, and just let her take it all in. If you start public access work and your puppy is immediately fearful, with a lowered tail, glued to your legs, looking petrified, stop it there. Go home. Wait awhile and build trust, then try again at a later date as she matures. Especially if she is undergoing a fear period.

If your puppy is uncertain about a specific thing when in public, a display for example, and she backs off, don't worry or panic. It's normal. Wait and give her a chance, watching her reaction. If she is saying, "absolutely not, I know for a fact a monster lives under that pile of towels," and is adamant she is going nowhere near them, don't force her. Let her take her own time. Instead of you both standing and staring at the object, it's better to keep her legs moving and the energy, enthusiasm and momentum up. Retreat slightly to a place where she is comfortable again, and you can resume playing with her and encouraging her to walk happily beside you.

Once she is settled, her tail is back up and she's relaxed and is engaged with you, very, very gradually advance back to the area where she stopped and was scared before. Be careful not to push her back into a fear response, where she is incapable of learning. As soon as you see her start to deflate, stop and don't go farther toward the object, but work in this new area which is just that little bit closer, parallel to it. Double your enthusiasm. That might be all you do. You don't need to get right up to whatever scared her, as long as you have managed to get her to advance a bit closer and to relax near the point she initially stopped and scared. Puppies get tired easily, and it's better to end there on a good note. Perhaps try conquering fears again another day, or just wait until she is older.

A puppy being scared of something is not the end of the world; what is more important is her reaction after she is frightened. We all get scared of things in our lives: you, me, Mazey, Ironman, your puppy. What I want to see is a puppy who starts to develop resilience and can think about the situation, put her trust in you, and start to tackle and overcome her fears. This happens best during her socialization period, which is why using it to your advantage is so very useful.

If a puppy gets a fright, but then immediately wants to go and investigate what scared her, that is a perfect response. If she gets a fright, has a think about it then advances on her own, or perhaps with some encouragement, this is also promising. What I do not like to see is a puppy who every five seconds sees something she is scared of and runs away, hiding behind her owner's legs and yelping, unable to regain her composure. This is a puppy who may be a challenge even as a pet, and is unlikely to live a happy, fulfilled life as a service dog. As a one-off, yes, that is normal, but repeated incidents of this type mean the training and life as a service dog will be stressful. This is not fair on the puppy.

Always try and set your puppy up for success by trying to create an experience that will be positive for both of you. This is why a confident temperament is so important for a service dog. With a genetically nervous, scared dog you are battling against her basic nature. She may ultimately make a great service dog in time, when you have a strong bond of trust and respect between you. This can take three or four years, not overnight. On the other hand she may not ever enjoy the job, and might be absolutely miserable in her work. How much easier it is with a puppy who from day one is bold and confident. For a service dog, temperament must come before looks.

Back to Mazey. As the weeks went by, we did more small exercises out and about. She was allowed to politely greet members of staff and members of the public who asked to pat her. She got to walk up and down several aisles, using a lure to encourage concentration on me. We practiced her impulse control, including the ability to leave dropped food, and also to lie calmly on the floor while I chatted to someone or pretended to use the checkout.

As time went on, Mazey went everywhere with me. She learned to wait patiently while I stopped to examine different products. I either carried a basket or pushed a shopping cart, and she learned to walk on either side of me. At this point I would take her to the checkouts and might buy one or two items. She had to learn to sit and stay while I was not directly watching her with my full attention. I did always keep her on-lead at this stage, but an important exercise for a service dog is to walk to heel if the lead is inadvertently dropped. They should learn to stay and not move, even when your back was turned. Mazey was not being watched and I was using two hands to pack groceries.

Mazey was about six to eight months old at this point, and I then started to do more basic formal obedience exercises. She already knew the basics: she had a great recall and good manners; she would sit, lie down, stay and walk on a loose lead on either side of me around distractions like people and other dogs. Around this age she earned her UK Kennel Club Bronze award, and a few months later, the Silver award. I taught Mazey some fun scent-work and tracking round about this time, and also did some showing classes. She won Best Puppy in Breed and Best of Breed at the Royal Cheshire show. Go, Mazey!

Life went on. When she was closer to one year old, I expanded Mazey's obedience to longer stays, including out of sight. I had already taught her a place command plus good manners around about doorways, so I expanded on these. I asked her to back up or step forward for a certain number of steps on command in a direction I signaled.

It was then time to start to teach her some basic task-work, including to walk in front of me, to block people from coming too close, to bark when asked, to switch on lights, to tell me when it was time for my medication, to open the cupboard door and to fetch my medicine bag. Pretty basic but useful stuff. She then earned her UK Kennel Club Gold award at just over one year.

Shortly thereafter, at about fourteen months, Mazey sat her public access test with a service dog charity that specializes in helping owners train dogs. By this stage, Mazey was ultra-reliable and fantastic to work in public, and within about six weeks after that, I taught her medical alert for me. Following that, I taught her some light guiding work for when I had an autistic meltdown, enabling her to lead me either to the checkout or to the exit of shops. I also played about with other skills, such as identifying and leading me to certain supermarket aisles using scent-work. She would always initially use her nose, then at around about the correct aisle, she would double-check with her eyes.

I don't eat out or really have any hobbies or interests other than dogs and the worship of cats, the two feline overlords who design to let me serve them. Nevertheless, every so often I would take Mazey into a cafe so she could have the chance to be taught to settle in an environment where food is being served. In addition, she accompanied me to appointments with my medical practitioners, including when I required x-rays, where her ability to stay when I was out of sight was put to the test, since she went behind the shielding with the nurses, and had to retain a ten-minute stay without moving or being able to see me, all on one command.

So that is the rough timeline of Mazey's service dog training. However, this was in many ways super quick, and most dogs cannot and should not be pushed to go at the same pace as Mazey. In many ways she was literally born to be a service dog, and with her very bold, people-orientated personality, she enjoys the work and finds it interesting and fun. Mina, on the other hand, has had many health issues, and is way, way behind the stage Mazey was at the same age. This is due mainly to Mina's personality and the fact she is a very large-boned, slow to mature bitch, both physically and mentally.

If your dog is not enjoying the work or is struggling, back off. Maybe give the dog some time away from public access work then start again. As I did so many play-based activities when my dogs were puppies, I felt that when it did come time to start more formal obedience-work, it progressed quickly. We understood each other so well, plus Mazey was keen to learn as she knew training sessions meant we would be having lots of fun together.

This type of public access training may not suit everyone, but what a lot of owner trainers lack more than anything else is confidence. They worry their dog will misbehave in some way, and they will be called an impostor or asked to leave a shop. For that reason, often people start public access work in pet shops and other dog friendly places, though this is the last place I would start to train a young puppy. These shops have lots of badly behaved dogs in them, not to mention dogs constantly urinate on products and displays as well as the floor, and if a puppy is not yet fully toilet trained....

When you feel up to trying public access work, approach some stores and ask if you can bring in your service dog in training. Legally, when in training, your dog should still have access rights, though in the U.S. this depends on the state, so always check the law where you live. In the UK it is the opposite, and service dogs in training have no rights at all. However, whether in the UK or U.S., most stores are receptive to young dogs coming in and learning their trade. The main things your dog needs to be proficient in are not toileting in store, not sniffing goods or grabbing things off shelves, and not jumping up on people. Training at home is great, but nothing beats training in the environment your dog will eventually be working in.

Mazey was very much a dog that enjoyed play and was not terribly interested in food rewards. In order to combat this, I did a lot of public access training in the middle of the night when no one was about, so I could reward her with a toy. Very gradually, both at home and during our training sessions, I was able to transition her to accepting food (as well as praise) as a reward. Once that was done, I phased out the toy reward as this was

Mazey enjoys being trained, particularly outdoors. Photo by the author (2022).

not a practical thing to reward her with. I do tend to carry food with me as a reward when working Mazey, but she is on an intermittent reward schedule, meaning she does not get a reward every time she does something I ask her to do. Only sometimes.

Food lures are great when teaching service dogs new skills, including heelwork in public, but at some point you do really need to phase them out. Not totally. Rewards should always be available for good behavior, and if you use food or a combination of food and verbal rewards, that's fantastic. However, it's hard to work a dog who expects constant food and will not work otherwise, either zoning out or getting disruptive and pushy to try and force food from the handler if it's not forthcoming. Also, a permanent heelwork position is not practical.

I have seen more and more service dog trainers who believe in coercing behavior via constant trickle feeding. Training sessions consist of ladling food down a dog's gullet for an entire twenty to thirty minutes, rewarding the dog for doing nothing more than walking to heel without pulling. We are not talking about young puppies or dogs undergoing behavioral rehabilitation, just adult dogs who would only concentrate and walk on a loose lead when offered food from the owner's hand every thirty seconds or so. This is not training a service dog, in my view.

As I have said, we are all different. If this is a method of working your dog that would suit you and your service dog on a permanent basis, who am I to say it is wrong? If you are recommended to train this way and it doesn't work for you, keep an open mind as regards other training options.

There are times where a dog needs to get into the habit of retaining concentration on the handler in increasingly busy environments. Lures may help establish a good pattern of behavior, but practically speaking, this can't go on forever. At some point when working a service dog in real life, you need to pick up and look at the goods you are purchasing, without covering them in particles of kibble dust or slime from raw chicken. This is not *Ghostbusters: Service Dog of the Marshmallow Man.* Ultimately your service dog needs to be your partner in crime, not a gangster dog holding you hostage for food.

Onto the unusual, if not the cruel. Depending on your lifestyle and where you live, there are some public access environments that can be a little weird and need special work and training. Service dogs, including puppies, tend to deal with elevators well but moving walkways and escalators can be remarkably scary for dogs. Personally I would wait until a dog is an adult to try and introduce her to moving walkways and escalators, both from my experience with Mazey and what I have seen with other service dogs.

There is a big supermarket Mazey and I frequent regularly that has uphill and downhill moving walkways where I trained Mazey in their use. I started by initially not asking her to go onto it, or even terribly close, but gauged where she was comfortable. We just worked on confidently walking past it. From the offset she didn't like it very much and kept as far back as possible, with a wary eye on it. I also did quite a bit of work on getting her used to the metal grating of the floor of the moving walkway. Mazey is a dog that, even to this day, always takes a good look at any unusual surface she stands on, and the metal grating material was something she had never encountered before.

As there was no way I could ask for the moving walkway to be stopped for training purposes, I decided it would also be prudent to teach Mazey the command to "step," when she came to something on the ground that she may need to pay particular attention to. There was nothing I could use in day-to-day life that simulated the walkway, so I simply used curbs or other things she needed to step onto or off of, just so she knew to pay attention to what was on the ground and about to be under her feet.

The preparation took a month or two as I did not want to rush her. On the big day, after a few sessions working right beside the moving walkway as usual, I plucked up courage and walked briskly to it in a matter of fact way. Mazey hesitated and then jumped onto it, happily standing on the metal grid to get some very high value pieces of cooked chicken just before jumping off. We went back down and left it there.

I had a chat with the supermarket security guard about the moving walkway on the way out (as he had started to clap when Mazey went onto it). He told me that a very large service dog charity brings its dogs into the store every six months to train on the walkway. Many dogs are afraid of it and won't go anywhere near it, even with the walkway shut off and not moving at all. I have more time than most service dog trainers to prepare my dog, so it's not surprising I was able to get Mazey onto it the first time I tried. We then moved onto an escalator, which Mazey also took in stride.

If you're going to use a lot of public transport, and if there are escalators or moving walkways that cannot be easily avoided, do some quality preparatory work beforehand. Some dogs will step on them the first time, but many will not. There would be nothing worse than missing your flight because your dog would not use an escalator or moving walkway at the airport and is too big to be carried.

Another place it may be worth training your dog to sit is the footwell of a car. In the UK, it's illegal to refuse a service dog entry into a taxi unless the driver has an exemption, but the driver may try and make you put your dog into the footwell and not allow the dog on the seat, even if you have a clean settle mat to cover it with. I had to do this when coming back

Mazey demonstrating for Mina how a ramp for the car should be used. Photo by the author (2020).

from the hospital after an emergency admission. I was just lucky Mazey is so willing, as it was very hard to squeeze her into the tiny car footwell. This should not be a problem with a small service dog, but with a giant or large one, it may be very difficult unless the dog understands what is being asked.

Once you are confident that your dog is behaving well in public, in all circumstances, it is then time to consider whether to take a public access test, even if only to boost your own confidence. Public access tests are not compulsory, though if you are training with a service dog charity/organization you may have to pass one before they will certify your service dog as fully qualified.

Some service dog charities/organizations prefer to have dogs complete a public access test before task-work, while others prefer to do it after. There are also now some private service dog trainers who offer public access tests and who can travel to you in order to complete the test individually on your home turf. Or you can complete it as part of a group on a certain date and location if you want to keep costs down.

Every public access test is different, though you should try and find one which reflects how you work your own service dog, which can be difficult as we all have such different needs. I never eat out, for example, so although I know Mazey behaves well in cafes on the odd occasions we have been in one, a public access test with lots of emphasis on eating out and squeezing under tables would be a waste of my time.

Instead, Mazey does a lot of work in supermarkets: she has a rock-solid stay and is able to be easily worked in all manner of scenarios that could crop up in a shop, including going on escalators and moving walkways, loud noises, bratty kids, etc. Similarly, I will never use public transport due to my disabilities, so have no need to spend a lot of time teaching her to curl up in a small ball to squeeze into gaps between seats, whereas this may be vital for other service dog teams to master.

Once you have completed (and passed!) your public access test or at least have some decent training under your belt with your dog's basic obedience down pat, it's time to start thinking about task training. Task training usually only starts once your service dog prospect is close to maturity, both physically and mentally. Your young dog, having done well in her public access training and having passed through puppyhood, may now need more of a challenge.

As I've said, I'm a firm believer in leaving puppies to be puppies. Smaller dogs will reach maturity and be ready to start task-work a lot quicker than large or giant breeds, which may not be fully physically mature until two years of age or slightly older. Your service dog should always be excited at the prospect of a training session even if it's "just" obedience, since any training session means doing a lot of things a dog will enjoy. Yes, there will be more and more formal obedience, but the training should still be enormous fun for your dog, with plenty of play and rewards.

I like to try and transition my service dog prospects from play and toy rewards toward appreciating mainly food rewards. Enthusiastic play is fantastic for teaching puppies and young dogs the basics, including getting your young dog bonded and engaged with you. This type of play is done at a higher level of arousal, and in a young puppy we are looking for a lot of movement and engagement with us. Once we have achieved this and we have a very strong bond with our young dog, it's time to calm things down a bit. Service dogs on the whole need to be calm and well behaved while working in public. Not looking like an unexploded bomb, eh, Mina?

Of course, every dog is different. Some dogs will always need to be trained with a massive amount of energy and enthusiasm in order to keep them confident, interested in and keen to work. These will mainly be lower-drive dogs who are not working breeds and who need to be persuaded that being a service dog is a good thing, that it's much better than lying on the sofa snoozing all day as was the fate of their littermates. Other dogs are permanently bouncing off the walls and need work to develop their patience and impulse control. As you have most probably guessed, these are working-line dogs of working breeds. Then we have dogs who are in between these two extremes. These often make the very best service dogs.

When starting task-work it's important to be clear and consistent with your young dog. This may be the first time you have taught the task in question to your dog, so in a sense you are both learning at the same time. Make sure you understand the various steps and how to link the behaviors together in order to eventually arrive at the entire task that you require. It's worth writing these steps down so you have a roadmap to come back to in the event you have problems, either with this task or another task later on which has similarities. It's incredibly easy to forget just how you have taught a dog something when training behaviors for the first time, particularly when six months down the road and teaching a different task with related skills.

Mistakes. Well, we've all had a few, but don't worry about them. I know that it's easy for me to sit here and say, "Don't beat yourself up for making mistakes." It really is true, though. We don't improve on ourselves as trainers or as human beings without making mistakes and learning from them. Sometimes it can be beneficial to go back several steps and take more time to teach a really solid foundation of skills. This can be especially true if you have been pushing forward quickly with a young and talented dog.

So if things are going great, why scale it back slightly? Well, service dogs often need to develop the ability to think for themselves and problem solve, particularly if their task-work is going to involve intelligent disobedience, which a working guide dog must master. This is also true where your dog may be placed in the scary position of having to do her job with no guidance—if for some reason you're unconscious—just when she needs it most. An example of this would be a service dog pushing a panic alarm in the home after her owner collapses.

If you never leave her to work out some aspects of skills for herself on her own initiative, she could flounder when you start to teach intelligent disobedience. She might understand the skill as taught but go to pieces when no handler input is forthcoming in a real-life scenario. I'm not saying to avoid meticulously training your dog and setting her up for success; just allow her to develop the habit of doing some thinking for herself, depending on the task-work you need.

Teaching these sorts of skills can take time. Sometimes you'll move forward quickly, other times you won't. There are no prizes for the quickest trained service dog. It really makes no difference if your dog takes one year or three years to fully train—what matters is her partnership and bond with you, her reliability, and her help in mitigating the majority of your disabilities, especially the ones for which you need the most help.

From the start, it's also worthwhile deciding on the specific words and/or hand signals you will use to help ensure commands are not mixed up. How easy is it for us to give dogs confusing instructions? Is there anyone reading who has not inadvertently told their dog to "sit down" when usually "sit" and "down" are two entirely different commands? I know I have! Also decide on whether you may continue to use a clicker (if you have been using one) or whether to transition to marker words.

I don't tend to use clicker training with my own dogs. I prefer to use marker words, since even adjustable clickers are too loud for me due to my noise sensitivities. I also find that when the dog arrives to the stage of learning task-work, very soon she will be out and about working in the real world as a bona fide service dog. Clickers are fantastic for teaching new skills in a controlled environment, but for me at least they are not so easy to use with a service dog doing her job in the real world.

I find it hard to remember my own head most days, never mind a clicker. Plus trying to click while holding a shopping basket as well as a lead is not so easy for my arthritic fingers. If it works for you, there's no reason to stop using one. In general, though, even with dogs well-suited to clickers during training, it's time to wean off clickers and opt for marker words when you start to perform task-work outside the training room. You do need to take time to master the use of a good marker word, though, bearing in mind the type of enthusiastic "yes" that many of us use will have people staring. And not in a good way. More a *When Harry Met Sally* way. Now that's a blast from the past.

Once you are confident with your task-work at home, there comes a time when you must start to train those tasks in the real world. With some tasks it's only in public that the final task can be fully and properly trained. For example, a dog may learn to touch a target stick, then to press with her nose a spot the target stick touches, the end task being to press the button for an automatic door to open and give wheelchair access, for example, which is only found at certain shops.

Dogs do not generalize well. Even though your dog may be performing certain tasks excellently at home, she may appear confused when asked to perform the exact same task in public. When teaching medical alert, I initially teach the dog basic scent-work in a training room, expanding into different rooms of the home. I then will train her in the garden, and then eventually in public places, taking it slowly, step by step so my dog has time to work out that she must indicate whenever she detects a certain smell, no matter her location or the activity we are enjoying together.

The discussion of medical alert training neatly leads us onto proofing our training. This is particularly important for all tasks, and none more so than that of medical alert tasks, where it's incredibly easy to inadvertently tell the dog the correct answer through your own body language. Take the story of the horse called Clever Hans. He had scientists and even his own owner convinced for many years that he could count as well as any calculator. He would give answers to sums by pawing the ground.

Hans could not, of course, count, but he perhaps had an even more impressive skill: deciphering the body language of humans to determine when they expected him to stop counting, whether it was his owner, an audience of admirers, or scientists sent to study him. It was only when Hans could not see anyone that his powers of addition, subtraction, multiplication and division failed him. One of the tasks I have taught Mazey is to bark when I move an eyebrow. This enables me to ask her to bark without a person knowing I have done this—say, for example, if they are invading my personal space, even with Mazey blocking them from trying to get too close.

If I was proofing medical alert scent-work, I would ask a friend to pass me a swab without knowing myself whether there was a scent on that swab that should trigger the dog to give a medical alert. If the dog does not alert when she should have (or vice versa), I may step back several stages in her training. It's possible I was giving the dog clues during her training, and she had been reading my body language and determining what I expected her reaction to be instead of genuinely reacting to the scent.

Once your public access training is sorted and your task-work is complete (though there is always more to teach) I think it's time for a big pat on the back, plus a tub of ice cream to congratulate yourself. You now have a fully trained service dog. Your dog's wonderful behavior is a testament to all of the blood, sweat, tears and sheer hard work you have put into her. Training a service dog is not easy, particularly when disabled and self-training, so don't downplay your achievement. Learn to bask in the admiring glances. And you never know; you may even find a new career for yourself. You will have many people stop you and ask you who trained your dog. If you can, enjoy it.

Chapter Eleven

Out and About

Many people think being able to take your service dog with you everywhere is wonderful. Some feel quite jealous of service dog handlers, wishing they could do the same with their pet dogs. In part, it's true. Every day I wake up and feel truly blessed to have Mazey in my life. I appreciate the chance to form a truly unique relationship and bond with a totally different species; a dog that accepts me for who I am, even though I often don't believe I deserve such love and devotion.

However, on the flip side of the coin, I only have Mazey because I need her in order to live as close to a normal life as possible. Being disabled brings a lot of challenges, and the reality of taking your dog everywhere you go is substantially different from what many pet owners may think it is. Service dog handlers put in a massive amount of work into the training of their dogs, in addition to the great responsibility they have for their dog's behavior in public, which is seen as a reflection of the disabled person themselves.

There are also some unexpected disadvantages to working a service dog out and about. The main one is being constantly stared at and secretly photographed without your consent. It's a bit like dating a Z-list celebrity, but without the looks, glamour, nice clothes and fat paycheck. Bah humbug. Mazey does sometimes get dog treats from kind passersby, but no one offers me chocolates.

My aim in this chapter is to give readers of this book a realistic glimpse into what it's like to be disabled and working a service dog in public, and why some service dog handlers may come across as entitled and narcissistic if approached. I also want to provide guidelines as to the type of behavior that should be expected from service dogs and their handlers. There's a lot of discussion these days about fake service dogs, but as we saw in preceding chapters, provided the handler meets the criteria for disability, and the (adult) dog can perform one task—which can be an incredibly simple task—then that dog **is** a legitimate service dog. It's not for anyone else to judge the worth of that task to the dog's disabled handler.

I do want to stress that it *is* a privilege to have a service dog. It just is. Not every country in the world allows service dogs, never mind permits owners to train their own service dog as is the case in both the U.S. and UK. In essence, we in the service dog community police ourselves in terms of our dog's conduct and behavior. Of course, our disabilities may be entirely unwanted, but those of us who are disabled and who have a service dog should not take for granted the ability to take our service dogs almost everywhere with us. Our service dogs don't have to be automatons with no character, but neither should they be disruptive and a nuisance to other people.

Not everyone likes dogs, and if I'm honest, I don't like badly behaved dogs myself, whether pets or service dogs. Nor do I like pushy service dog handlers taking advantage of the law and order to gain special treatment that they feel entitled to but that they deserve no more and no less than anyone else. Some of these handlers seem to take pleasure in spoiling the enjoyment of members of the public who do not appreciate their badly behaved service dog. These handlers are in the minority, but as self-training is growing, so are the number of entitled brats who want to push their service dog down everyone's throat.

More and more I see service dogs being given license to misbehave under the guise of "working" when in many cases they are not performing task-work. They are simply being naughty or have had no training at all and may be acting out of confusion or fear. Just have a look at the social media accounts of a range of service dog handlers, and you'll see a few absolutely amazing service dogs, but also a plethora of barking, growling, lunging dogs. More often than not they are described as giving a "medical alert" to strangers as an excuse for their dog barking, lunging and jumping up on these passersby.

Such service dogs are not giving medical alerts; rather, the dog is reacting to strangers and is out of control. Saying the dog is "sensitive to the needs of others" and is "giving a medical alert so she can save the lives of people with undiagnosed medical conditions" is fantasy, more akin to something that comes out of a bull's behind. It's not real. Service dogs are just that: dogs. There are occasions where pet dogs or service dogs will detect biochemical changes in their owners or in strangers, perhaps repeatedly sniffing a certain body part that is then found to have a tumor at a later date. But that generally occurs when the dog is in close contact with the person for a period of time. This is very different from a service dog walking up to a random person in a shop and suddenly jumping up on them.

Now it's not for me or anyone else to rain on someone's parade and call them out individually when I see this sort of video online. Being disabled is a nightmare at times, and depression runs rife, particularly with young service dog handlers who may never find a job or live even a remotely normal life. If a handler is so desperate for validation from strangers online that he needs to post a video of his dog misbehaving and claim his dog is "saving lives," then there's a lot going on under the surface. People can and do get bullied into suicide. If you see a far-fetched video that looks entirely fake, just grit your teeth and scroll past.

Oh dear, it does seem I woke up on the wrong side of the bed this morning. Ranty ranty and it's only 9 a.m.! I suppose it's because this subject is extremely dear to my heart. Those of us who have legitimate service dogs that behave well in public get tired of business owners who, having previous bad experiences with poorly behaved service dogs, then take it out on us. We are left having to defend ourselves and our access rights.

The plague of fake, badly behaved service dogs has long-term consequences. It's playing right into the hands of some of the national and international service dog organizations who would like nothing more than to stage a coup and take over the entire industry and do away with owner-trained service dogs and freedom of choice. This would leave me housebound, so I will fight it until my dying breath and then onward as a particularly mischievous poltergeist.

So how should service dogs behave in public? The answer is they should behave well. They should walk where their handler asks them to, whether that be by their handler's side, in front of their handler, or occasionally behind them. Service dogs should not approach or jump up on people, nor sniff or pick up goods in a shop unless their handler specifically asks them to do so. Being a service dog involves a lot of hanging around, so they should have the ability to wait patiently for their handler without barking, whining or otherwise causing a fuss. All service dogs should be fully house trained and should not toilet in shops or other indoor areas. Many are trained to toilet on command and will have been asked to go to the toilet before working, though like us humans, it is possible to get caught out once in a while.

Most service dog trainers recommend that you always have hold of your dog's lead in some way. However, this doesn't reflect real life. In lots of circumstances, both indoors and outdoors, there is simply not enough space to walk side by side with your service dog. Architects do not design with the disabled in mind. There are different ways of tackling these issues, such as using an extendable lead. Other people like me find it much easier to work our service dog off-lead at times. When I do this, I tuck Mazey's lead into the handle of her harness so it's not trailing on the ground.

On those occasions when I do need to work Mazey off-lead, I will then usually ask her to perform a send-away. This is where I will point in the direction I want her to go, give the command, whereby she will set off at a steady trot in that direction. When I want her to stop, I will ask her to sit/down, then to stay. She will remain in that spot until I can catch up with her and give her a release command, where I then ask her to heel by my side. I usually use a send-away in very narrow corridors or spaces, or narrow paths outdoors where there are no other people around so no one is disturbed to see a large Rottweiler advancing on them. Alone.

If there are too many people around for a send-away, I typically ask Mazey to "go first," which means she puts herself about one Rottweiler length in front of me, squeezing through spaces or gaps between people ahead of me, all the while still on-lead. This is fine for weaving our way through dense crowds, though great care has to be taken that the lead does not get tangled around anyone's legs. Mazey is a large dog with a lot of confidence and presence, so she can easily make space for herself, but smaller or less experienced large dogs would struggle with such an exercise. However, small dogs do have the advantage of being able to be temporarily picked up, or to jump onto their handler's lap if in a wheelchair.

Most service dog trainers will also tell you that your dog must maintain a heel position at your side at all times and that they must always be on a loose lead. This is a preconceived notion of how service dogs should work. It is then thrust onto disabled handlers by trainers with no disability themselves, without consideration for what the individual needs are of some service dog handlers, especially people with psychiatric service dogs.

As part of her task-work, Mazey always walks slightly ahead of me, her tail just beside my legs and to the side of me, with a slightly taut lead. Mazey is not being disobedient and pulling on her lead—though she will if I ask her to—for example, to assist pulling me up a steep hill. Rather, I have the lead with a certain degree of tightness to give me confidence that Mazey is there supporting me and that we are a team, taking on the world together. It's similar to holding a child's hand, or riding a horse and having a contact with the reins.

Mazey wears a harness so this contact is not uncomfortable for her, and she will immediately come back into a heelwork position at my side with a loose lead whenever asked. I find that many people with psychiatric service dogs have this preference when working their dog, particularly people with PTSD, anxiety, and autism, so if you see a service dog working this way, please do not assume it is a disobedient dog with poor heelwork.

Due to the arthritis in my hands and fingers, I often struggle to hold Mazey's lead when handling multiple items, such as objects in a shop I have picked up to inspect. At the checkout I always work her off-lead when putting goods onto a conveyor belt, getting my wallet from my bag to pay, and packing goods into my bag. Mazey has an excellent stay, so I can trust her to remain where she is at my feet, not moving a muscle, even though I have my back turned to her and am not paying her any attention whatsoever.

Retaining a stay in this way is an important thing for a service dog to learn. And for a friendly dog like Mazey, it's essential she understands she is not to give into temptation and break her stay to go over to people who may be making kissy noises at her or otherwise trying to encourage her over to them for a pat and cuddle. It is at these times, when your back is turned, that people will typically try and go for a cheeky pat or hug with your service dog.

Other disabled handlers are the total opposite to me and prefer not to have their dog off-lead ever, using extendable leads for times when it's impossible to walk side by side, in addition to using belts and harness, such as those used in canicross, to tether the dog to themselves or to their wheelchair. Still others prefer to never have their dog on-lead at all, though even with a very well behaved, reliable dog like Mazey, I would be petrified to do this. I would not recommend it for the vast majority of service dog teams, particularly outside where there are a lot of temptations. In the UK, many people tie up their dogs outside the door to shops, and if your off-lead service dog is attacked, it's much easier to separate two fighting dogs if both at least have a lead on.

The reason some service dog handlers mainly work their service dog off-lead, and indeed there are times when this is advisable, is if the handler is susceptible to seizures. Once such a service dog has given a medical

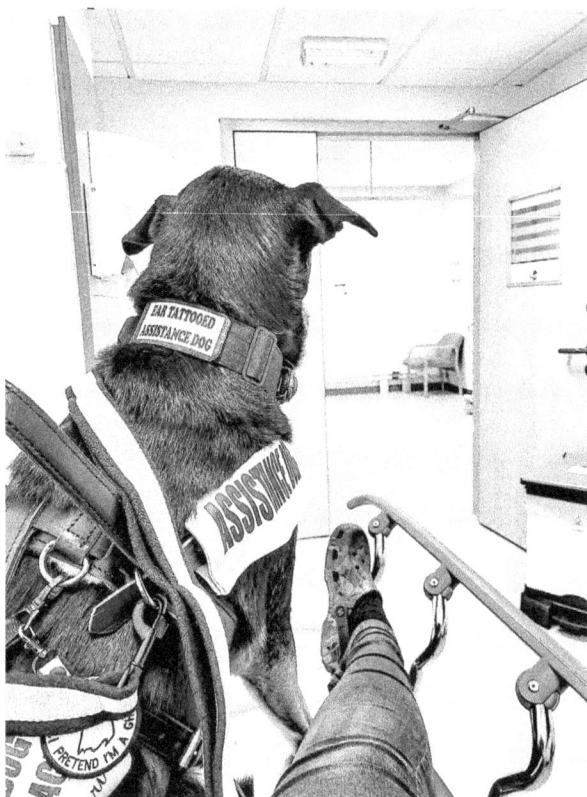

Service dog Ezra doing an amazing job assisting his owner when she was admitted to the hospital. Photo by Ashley Tysall, his owner and trainer (2022). Reproduced by permission of the photographer.

alert and a seizure is on its way, it's recommended that the service dog is not tethered to the handler, or otherwise restrained by them. Instead, the dog should be able to move out of the way when their owner is fitting to avoid potentially striking the dog with uncontrollable body movements.

If you see a service dog working while out and about, she should be unobtrusive, although a lot will depend on the tasks required of the dog and the handler's preference. I like Mazey to give an initial medical alert by moving in front of me, laying her head firmly against my leg, and making eye contact with me. If I'm starting to dissociate and I ignore her, she will then move to a second stage of alert and bark to get my attention.

I'm a private person, so I prefer not to have people staring at me. We are all different in both our personalities and our needs. Some service dogs will be taught to give a medical alert by repeatedly barking loudly and spinning round and round in circles in front of their handler. I would absolutely hate this and feel mortified at the disruption. But I can understand the point of it: should you fall ill, your service dog will alert you and any passersby within a ten-mile radius. This may prove very useful indeed.

Service dogs are remarkable, but they are not robots. Dogs are dogs, and as such they will have off days. In addition, all service dogs all have very different personalities. There are service dogs who will totally mind their own business, concentrating solely on their handler, oblivious to whatever else is going on around them. Other service dogs have much more gregarious, inquisitive natures and like nothing more than to say "hello" to everyone they may meet when out working. Mazey falls distinctly into the latter category.

I'm a bit of a recluse and very rarely go places such as restaurants or cafes, but if I have to eat out, Mazey will happily tuck under a cafe table and snooze. Mazey's main job in public is working in shops, or occasionally coming to medical appointments with me, including overnight stays in the hospital. If you're being admitted to the hospital as a planned stay and intend to take your service dog with you, always discuss it with hospital staff beforehand and ask to see a copy of the hospital's policy on service dogs if one exists.

You may find hospitals that are anti service dog. They will demand a whole series of hoops are jumped through in order to try and put you off bringing your service dog with you. They may want to carry out a risk assessment on you and your individual service dog, which would typically include proof of vaccination, worming and flea treatments, and also proof that you hold adequate third-party liability insurance for a specified minimum amount or that the dog has undergone certain training. Other hospitals have an entirely different attitude and offer dog beds, food and water bowls, plus emergency dog food supplies, all ready and waiting for service dogs who are admitted unexpectedly along with their handler.

I can't speak on the legality of forcing the owners of service dogs in the U.S. to comply with certain health, training and insurance requirements, so if you encounter significant problems that seem unreasonable, it would be best to consult with an attorney. In the UK, unfortunately many hospitals have illegal service dog policies, merrily breaking the law as though the hospital is its own nation-state.

This is due to medical organizations, which shall not be named, giving advice that directly contradicts both the Equality Act and the policy documents written by the UK Commission on Equality and Human Rights. The commission is aware of the problem but can't afford to enforce the law against individual hospitals. Damages for disability discrimination are so low in the UK that solicitors will not take on cases without very high retainers paid upfront, leaving ordinary people with no legal recourse whatsoever. I almost died of sepsis once due to the actions of my local hospital, but that would be a book all in itself.

Regarding service dog behavior in the hospital, some hospital staff prefer to know where a service dog is and have encouraged me to allow Mazey to sleep on my bed with me, for the comfort of us both, and also so they know she has not gone off exploring. Mazey would not do this, but many other service dogs will, particularly when their handler is fast asleep and visitors are offering her biscuits.

Mazey has also slept under my bed, though this can be a double-edged sword. One older lady had not realized Mazey was with me. When she saw a large Rottweiler suddenly appear from the ground (i.e., from under my bed), she started screaming and thought a demon had come to take her to hell. It was funny, but also not funny, and it makes you wonder what bad deeds in her life made her think she was going to hell. She lightened up when she saw that Mazey was real and subsequently enjoyed some cuddles with her.

The main thing is, wherever you go, your service dog should not disturb other people unnecessarily. In addition to behaving around people, they should not be kicking off, barking and growling at other service dogs. I would say out of all the service dogs we have met in public, this has been 50:50 in terms of quiet versus reactive. Sometimes a dog will give a bark of surprise if you bump into each other round a corner, or a young service dog may whine slightly as she may want to play. They are dogs. It happens. It's fine. What is unacceptable, however, are untrained, scared, disruptive or aggressive service dogs screaming, lunging and barking repeatedly at another service dog that had the audacity to quietly walk by.

As I said, I don't eat out much. But if you do, be considerate and don't go for a meal until your dog can behave suitably in such a public setting. Your service dog should not be asked to settle in a place where servers and members of the public are going to trip over her, or her trailing lead, or the corner of any settle mat you may have provided for her. Both your dog and her gear need to be safely out of the way, which is usually under the table if she will fit. Not all breeds will, and if you have a big dog, serving staff should try and find you a suitable table where you can eat in a relaxed way without worrying your dog may become a trip hazard.

Most large service dogs are adept at curling up out of the way below chairs or tucked in right beside their handlers. Small service dogs are no different and belong on the ground in a restaurant/cafe/bus/train just as much as a larger service dog does. Their lesser stature does not give small service dogs license to sit on tables or on chairs beside their owner. If you have a settle mat that is not going to cover items with dog hair, then by all means ask whoever is in charge if it's ok to sit your small dog on a chair beside you. But don't expect it as your God-given right. If they say yes, happy days, but don't assume they have to make this adaptation for you.

I know it can be hard working a small service dog in busy shops where they may potentially be stood on, and it's a legitimate worry for a great many handlers that their small dog will be injured. To offset this, many owners plonk their small service dogs into shopping baskets or in the child seat of shopping carts. I see this all the time where I live. Often the dog is not even placed on a settle mat to stop hair going everywhere. Some supermarkets are accepting of a dog on a settle mat, and the cart is then put aside by staff for cleaning after use, but always check. Putting your dog directly in a cart or basket, where dog hair may then contaminate the next person's shopping, is just not cool, and it can even be illegal. In the U.S. the DOJ advises that small dogs not be placed in carts but rather be carried by their owners.

I have seen a variety of excuses for placing small service dogs in shopping carts and baskets, or for sitting them beside their handlers on chairs in restaurants and cafes. I have even seen them placed on the table itself. The insidious online service dog groups and forums that preach entitlement advise handlers to tell people that their small service dog has to smell the owner's breath from directly inside of their mouth in order to give a medical alert, leading to the handler gormlessly unhinging their jaw like a snake in order to prove the dog needs to stick their snout directly into their oral cavity. Obviously a display of that sort shuts up anyone who suspects the dog does not need to sit on a chair or even on the tablecloth.

I accept that some service dogs like to put their nose right up to their handler's face when "checking in" and searching for a scent. Nothing wrong with that. All dogs work in different ways. However, training a dog in this way, or permitting a dog this preference, does *not* entitle the handler to insist their dog must permanently sit inches away from their mouth at all times. A dog's sense of smell is amazing. It's quite literally their superpower, and they do not need to tickle their handler's tonsils in order to smell changes in the chemical composition of saliva. A handler can bend down to let their dog "check in" every so often as the owner of a large dog would do, or they can use swabs to put the saliva on, or heaven forbid, a well-trained dog will quickly and easily detect the scent from the ground several feet away with no issues whatsoever.

If the dog does need to get that close and personal, and must hover within inches of their handler's mouth at all times or can't otherwise do their job, then in my view the dog is quite simply not up to the job. She may be too inexperienced or she has not yet developed sufficient sensitivity in order to safely perform medical alert in public places. Or the dog may not be suitable for medical alert task-work. Not all dogs have the drive and concentration for this type of work, and there's absolutely no shame in that. When owners insist the dog needs to go mouth-to-mouth with them, it is usually because the dog picked up medical alerts on their own and have never been formally and methodically trained to perform it as a proper task. More often than not the alert is the dog licking the handler's lips and mouth, which may be backed up by "a certain look in her eye."

Some of these alerts are fake. But many are not fake, and the dog has legitimately used her acute intelligence to learn the job of medical alert all on her own and has found licking her handler's mouth an effective way of simultaneously confirming the scent (as she has generally smelt it from the ground first) and gaining her handler's immediate attention. With such a dog I would tend to train a more effective alert that does not risk infecting the handler with tapeworm or other zoonotic nasties from your dog's behind, which we all know dogs enjoy licking frequently. But each to their own.

In conclusion, if you're a business owner who sees a small service dog sitting on your nice clean tablecloth, sipping tea from your best bone china cups, this is not appropriate behavior. You do not have to put up with it, and you can ask that the dog be placed on the ground, regardless of wails to the contrary. If the handler is so concerned about the dog having direct access to their mouth at all times, then a baby carrier can be used instead, or if that is not feasible, they can simply "check in" with the dog at frequent intervals, as I described above.

Be careful, though, of being respectful when discussing service dogs and any alleged misbehavior. In the U.S., you may only ask two questions of the handler as regards the legitimacy of their service dog. Those questions are (a) is the dog a service dog who is required because of a disability on the part of the handler? and (b) what work or task has the dog been trained to perform? That's it. You cannot ask for any documentation regarding training or certification, nor proof of the owner's medical conditions. In the UK, things are less clear-cut as regards what you can and cannot say to a handler, and I would advise all business owners to read the advice given by the Equality and Human Rights Commission.

There, I've said it. I will wait for the parcel bombs in the mail from the owners of lip-licking service dogs, both large and small. Before we leave the topic of working dogs in places with seating and tables: if you do have your service dog with you in a cafe or restaurant, please don't let them sit and stare at other people eating their food, more often than not producing copious saliva to drip onto the floor. It can be unsettling for anyone to be stared at by a dog while they're eating and trying to enjoy a meal, plus people with eating disorders can be very negatively affected by being watched while they eat. Yes, even by a dog.

So, the dog should be well behaved, but what about the old chestnut of service dogs ignoring all and sundry while working? My service dog, my beloved Mazey, has a "personality," and I adore that about her. She's extremely intelligent and quite simply loves life. She takes a keen interest in whatever is going on around her. Mazey's tail is always up in the air, curved like a saber, happily wagging. Her eyes are bright as buttons, full of fun and goodwill, and she has a bounce in her step. Service dogs need

Cute though she is, would you want Mina preparing to eat your lunch? I think not! Photo by the author (2021).

to look where they are going. It's not feasible to work them in an obedience position, constantly trying to make eye contact with their handler. Mazey walks close by my side, or more often than not, slightly in front of me, looking about her as she pleases.

As Mazey is an extremely gregarious dog, she often attempts to make eye contact with any person she feels may fall for her obvious charms, hoping they will ask me if they can pet her. This usually occurs when my attention is elsewhere—for example, if I'm in a shop looking at the labels on products, or at the checkout, paying for and packing goods, at which point Mazey will be sitting by my side. Don't get me wrong, Mazey will not move toward anyone that returns her gaze, but she will initiate eye contact and wag her tail appealingly.

In most service dog circles this innocuous behavior is frowned upon and is called "soliciting attention." It's considered a big no-no for a service dog, but there's never any explanation as to *why* this is such a heinous crime. I'm not most people, and I'm not going to upset my dog in order to obey a pointless rule that makes no sense to me. I really don't mind at all if Mazey makes lovey-dovey eyes at passersby. If they don't want to return her gaze, then they can keep walking and ignore her. A cat, or rather a dog, can look at a king. Or a Walmart shopper, as the case may be.

Mazey is who she is. I'm never going to punish her for being a friendly dog who is relaxed and happy in her job, living her best life. She's experienced at what she does, and she has no need to fix me with a stare of death in order to tell whether or not a

I'm lucky to have two super friendly dogs who introduce me to a lot of people and help me feel less lonely, although here, Mazey does not look amused at Mina photobombing a pic that should have been all about her. Photo by the author (2021).

medical alert may be imminent. Her nose does the talking in this scenario. Where people don't like Mazey, they barely notice her. Other individuals who can't resist Mazey's big Rottweiler smile and helicoptering tail are perfectly welcome to ask if they can say hello to her. Mostly I say yes. Mazey enjoys the break, and I do too.

Now of course I understand why many service dog handlers hate it when strangers approach them and ask to stroke their service dog. I get it. People have all sorts of trauma in their lives and seeing a strange person approach can be extremely threatening and intimidating. When you've been brutalized in the past, it doesn't matter how objectively safe your surroundings are, that terror can kick in at any time.

Other service dog handlers may not particularly like other humans very much, especially humans they have never met before. Again, I totally understand. Meeting new people and not knowing what to say can be extremely awkward. Or a handler may be in a hurry with no time to stop for a chit chat with a stranger. Or they may have suffered a bereavement and be on the verge of breaking down in tears or bordering on a panic attack because they are in a busy public place. There are any number of reasons why a handler may not want to be approached by a stranger wanting to love on their service dog.

Some young service dogs, if excited or distracted by a person patting them, may then struggle to get back into the swing of their work. For many tasks, this is simply annoying, but for others, this can be legitimately dangerous for the handler. If a guide dog does not stop at a curb, their handler could break a leg from the unexpected step. Similarly a dog that misses a medical alert could cause their handler to fall and hit their head because the handler didn't have enough warning to get themselves settled. Plus, as I said in Chapter Two, in many U.S. states it's a crime to distract a service dog.

This may seem far-fetched, but it happens. Yes, maybe it could be argued that a service dog who is so inexperienced or poorly trained that a simple pat distracts her sufficiently to put her handler in danger is not up to the job. Did you do your own job perfectly when you were new to it? Probably not. It takes time for a service dog to properly learn their trade. Would you want it on your conscience that someone died because you could not resist a pat?

A service dog is not public property. Disabled people are just that: people. They have the same emotions, fears, hopes and dreams as everyone else. And as individuals their view of the world may differ from yours. They don't need to justify why they may not want their dog patted, or why they may not appreciate being approached and shamed into allowing it. Ask yourself: would you go up to a person in a wheelchair and start asking questions about their medical condition, the type of wheelchair they have, or whatever else, based on curiosity about the wheelchair? I suspect not. A service dog is no different. She is a medical aid, not a pet. Don't ask cheeky questions that are none of your business. If you do, expect cheeky answers.

If you do see a service dog like Mazey, one who's inviting attention, look at what the handler is doing first and whether it's likely they may welcome a conversation. If the handler avoids eye contact, deliberately looks away and ignores you, or worse still gives you a scowl worthy of Miss Trunchbull to your Matilda, chances are they *do not* want to be disturbed! Leave. Them. Alone. If, however, the handler smiles and initiates a conversation, then just ask if it's fine to say hello to their service dog. They may say "yes" or they may say "no." Don't get salty if you're turned down. Everyone has a life, and other people have no obligation to strike up a conversation with a perfect stranger, even if they are polite to you.

My advice, then: if you see a service dog, err very strongly on the side of caution. If you're close enough, read the labeling on the service dog's vest/cape/lead sleeve, but don't shimmy up to the dog just to get close enough to do so, accidentally trailing your hand over the dog's head. If a dog is plastered with labels that say "do not distract" as most are, then heed that warning. Don't even ask to pat the dog. I can guarantee the handler will have noticed your approach, and if he offers to let you say hello to his service dog, all well and good. Go for it. But just try to be respectful and don't ask to pat a service dog when the handler clearly wants to be left alone.

If you do get a good response and start chatting with a person with a service dog, be mindful that they are a human being with feelings just like anyone else. Do not be rude and ask intrusive, intimate questions you probably would hesitate to ask a third date, never mind a total stranger. One of the most common questions I get is people trying to find out what my disability is. This is rude!!!! How would you feel if I had never met you, yet started asking what your medical history was? Or I asked you about your salary as I saw you getting out of a fancy car and was curious. You would not like it at all, would you? Similarly, service dog handlers do not enjoy being asked about their disabilities.

I don't want everyone to know what my medical conditions are. Some service dog charities/organizations will advertise what disability/medical condition is represented on the service dog's cape/vest/jacket, either explicitly or easily ascertainable via the name of the charity/organization. I don't like this. When Mazey was part of a service dog charity/organization, out of principle I never worked her in her vest.

Often the question about disability will come in a roundabout way. People will ask me, "what does she do for you?", instead of being direct and asking what my disabilities are. My answer will depend on the person. Sometimes people don't approve of Mazey because she's a Rottweiler, and despite her excellent behavior, they assume she's a fake service dog and are trying to catch me out.

So, if I'm asked, "what does she do for you?", I may answer, "she helps me." If they then say, "how does she help you," I might reply, "she mitigates my disabilities." After a few of these types of questions and vague answers, usually people will recognize they are being rude and apologize. Or they will get aggressive and double down, pressing me with stupid questions, even though by this stage they realize such questions are not going to be answered.

If the person in question is nice and has made a genuine mistake of being rude out of sheer curiosity and thoughtlessness, then I may say Mazey does medical alert for me and leave it there. If we chat some more and they are being genuinely friendly, I may explain I have quite severe autism, have arthritis, etc., and describe to them some of the tasks Mazey does for me, such as switching on lights, reminding me to take my medication, picking things up that I drop, etc. I find that the people who may initially have been the most inadvertently rude often feel they would benefit from their own service dog, but don't know how to go about getting one. They see Mazey and it's like a cat spotting a mouse. They gather up their energy and pounce.

I'm a non-confrontational person, so when vague answers rile people and they start to get aggressive, I'll be more polite than they deserve, saying it was nice to chat with them but I have to go. I will then ignore them, turn and leave. If they try and stop me in any way, I will ask Mazey to get between us and to block them from getting close to me. This is one of Mazey's tasks, a common one for psychiatric service dogs. Because she's a Rottweiler, very confident and solid in build, no one has yet tried to skip past Mazey to accost me further.

If I'm feeling scared or threatened about such an encounter, particularly if the person in question starts to follow me—and you would be surprised how many people will do this if you refuse to engage further—then if in a shop I will find a member of staff and let them know that I'm being harassed. Do not hesitate to do this. Your safety comes first, and most stores will have CCTV and will call the police if a person persists in stalking you. If you're outside and feel scared to go back to your car alone, again find a shop and let the staff know what is happening. Most store personnel are happy to send security/another staff member with you if you're parked nearby or call the police if the store is small and there's a chance the person is trying to hide but is really lying in wait outside.

I have only had this happen once, when a guy was waiting for me outside a supermarket. Thank goodness I had asked security to escort me to my car. The guy took one look at security, then legged it. However, I have had people follow me around a store on more than one occasion. One lady even tried again and again to ram into Mazey with her buggy before she was asked by the store manager to leave after knocking over a display. Really, what gets into people?

This sort of behavior is sadly why more and more people want a service dog who is also trained in personal protection, which I personally think has too much potential for going terribly wrong, unless, of course, the handler is an expert in this field and is regularly training the dog themselves in personal protection work. Most of the time the fierce—well, okay, adorable—look of a Rottweiler, German Shepherd or Belgian Malinois is enough to deter people out for trouble. But these breeds also come with a lot of responsibility and require a great deal of exercise and training all of their lives.

As well as blocking people from getting too close as part of their task-work, a service dog can also be taught to rhythmically bark at them, as Mazey does. Barking in addition to blocking is something I would only use if I felt under imminent, real danger from a person, as it could be easily misinterpreted and get Mazey into trouble in the UK for acting "dangerously out of control." I would rather just squirt such a person in the eyes with dog deterrent spray if under attack than get Mazey involved at all.

For those of you considering a service dog, please don't be put off too much at the thought of being stalked or otherwise harassed. There are bad people in all walks of life, and you're going to end up meeting some of them whether you have a service dog or not. The key to deterring unwanted attention after it has started is advance preparation. In addition to putting plenty of "do not disturb" patches on your dog's vest/cape, I would also advise to have a ready-made list of words and phrases to say to people when they want to pat your service dog and you just want to be left alone. You can also carry some laminated pre-printed cards to show people if, like me, you can become overwhelmed and nonverbal. This can be extremely effective as it makes people sit back and check their entitlement to intrude on your time, space and service dog.

I find honesty is often the best policy. If you're busy or want your own space, say just that. Should you have to be apologetic for not wanting someone to pat your service dog? No, absolutely not. But as the old saying goes, you catch more bees with honey than vinegar. Or something like that. Was it wasps, or even murder hornets? I hope not. Bear in mind I am a Brit, and we do have a dreadful habit of apologizing, even when we shouldn't have to.

If you really want to disarm someone, you could mention you're upset over a recent bereavement, and need some space or you'll start crying. Or you could bring up the fact that you need a kidney donor and inquire about their blood type, as they seem such a kind, giving person. Maybe they would like to donate to your Go Fund Me for a tattoo of Satan, or perhaps they want to have a conversation about Jesus/veganism/joining the local knit and natter group/a discussion on purely positive training versus balanced training /Brazilian butt lifts/the pros and cons of a back, crack and sack wax, or whatever you think may alarm them the most. Anyway, you get the idea: if in doubt, overshare.

No matter the vast amount of patches you have on your service dog's vest/cape, or how good your resting bitch face is, certain individuals will not even try to strike up a conversation but will come up, totally ignore you and commence patting your dog or otherwise distracting her. This is not the worst of it. People think nothing of taking photographs and video footage of you and your service dog without asking for your permission. Some look embarrassed if the flash goes off by mistake and you catch them in the act; others have not a care in the world.

Sadly, I don't think there is anything you can do to prevent these sorts of things from happening. It is part and parcel of life with a service dog. When you become an actor or actress, you may not want fame, but it comes with the lifestyle and job description. The same can be said for owning and working a service dog. Disabled people with service dogs do not ask to be the subject of curiosity of all and sundry, but this is what happens. And it can be a deal breaker for many people.

If you do not believe you can cope with the constant attention, or somehow work around it, then a service dog may not be for you. I should not have to write this but it needs to be said, as it saddens me when people give up working their service dog in public because they cannot cope with the hassle. Although passersby may in many countries be breaking the law by distracting your service dog, it does not in practice give the protection it does in theory. You do tend to get used to it in time, though. I'm a shy sort of person myself, and now I hardly notice the constant stares and chatter when people see me and Mazey out together.

If you're on the fence about getting a service dog, see if you can find a willing individual to let you observe their service dog partnership for a few hours. If possible, try working the dog a little on your own, perhaps with the handler walking just behind. Two people together give a false impression, and I have always found that if I am out with a care worker and Mazey, the chatter about us quiets. No one tries to take photographs, and it's infrequent for people to approach and ask to pat her.

Another way to mitigate attention that I found useful was to go shopping in the middle of the night when it's quiet. Another tactic you could use to repel people is to keep up a constant stream of conversation with your dog. I do this with Mazey as if she was a person. This may make me seem crazy, but I love Mazey and I like to speak to her.

However, this can backfire. One staff member in a supermarket told me I needed to "behave like a normal disabled person," because apparently chatting away to Mazey was not the normal thing and someone had complained! I wasn't belting out the greatest country anthems of 1965, just minding my own business and asking Mazey questions, such as whether she wanted lamb mince or beef stew for tea. This was demeaning in the extreme, and it's one of the few occasions I complained to a company's head office about the conduct of a staff member.

Ironically, when you find yourself secretly filmed it is by other members of the service dog community. A small minority of service dog handlers can be extremely poisonous, hunting for people they do not approve of. Some even take day trips to where that person lives to hang around their homes and the shops they frequent, all so they can film them working their service dog. The footage is then unfairly edited and plastered over the internet in fake service dog groups. Yes, people really do have so little to do with their time that they go on these groups.

To my knowledge this has not happened to me, or of it has, none of my friends and acquaintances have told me about it. I'm not a member of any of these groups and have left even many of the more positive service dog groups and forums I have been on because there seems to be a lot of self-righteous anger in them these days. Instead of being safe places to learn and discuss working and training our dogs, they have become a place where witch hunts and in-fighting are common. I'm not a drama llama, so off I toddled.

By now you may be running for the hills, determined not to touch a service dog with a bargepole. Or, if you have a narcissistic personality and dream of a poodle dyed every color under the sun, with a clip like a stegosaurus, you're imaging all the admiration you may get. The attention a service dog attracts when out in public is not all bad news though. I have met some remarkably nice people when chatting out and about. I have also found that on the whole people treat me better when I have Mazey with me.

Autism, as with other invisible disabilities such as anxiety, depression, seizures, irritable bowel syndrome, rheumatoid arthritis or whatever else, makes life incredibly tough, and people can be cruel and intolerant. Being different is not as celebrated in real life as it may appear online or in the movies, where the geek gets the girl and the jock is left on the shelf. I have always been bullied for being different, even in shops where sales assistants look down their nose at me for something as minor as mismatched socks, or wearing a T-shirt with cats on it. Mazey's presence alerts people to the fact that I do have a disability, and even though I don't advertise what my disabilities are, people do now stop and think before automatically judging me. It helps. It helps a lot.

One of the urban myths that abounds on the internet is that if you see a service dog on their own, their handler is lying unconscious in a ditch somewhere and the dog has been trained to go and find help. Unless the service dog is quite obviously a reincarnation of Rin Tin Tin or Lassie, this is probably not correct. Most service dogs are trained to stay with their handlers in the event of a medical emergency, not to go AWOL to find a passerby and lead them back to the injured handler.

If a service dog has acted on her own initiative and you meet her alone, and she tries to lead you in a certain direction, by all means follow her if you can. Dogs have been known to do this. Otherwise, if the dog is lost or scared, a much better bet is to try calling the phone number on the dog's name tag. If there is no answer, or the dog has no tag, then don't hesitate to call 911/999 and report that you have found a loose service dog. It's then up to the police to deal with the matter. Hopefully they will send an officer to collect the service dog and organize a search for the owner.

If you see a service dog giving a medical alert in public or see the handler sitting or lying on the ground, be led by their instructions if they are conscious. If they're unresponsive, don't try and lead the service dog away from them. This can cause great distress when the person wakes up and finds their service dog gone.

You may find details of the handler's medical conditions with the dog, perhaps in a barrel tag or in a saddlebag attached to her harness, or the handler may be wearing a medical alert bracelet. Some handlers who frequently lose consciousness take with them a pre-printed laminated card that they will place beside themselves before they lose consciousness, letting passersby know the best course of action—for example, not to call an ambulance and not to try to remove their service dog from their side.

Having covered all of that, let's move on. Some of us with service dogs do work or are lucky enough to be able to afford to go on holiday. If you are traveling and staying away from home, you do have the right to bring your service dog with you to stay in hotels and other accommodation that otherwise does not permit dogs. You should not be charged extra for bringing your service dog, but check state laws just in case. In the UK, some hotel chains specify that service dogs are exempt from additional charges. I would always go for a hotel chain that accepts service dogs and make it clear I am bringing one. Irrespective of protection the law may give you, it does not give you a bed to sleep in if you are turned away, so always err on the side of caution.

If traveling on holiday, bear in mind that you cannot go out and leave your service dog alone in the hotel room. Your service dog is there as a medical device, and as such needs to always be with you. So if you're planning a family vacation and may be going places service dogs are not welcome such as a zoo, then find accommodation that is dog friendly and will allow you to leave your service dog alone in your room for short periods of time.

Alas, we are almost at the end of this chapter, and what better way to finish than by taking a look at access issues. This is something almost every service dog handler will encounter at one time or another. There is nothing worse than happily going about your day and then suddenly you have a big bloke step right in front of you, tell you he's in charge of security and has been watching you, and since you're clearly not blind you have to get out of the shop/hospital/cafe or wherever you might be hanging. Unfortunately, there are still some employees who are ignorant of the law on service dogs and think only blind people are entitled to one. If it wasn't for the lack of enthusiasm on the part of the UK legal system to punish this sort of thing, I'd be a millionaire several times over.

In this day and age there really is no excuse for refusing you access when working your service dog in public. The thing to do if you are stopped is to keep calm. If you have a phone, you may want to consider recording the interaction if it's legal in your location. In the U.S., as I mentioned earlier in this chapter, the questions you can be asked regarding your service dog are very limited indeed. If they ask anything else, they are breaking the law. Only an attorney who is familiar with this area of law would have a good idea of how easy it is to sue, and how worthwhile it would be given how stressful and expensive lawsuits can be.

The UK is a whole other story. Although we have legislation, there is no black and white law to break as regards what can and cannot be asked regarding your service dog, though the Equality and Human Rights Commission does provide a guide to businesses. In addition, many businesses in the UK such as supermarkets and hospitals knowingly break the law with impunity, well aware it is nigh on impossible for them to be sued. And even if they were sued and lost, the damages would be tiny. This is not how it should be, but multiple other service dog handlers and I have tried to take legal action over very serious breaches of the law and have gotten nowhere.

If someone is nice and genuinely not trying to cause trouble when they stop me, then I will explain the law and if required pull out my printed guide to the relevant legislation: not the Act of Parliament itself but rather the Equality and Human Rights Commission Guide to Service Dogs. For those of you in the U.S., the Department of Justice FAQ page is useful. I also have the relevant websites bookmarked on my phone, but since I enjoy being unreachable, I don't always take my phone with me when I go out, hence also carrying paper copies. I'm not a handbag sort of girl, and I carry my rucksack with me everywhere, so stuffing the paper copies in the bottom suits me.

In the UK there is also something called an Access Card,[1] which can be purchased online. Among other things, the card gives details about your disabilities, any adjustments you may require—for example, a hearing loop—and, of course, the fact that you have a service dog. I don't have one myself, but other people have told me that they find them very useful.

Because I become extremely distressed when stopped and/or followed by security guards in shops and other places, I can become nonverbal. I therefore carry a very small selection of pre-printed laminated cards that I can use to communicate with people. This saves me from having to try and write out sentences with a pen and paper or on my phone, which is not easy when I'm upset and my hands are shaking, never mind the arthritis in my fingers and my admittedly appalling handwriting.

You can source these cards online or make your own. Mine have basic phrases explaining I am currently nonverbal, that Mazey is my service dog and that she performs medical alert and other tasks for me. I also have cards that state I have autism, to please leave me alone, to not touch Mazey, to not summon a first aider or an ambulance, and—when I want to unleash my inner Karen—to please call the manager. As you can see, the phrases you carry are really only limited by your imagination.

For those of you in the UK (and elsewhere) who may need to battle with hospital administrators in case of an emergency admission, or if flying and the legitimacy of your service dog is queried, it can be useful to always carry with you on your phone or in hard copy some pertinent details about your service dog. I would recommend scans of your service dog's vaccination certificates/titer test results, training logbook and other appropriate training documentation/tests passed, details of any service dog charity/organization membership, and also your third-party insurance documentation. You should not *need* to do any of this, but sadly in the UK it's better to be safe than sorry.

As a matter of routine, depending on your disabilities, you should consider whether you need to carry with you your emergency contacts and details of your next of kin, not forgetting pet sitters or boarding kennels who can take your service dog or any pets you own should you be in a serious accident. Although service dogs are permitted in hospitals, they are not allowed in sterile surgical units, or ICU/CCU where you would be too unwell to ask her to perform task-work or to look after her anyway. Her care is your responsibility and not that of medical staff.

It's always best to ensure your animals will be cared for in the event of an accident. This applies to everyone, not just people with service dogs. I mean, cats in particular have to be looked after in the manner to which they have become accustomed. They would never forgive you if they ever had to slum it with no staff. Even overnight.

Lastly, on a similar but glum note, it's never too early to make a will. No matter your age, make a will and set down exactly what you want to happen to your service dog and other animals. You may want your service dog to live out her life with suitable family members, or you may want her to go to work for another disabled person, doing the job she loves so very much and changing the life of another person, just as she did yours.

CHAPTER TWELVE

Service Dog Gear

There's a wide range of gear you can use with either a pet or a service dog. Much will depend on your dog, your disabilities, your purse strings, and of course your love of shopping. I'm quite minimalist myself, and due to my autism, I hate shopping. If I like something, I tend to buy about five identical items, hoping it will be years before they wear out. I sometimes do the same for Mazey and Mina's gear and toys (for training purposes). Therefore, Mina and Mazey sometimes dress like identical twins, which could get a tad creepy—like those sisters in *The Shining*—though luckily Mina is taller than Mazey so they don't look quite so identically sinister. Also, it has to be said: I'm a pretty basic girl, so I stick to pretty basic gear. Ha!

Most service dogs wear a collar, a lead, plus an identity tag if that is applicable where you live. Mazey, Mina and I reside in the UK, so legally my dogs must wear an identity tag when out in public. The tag records my name and address and, in addition to their microchips, helps get them home should they ever get lost. Legally the tag must have my surname, postcode and house number, though I also include my dog's name and my telephone number, as I would want to be contacted ASAP should either of my dogs go missing. You should check your local laws as regards both identity tags and microchips. This will vary from country to country and, if you live in the U.S., from state to state.

Collars can be made in a wide variety of designs, the simplest being flat-collar, which can be made in a multitude of different materials and styles. As I work Mazey on a harness, her collar is used to carry her identity tag. She has a beautiful rolled collar made from bridle leather, with brass fittings to match her fleek brows and tan points. I prefer nut brown leather, though many people would rather see a black collar on a black dog. The only real disadvantage with leather is that it can get stiff and hard when wet, so you may prefer a leather collar for pleasant summer days and a collar of another material for winter. Or all year in the UK.

It's also possible to get collars with a handle on them, which can be handy to grab onto if you have a young dog and need a bit more control, or if you need to use the handle to temporarily thread your lead through so it doesn't drag on the ground. Make sure the handle is wide enough for your own hand and easy to take hold of. Also check to see whether the collar is well balanced. I tried one on Mina not so long ago and because the handle was very well padded, it meant the handle was actually the heaviest part of the collar. Instead of the handle sitting on top of her neck where it could be easily grabbed, it slipped round and sat underneath her neck, meaning the handle would have been useless if I had needed to take hold of it in a hurry or tuck the lead into it.

As part of your winter outfit, an LED collar that lights up the darkness is very handy indeed. Some of these collars are lit up the entire way around the collar; others have alternate light and dark patterns. Some flash with two or more speeds; others just stay permanently lit around the whole collar. You can also buy LED tags if you don't want the expense of a new collar, though these would mainly be of benefit when your dog is on-lead and you want them more easily visible to drivers and other pedestrians. Off-lead, they are only visible if your dog is extremely close to you.

It's also possible to buy a collar identity tag that comes in the shape of a little barrel, with a top that screws off, in which you can put a piece of paper. Although traditionally used for name and address, this is a cheap and easy way to put any pertinent medical details about your own medical condition, emergency contact details, etc., etc. Other additions to your collar could include a GPS tracker. Your service dog will have an outstanding recall—won't they, Mazey—but you never know in life. Should you collapse somewhere remote and your dog wanders off to catch a rabbit for supper, a GPS locator may help searchers find your dog.

Don't sigh with relief yet. We're not done with collars. In fact, far from it. Who would have thought it was possible to say so much about the humble dog collar? If you're a manager of a doggy daycare, this would make an excellent interview question: "Tell me everything you can about dog collars in five minutes." That would sort the wheat from the chaff. Personally I would give bonus points for the inclusion of

Mina wears a martingale collar: not as a device of torture, but as a collar loose enough to put on all by herself that I can tighten to stop it falling off her head. Photo by the author (2021).

clerical dog collars, though I would draw the line at the types of collars observed in *Fifty Shades of Grey* lest you be sued for sexual harassment. Or hit on. Or both.

Anyway, I digress and for good reason. We've covered the non-controversial section on flat collars, and now we proceed to a discussion on other types of collars. A discussion that can get very heated indeed, though I have already rattled on enough in previous chapters about maintaining choice in the use of training tools.

So, my beautiful Service Dog Mazey works on a harness and wears a rolled leather collar to carry her identity tag. Mina wears a flat leather collar with her identity tag, in addition to a martingale collar, to which her lead is attached. Although Mina has a typical Rottweiler neck, being very thick and muscular, she has a small, narrow head with extremely flexible ears(!). It's easy for a normal flat collar to come up and over Mina's ears should she suddenly stop to sniff something delicious. With my slow reactions, I accidentally keep on walking, and the lead goes taut then up up and away, soaring off and over Mina's head. The martingale is a good choice of collar for Mina. She can wear it in a way that suits her, while giving me peace of mind that her collar can't just slip off her should she suddenly stop for whatever reason. If I used a flat collar adjusted tight enough so that it could never come off, it would need to sit very high up on her neck, just underneath her ears where her neck is the narrowest. It would be so tight as to be constantly choking the life out of her. This would be downright painful, and not something I would ever do to Mina or any other dog.

Another collar type commonly worn by large breed dogs, especially hairy ones, is a collar made of metal links called a fur saver. A collar/lead combination that usually continues to tighten, from which the lead element can't be detached, is called a slip lead. Usually made from cord or rope, a slip lead has a handle on one end and a loop on the other that fits over the dog's head. Some slip leads can be adjusted not to tighten fully, as with Mina's martingale. I tend to carry a light slip lead in my backpack wherever I go, just in case I come across a lost dog on my travels. The noose end can be made very large, so it's easy to place over the head of a frightened dog while ensuring the dog can't then back out of the slip lead and run away again.

Related to the slip lead is the choke chain. As the name implies, it is simply a chain link collar with a loop for the lead. The chain will keep tightening on the dog's neck as long as the dog and/or handler keeps pulling.

Prong collars we've mentioned, and although some readers with powerful dogs may need them, most service dogs will not. The collar is not as fearsome as it looks. It distributes pressure evenly around the collar instead of on one spot as more traditional collars can do, which can damage the larynx/trachea of stronger dogs who pull heavily into their collars.

Another more controversial collar for service dogs is the e-collar. These have come a long way since their early development as "shock" collars, which is a total and utter incorrect use of the term these days. There is now a wide variety of e-collars on the market, their primary use being to control a dog while off-lead. Some people also use e-collars for exercising deaf dogs: a beep, vibration or stimulation is a signal to look to the handler for signing instructions.

Before we finish with collars and go onto leads, glorious leads, let's have a quick look at head-collars. I have to admit, head-collars are not my favorite tool. I personally find them harsh, hard to put on and take off, and disliked by many dogs. However, I'm all for any tool if it suits the service dog and handler in question. Do I like service dog charities/organizations increasingly wanting to foist head-collars onto every service dog in all of creation? Noooooo. Why? For what purpose? Is there something I'm missing? Does a head-collar provide a direct link to the mothership?

A head-collar has a strap around the nose and another that goes around the back of the head. Dogs with short muzzles like Rottweilers can generally remove a head-collar in milliseconds. The nose strap, which tightens when the head-collar is being used, is problematic, not just from the perspective of pressing on nerves and fascia. We all know that dogs don't like to have their muzzles gripped and their mouths held shut from a psychological viewpoint. Strapping a dog's jaws together removes their only means of defending themselves, leaving them feeling vulnerable.

Once the head-collar is on, a dog is well aware that they are defenseless without their teeth. Some will initially fight; others immediately shut down and give up trying. Of course this is good from an obedience perspective, but what does it tell you about how your dog feels when you strap her muzzle shut with a head-collar? In dog terms, grabbing her muzzle is plain rude, if not an outright sign of aggression, akin to an alpha roll. Thus, a head-collar is not appreciated by many dogs.

I will admit I have seen some dogs undergo a great transformation after a head-collar was gently introduced over time. Engagement was worked on and then pressure and release was properly taught to the dog, so don't rule one out. Just because I hate them doesn't mean you have to as well.

The natural place to follow on from collars is, of course, the lead. There is not too much to say about them. Thank the Lord, I am sure you are uttering. Like collars, they come in a wondrous variety of materials with different buckles, clips, loops, lengths, and all sorts of adaptions in a wide variety of places.

I prefer a riot lead, which is a lead with two loops, one very close to the buckle that attaches to the dog's collar/harness, the other at the end of the lead as normal. I use a stiff cord riot lead, as the short loop is great for close control and keeping Mazey tight to me, whereas the regular loop at the end is great for when she is on a longer lead. My riot lead is very stiff at the handle/short loop which means I can use it for light guiding work, though most riot leads are not as stiff as mine at the bottom, so don't buy one expecting it to be suitable for this purpose.

I find lead length is personal preference and also dependent on what you are doing. I like a longer lead, and if I do need to work my dog off-lead as I described above, then I will loop it through the handle on Mazey's harness. You may prefer a shorter lead that doesn't drag on the ground so isn't a trip hazard. If using a loose lead that may drag on the ground, my preference is to have no loop on the end so the dog can't accidentally get a leg caught in it.

There are specialty lead sets for other activities such as canicross. Some handlers find them useful for day-to-day work with their service dog, as it allows them to have free use of their hands, but still have the dog on the lead. I have never tried such a set up myself, though I can see a lot of advantages to it. There is such a wide variety of materials, clips, buckles, loops and lengths of leads, with so many uses depending on task, I can't do it justice here. Mainly leads are really a matter of personal preference and what works for you and your disability.

One thing you may consider very useful to put on your lead is a lead sleeve. Usually very brightly colored—for example, luminous yellow or orange (with appropriate text)—the lead sleeve will clearly tell people your dog is a service dog in training, the scenario they are most often used for. I find lead sleeves get in the way of my hands when I'm shortening the lead so I don't use them myself, nor did I use them when Mazey was still in training. But horses for courses and all that.

Head done: check. Neck done: check. We now come to harnesses, followed by capes and vests. There is a wide array of harnesses out there, and much will depend on the tasks your dog is performing and your own preference. I attach Mazey's lead to her harness instead of a collar because I occasionally use Mazey for light guiding work. The type of harness I use has Velcro strips to which I can easily attach patches identifying Mazey as a service dog. I don't like vests or capes as they have no way of sitting on top of a harness because they are primarily designed for dogs working on a collar. Plus, when it's hot I don't want Mazey under the extra coverage of a cape or vest. She's cooler working in just her harness.

Guide dogs will need a harness with an attachment for a handle, which gives a good feel between the dog and handler. There are specific manufacturers of guide dog harnesses that will make a harness to fit you and your dog in a bespoke way, but these are very expensive. Other people use quite standard type harnesses whose manufacturers make a handle for guiding use, the harness being very similar in design to the harnesses used by guide dog charities. Generally these harnesses have a little saddle that sits on the dogs body, with a strap that goes across the chest and another underneath the stomach.

If your dog is regularly required to pull any sort of weight into the harness, look at those designed for this purpose. Have it properly fitted, and make sure it works for you and your dog. I very occasionally ask Mazey to help assist me walking up hills. She has quite a bog standard harness not designed for pulling heavy loads, but for very light assistance up hills, on a rare basis, it is fine.

Most harnesses have a clip on the top, to which the lead is attached. Some have a clip at the front, which is often called a "no pull harness." If it works for you, fine, but no pull harnesses are in no way kinder than a collar and lead. They work by restricting the movement of your dog's legs, which is, of course, uncomfortable. Beware: for a very strong, pulling dog; the straps of a front pull harness can injure the chest muscles/rub off the hair, as any tool can injure a dog if not used correctly.

I don't like no pull harnesses. I find the concept of manipulating different straps and leads attached to different clips in different places at different times too much for my hands (and small brain). I may be British, but I'm no Charlotte Dujardin. Some people have a lead attached to a ring top, a lead attached to the front ring, and a lead attached to the collar—pressure used on different leads at different times. Eeekkk. A collar and one lead are fine for me if correcting a dog that pulls on the lead. You are not me, though, and if it toots your horn, who am I to tell you not to have three leads?

Most people working their service dog in public, particularly if the dog is worked on a collar and lead, will also put a cape or vest on their dog. This simply is composed of a little jacket, rug, dress—however you want to describe it—that sits on your dog's back and buckles round the stomach and chest. Materials may differ, though they tend to be made of nylon in order to be hard-wearing and waterproof. The reason a dog is in a cape/vest is so it's easy to identify them as service dogs, and, as such, capes/vests will have a variety of text or patches on them.

The big question is what to put on your cape/vest? Some can be pre-ordered with the text you want already stitched on; others will have Velcro patches so you can design your own and swap it about according to your mood. Some people like to have their disability visible on their dog's cape/vest, such as "Autism Service Dog" or what their dog does—for example, "Medical Alert Service Dog." I did this for a little while, using removable patches on Mazey's harness, but for now, I quite like just plain "Service Dog." Not everyone needs to know my business.

The vast majority of service dog owners like to have patches or text on their cape/vest that asks people not to touch or disturb their dog. Sadly, no matter what wording you use, it never seems to work. People are attracted to service dogs as bees are to honey, as ducks to water, as psychopathic ghosts are to isolated houses wherein groups of scantily clad teenage girls are playing with a Ouija Board. You get the idea. People will make kissy noises, eye contact, or just walk up and start patting your service dog, no matter what is on the cape/vest. Expletives are best avoided, as are jokes. It's tempting to go with expletives, but they probably attract more attention, plus hostility.

It's not compulsory to tell people to leave you and your dog alone. As patches rarely work, I just go with "Service Dog" on Mazey's harness, and in actual fact, mostly I don't mind people asking to stroke her. I'm pretty sociable, and Mazey loves everyone, particularly kids. I mean, Mazey would adore the secret lovechild of Chucky and Annabelle. This is my dog's personality, and it's really important to me that Mazey is happy in her work. If I never let Mazey greet any of her fans or her friends who work in shops we frequent, she would be deeply unhappy.

In addition to your dog's working cape/vest, many people also have a separate one for exercise, which identifies their dog as a service dog who is off duty. This can be worn off-lead, or on-lead when enjoying enrichment activities. A cape/vest/bandanna of this type can reassure people and let them know that your dog is likely to be friendly. I have often heard people in such a situation tell small children not to be scared as Mazey is a service dog and won't jump up on them. It's a sad reflection that at some time other pet dogs have clearly done this in the past and scared a child.

This covers the main service dog-specific gear people have. We all, of course, should be carrying poo bags and, if going out for a long period, water and a bowl. I have a collapsible bowl that I keep permanently in my rucksack, and I either bring along water or buy it if needed should I tarry out longer than expected and Mazey asks for a drink. If she is thirsty, she will ask me for a drink, usually by taking me in the direction of a toilet for disabled individuals, since we have very regular routes and she knows where water can be sourced.

Some people will use booties in hot weather to protect paw pads from being burned. I am not a day person, so when it's hot enough to burn paws on concrete, then I stay inside. Once it's not so hot, then we do go out. I have trained Mazey to avoid metal drains and manholes, as they get dangerously hot and stay that way for long into the day. Even when concrete is not too hot to the touch, metal can be. Also watch for artificial grass if crossing play areas because it can also get extremely hot. In addition to booties for hot weather, some service dogs will wear specially designed sun-goggles. White dogs with pink skin may need sunscreen on ear tips and on their noses. Much is going to depend on where you live and your lifestyle.

Lastly, a quick note on toys. Use toys your dog likes, whether that be squeaky ball, a ball on a rope, a frisbee or a tug toy. Toys may float, or they may not. Mazey likes a ball that floats so she can dunk it. I carry a ball on a rope/a tug with me for

Mina, and Mazey prefers to carry her ball herself. I like to do a lot of playing on walks, so we always have some sort of toy with us.

Not only your service dog has gear. You may also have some gear for work and for training, such as a clicker. If you like clickers, choose a "click" of a volume you are comfortable with. I have autism and need a very gentle, low "click." Also, how could we forget food, glorious food? For the dogs, I mean. Though if carrying high value treats such as chicken, admittedly we have shared…. What I am saying is what would we do without something in which to carry our training treats?

I have a small pouch that is permanently attached to my rucksack strap that I can easily reach into while my rucksack is over my shoulder. I also have a dog training jacket that has large pockets for training treats and also, very importantly, toys. There are lots of treat pouches, made from a wide variety of different materials that can strap round your waist, hang from your bag or your belt, or be attached by our good old friend Velcro on your training jacket. It's up to your preference and imagination.

I do like having a training jacket myself. I pooh-poohed them as pretentious until I got my own, and since then it has rarely been off my back. I wear it while walking the dogs and while working Mazey, unless I need to go somewhere reasonably smart. Don't worry. I live near Birkenhead. Pajamas and slippers are the norm, so actual clothes and a dirty, smelly dog training jacket does not make me a candidate for it being swapped for a straitjacket. A good training jacket has loads, and I mean loads, of pockets, on the front, to the side, and even in the back. More than enough room for toys, treats, poo bags, leads and human stuff like phones, wallets and keys.

Other gear (for humans) you may wish to also carry I discussed in Chapter Eleven. This would include information on the law and access rights, details of next of kin and/or pet sitters, and pre-printed laminated cards for when you may be rendered nonverbal or need to give instructions as regards your service dog when you cannot do so yourself.

A piece of equipment that may be useful for you if you sometimes struggle to give a high-energy dog enough exercise is a dog treadmill. There are many designs, though most are slatted treadmills with the dog in control of how fast they go. Once they understand how it works, many dogs enjoy exercising on a treadmill, in the same way cats do on an exercise wheel, or hamsters on their little wheels. It's their choice to run, for how long and how fast.

Finally, we finish rambling about gear for your dog and for yourself. What a long chapter it turned out to be. And an abrupt end.

CHAPTER THIRTEEN

Traveling with Your Service Dog

Traveling with your service dog should be easy peasy. In some jurisdictions it absolutely is like a long, cool glass of lemonade on a hot summer's day, lounging on a giant inflatable rubber ducky in your pristine swimming pool. In other places (hint: the UK) it's like sitting on the cold, rainy, windswept beach, with sand down your knickers (or briefs), slurping lemonade made with all of the lemons but none of the sugar. I'll take a peek at the most common travel options when going on an adventure with your service dog, though this chapter will mainly concentrate on international air travel, since this is far and away where most problems arise. Famous last words, I fear.

If you intend to use public transport regularly in the area in which you live, then you should familiarize yourself with your local public transport operators and how they treat service dogs to make this process as easy as possible. In the U.S., you are protected by federal law, namely the ADA, as we have discussed in previous chapters.

Nevertheless, no one wants the hassle of being stopped and questioned, which will invariably occur when you are late for an important appointment. In New York City, for example, there are strict rules relating to the transportation of pets on the subway, and for convenience you may opt to get yourself a Service Animal Voluntary ID Card to speed things along, even though obtaining such a card is purely voluntary and not essential.[1]

When traveling outside your hometown, even where you're not going to cross any international borders, it's best to do your research well in advance. As the Boy Scouts always say, "be prepared." Nothing ruins a business trip or holiday more than being harassed and interrogated for simply minding your own business and going about your day.

Despite the ADA's protection, police officers or other officials may make value judgments about you and your service dog's training. This could result in your removal from public transport, even though this may be based purely on their own prejudices and have nothing to do with your service dog's behavior. A Pitbull Terrier service dog could, for example, be seen as "posing a threat" to public transport passengers based on breed alone, even though this is entirely unfair and illegal. This sort of attitude was seen in 2018 when MTA Chairman Joe Lhota stated, "bringing a Pitbull on board any of our subway systems is a violation of the law and a person who does that should be prosecuted to the full extent of the law." No, Joe, you got that one wrong.[2] Service dogs are not pets.

This statement followed an incident involving a Pitbull Terrier service dog who bit a woman's shoe on the subway after she pushed him off a seat, and then hit his owner (after he hit her first for repeatedly pushing his dog). There was human fault on both sides, and the dog in question had no charges brought against him by the police or animal control, though the owner was charged with assault and reckless endangerment. Irrespective of the dog being exonerated of fault, and in fact being a legitimate service dog, Joe Lhota was very clearly prejudiced against the dog's breed.

Here in the UK, we do not have anything like the protection of the ADA. Police officers and operators of public transport can and do ask whatever questions they like, no matter how intrusive or humiliating. Although under the strict letter of the law they are prohibited from discriminating against a disabled person, either directly or indirectly, enforcing the law or getting compensation when the law is breached is nigh on impossible. Disability law has no teeth, like an elderly Papillon with one tooth trying to gum you to death. Things are improving in some sectors, but transport and in particular air transport remain problematic for UK service dog owners.

Whether you are in the U.S. or the UK, the real key to having a stress-free journey on public transport with your service dog is preparation. This is helpful if using an unfamiliar route or going on a long journey as opposed to a hop, skip and a jump across town. Plan your journey as far in advance as you can, ideally booking your bus or train tickets several months ahead, making sure to specify that you're disabled, and that you will be traveling with your service dog. If you can't find an easy option to do this online and if you are able (and I'm a bit phone phobic myself), use your phone and try to speak to a real live person with an actual heartbeat.

Bus and train companies should provide you with disabled seating with extra legroom at no additional cost if you are traveling with your service dog. However, if you have a large dog, others may try to charge you for two seats if your dog cannot fit beside/underneath one seat. In addition to better seating, when traveling with your service dog you may also be provided with priority boarding and a complementary porter service to assist you with your luggage. This is always helpful when bringing not only your own luggage, but the luggage of your service dog too. If you're anything like me, the latter exceeds the former.

Prebooking your tickets should also help ensure you have no issues with access. More often than not it will be noted on your ticket that you are traveling with your service dog, whether such ticket is in paper or electronic format. Although you should not need to prove your dog is indeed a service dog, nor be interrogated about her, it's better to be safe than sorry. The law may be on your side, but that's no comfort if you miss your bus or train due to a stickler employee harassing you.

In addition to prebooking tickets, make sure you're familiar with the facilities at all of the train or bus stations you will pass through, and that you have enough time to navigate your way around, particularly if your service dog will need a toilet break or is not used to using escalators or moving walkways. If using a train or bus, you may have to find a convenient place outside for your service dog to toilet if it's a long trip. Most of this type of information is available online, but if it's not or the information is missing or vague, it's better to be prepared and double-check.

When traveling by public transport, it's always useful to know if there are any shops or cafes along your journey where you can buy water or food for your service dog. I prefer traveling light, so I only take a small bottle of water for Mazey, purchasing any extra I may require if on a long journey. Some restrooms may have suitable water from the taps to refill your water bottle, but in others the water is not drinkable.

Never assume you can rely on this option. Also check whether you can purchase the correct dog food you require at your destination. It's never a good idea to suddenly switch food, so if your dog is on a specialized diet not available at your destination, you may have to take all of her food for the entire trip, or gradually switch to a readily available food two weeks before travel.

If you are on a long journey with your service dog, it's worth bringing a settle mat, which your service dog can comfortably lie on. Don't forget an ample supply of poo bags, and at a minimum a portable water bowl, plus bottled water. Depending on the length of the journey you may also wish to give your dog a small meal, provided she is not prone to being travel sick. If travel sickness is a problem, speak to your veterinarian several days before you travel about the possibility of any medications.

Having quickly covered traveling by public transport, let's move on to transporting your dog by car, which for once is more regulated in the UK than the U.S., though laws will differ by state. In the UK dogs and other animals must be "suitably restrained" while traveling in a car, by virtue of Rule 57 of the Highway Code. This is pretty vague, but it's generally accepted that to comply with the law your dog, and this includes your service dog, should not be loose in the car and so have no potential to become a dog-shaped missile in the event of an accident.

Finally we come to air travel, a big bone of contention for those of us living in the UK with service dogs, where it can be easier to fly out of the country with a racehorse than a service dog. So bad is the airline industry in catering to service dogs that many disabled people are forced to leave the UK via ferry or the Eurotunnel, and then catch a flight from Paris or whichever ferry port is best for onward travel to their final destination. It sounds ludicrous, and looks ludicrous as I type it, but such is the laxity of

Mina as a puppy, dreaming of flying far, far away. Photo by the author (2021).

the government in enforcing the Equality Act in the UK. This is the situation we find ourselves in.

If you are a UK national and are flying, or at least attempting to fly with your service dog out of the UK, then you need to put in as much advance preparation as possible. You should speak to the airline extensively beforehand and put together a folder with full details of doctor's letters, plus certificates from service dog trainers and a logbook of all the training, certifications and behavioral assessments your dog has passed, in addition to insurance certificates, vaccination cards, certificates of health and any items for the airline's own specific requirements for traveling dogs.

The Civil Aviation Authority ("CAA") does state all airlines *must* take *all* service dogs without additional charge,[3] but in practice this is not what is happening. Service dog owners who have prepared correctly are being turned away at the airport. This is due to the CAA loophole that states that airlines may ask for proof that the dog has been trained to a standard that allows it to safely travel by air. Some airlines have interpreted this as allowing them to only permit service dogs registered and trained with ADUK, no matter the level of experience or training of the service dog. Thankfully other airlines do allow UK service dogs that are owner trained, or with a non ADUK charity/organization, but this obviously restricts the flights and destinations available.

Restricting flights to only ADUK dogs is not in reality about the standard of training; rather, it vastly limits the number of dogs eligible to go onto flights for free, meaning the majority of UK service dogs must either fly in the hold along with pets at a massive cost or leave the UK by another route as described above. There are owner-trained service dog groups campaigning against this loophole, but they have little to no funding and it's a long, uphill battle.

Thankfully, many readers of this book will not be subject to the trials and tribulations of the UK airline industry! Well, unless you want to visit the UK. In the U.S., there were a lot of problems with domestic air travel and people traveling with ESAs such as birds, reptiles, and other animals. This ended in March 2021, with few U.S. airlines now permitting ESAs on domestic flights, although some international flights may take smaller emotional support dogs. This is, however, a book about service dogs, not ESAs, so we shall concentrate on service dogs.

When you are flying internationally with your service dog, once again the key is preparation. It's essential to check the regulations for flying at both ends of the trip. To start with, speak to the airline you are going to use, and determine what paperwork is required for your service dog to fly out of the U.S. All airlines are different. Just because you have flown once with one airline, don't assume another airline will have the same rules, or indeed that the rules have not changed with the airline you have flown with in the past.

There's a whole lot of paperwork involved with flying a service dog that may well be in addition to the paperwork required when transporting a pet dog in the cargo hold. Often the timeframes for submitting the paperwork are precise. Confirm whether you can fill in parts of the paperwork yourself, or if some of the health checks must be completed by a veterinarian and whether that veterinarian requires certain qualifications. It may be that the airline imposes additional checks on top of what the federal/national regulations specify. And it may be that the country you are flying into has unusually stringent requirements, such as not only requiring a rabies vaccine, but also a titer test confirming the service dog has an adequate level of immunity. Always check the destination country's conditions for entry and exit.

In the U.S., Air Carrier Access Act prohibits discrimination on the basis of disability in air travel, but you still must abide by the terms of the ADA and also the Department of Transportation ("DOT"). For all flights, the DOT Service Animal Air Transport Form must be filled in. Check all forms are up to date! The form requires the handler's details, basic details of the Service Dog, including a statement regarding their health, training and behavior. The health statement can be signed by yourself, and you can list yourself as the dog's trainer.

If your flight is over eight hours, you will also need to fill in a DOT Relief Attestation Form,[4] which details how you are going to go about dealing with your dog's requirement to toilet on the flight. Either you must be able to deal with this in a sanitary way, or you must confirm that your dog will not need to toilet for the duration of the flight. Some airports in the USA are extremely dog friendly, and even have special toilet areas for dogs, so if your dog is trained to toilet on command, ensure you make use of any such facilities as close to boarding as possible.

The airline should be able to advise you on their own policies and procedures on the outbound flight, and any local rules as regards the airport you are flying out of. However, you must check yourself that you will comply with the laws of the country into which you are flying, both when you fly in and also when you want to fly out again. If you're flying into the UK from the U.S., for example, you will need to have contacted and received approval from the UK Animal Reception Center before you fly out of the U.S.[5] You need to do this, not the airline. If you do not, then your service dog may enter the UK but not be accepted back onto the aircraft to return to the U.S. That would be a big problem.

In addition to the regulations regarding flying with service dogs, you will need to check the status of whether your particular service dog is even permitted entry into all of the countries you may intend to visit, not to mention whether your dog is eligible to be worked as a service dog. Some countries, including the UK, have breed-specific legislation, meaning you would not be able to enter the UK with your Pitbull Terrier service dog without her potentially being seized by the police, never mind work her as a service dog.

Some countries do not have any laws pertaining to service dogs and do not recognize them at all. Yet others only permit service dogs trained and certified by their own national service dog charity/organization in order to work in public. If your service dog is owner trained, and is not registered with any national or international service dog organization, you may not be allowed to work her or take her into accommodation in which only service dogs are permitted.

If you can, it's a good idea to check your dog's eligibility to work in public in the country you are flying into and whether she will need any additional patches or identification, particularly if working her in a non–English-speaking country. If you contact the country's embassy, it may be able to give you some advice or refer you to one of the national organizations that deals with service dogs in that country.

There are many businesses that deal with the international air transport of pets that, for a substantial fee, will be able to help you with the basic legislation and regulations that apply to the transportation of your service dog. Make sure they also have experience dealing with dogs traveling in the cabin of aircraft, and in particular service dogs traveling in this way, since a service dog may be much larger and heavier than the small dogs typically permitted to travel in the cabin. These dogs are often restrained in a pet carrier, unlike your service dog who may have to wear a harness and some sort of seat belt restraint, but who will not be in an actual container.

I rather suspect that if all the above has not put you off visiting the UK with your service dog, nothing will. There are lots of other great countries to visit in Europe that are dog friendly, though just watch out for breed-specific legislation. I have resigned myself to a life with no holidays ever again, which is really rather sad, as I used to be an enthusiastic traveler. Well, perhaps one day I will win the lottery and can buy my own private jet. That would be nice. Mazey and Mina could have matching food and water bowls made of gold to match their brows. Ah, we can only dream.

Chapter Fourteen

Bringing Your Service Dog to Work

This is not intended to be a dusty legal tome, outlining employment laws and how they tie in with disability legislation. Rather, this chapter looks at practical aspects of bringing your service dog to work. Just as there are restrictions on where you can work a service dog in public, similarly there are some jobs which are just not practicable when you have a service dog. A brain surgeon is not going to be able to bring their service dog into a sterile operating room, and a zookeeper would not want their service dog around while shoveling manure in the elephant enclosure or when feeding the lions. Chefs cannot have their service dog helping to prepare "Lasagna à la doghair."

Unfortunately, bringing your service dog into work, even in an office environment, is frowned on by the majority of employers. This can make it incredibly hard for a disabled person to find employment, as you're damned if you do and damned if you don't. Going to an interview without your service dog, then popping up with her on day one, is not going to go down well, and some employers will find a way to terminate your employment at some point in the near(ish) future. Ostensibly not due to your service dog, and certainly not in any way you can file a discrimination lawsuit, but it will somehow happen all the same.

On the other hand, going to an interview with your service dog in tow is a sure way not to get the job, unless it's for a very obviously pro-dog employer who already has pet dogs in the office, plus insurance to cover this. Given today's job market and the number of highly skilled people looking for work, it's exceptionally hard to prove an employer discriminated against you and did not award you a job due to you having a service dog. The lack of flexibility of many employers regarding employees bringing their service dog to work with them leaves many disabled people with very limited life opportunities, as if being disabled was not hard enough.

If you're lucky enough to have a job where your service dog is welcome, then there are some basic adjustments your employer should be able to make in order to accommodate you and your service dog. A lot will depend on your office layout. Back in the day offices used to be, well, offices. Everyone had their own office, or at most, shared with one other person, so having a service dog in the office would have been no big deal.

These days, offices are mainly open, with mean, cramped little cubicles crushed close together. There is always going to be one person who complains that they're allergic to dogs, which means in practice the employer must accommodate both parties, which could prove difficult. Allergies are *not* a legitimate reason for prohibiting service dogs from a workplace. Nor are religious preferences and dislike and/ or fear of dogs, but you can see how an employer could be entering a veritable minefield with so many competing interests, all of which have some degree of protection under the law, with any disgruntled employee only too quick to make accusations of discrimination.

Whatever your office layout, your service dog needs to be able to relax in her own space and be unobtrusive and quiet while you're working. If the office is big enough, this may be in her own crate or in a sectioned-off area of a room that would keep her safely out of harm's way. This area can contain her bed, her water bowl, and any other amenities she may require. Your service dog's crate/bed should be placed in an area where there are no drafts, out of direct sunlight. It should also be large enough for her to comfortably lie down as well as stand up and turn around. Your service dog should be able to see you and, if she performs medical alert, close enough to easily smell you.

A risk assessment will need to be done as regards where your service dog and her bed/crate is situated in relation to your own desk or workstation, in addition to making sure there's easy access for both of you to any emergency exits in the event of a fire or other evacuation. Ideally there's a nearby toilet for disabled individuals that can accommodate both of you at the same time.

There will also need to be discussions as regards your access to any office kitchen facilities where food is being prepared. If you're going to keep your service dog's food in the communal fridge, make sure you have permission and it's well sealed and properly identified. It may seem funny to trick Scott from IT, who has a habit of stealing other people's lunch, into eating dog food pie, but I suspect he would not be best amused.

Mina says being cute is hard work. Photo by the author (2021).

Risk assessments should be particularly thorough for those service dog users who use a wheelchair, as it's essential that emergency exits are easily accessible, as are toilets for disabled people. Corridors should be wide enough for you and your service dog to walk easily beside each other. Internal elevators, external elevators, or ramps going into/out of the building must be able to comfortably accommodate you and your service dog safely side by side. I did see online a wonderfully swish modern wheelchair lift outside a very grand London Hotel, which was a terrible design for any wheelchair user who also had a service dog. It's a real shame that in this day and age, form is still taking priority over function.

For many employers, one concern with letting a service dog into the office is dog-mad employees with no self-control popping in to see and pat your service dog every ten minutes or so. If you're lucky, this could lead you to getting your own office, which would be a massive bonus for me but may feel isolating for other people. It's important, therefore, to have an open and honest conversation with your boss and colleagues regarding what is and is not appropriate as regards spending time with and/or distracting your service dog from her own work.

Most service dogs toilet on command, so should not need more than one bathroom break during your shift, unless you're working overtime or have particularly long hours. The ideal would be, of course, for you to have a sufficiently long lunch break for you to eat yourself, and for you to take your service dog for a short walk in order to stretch her legs. Some employers may also be happy for you to take her out for a short toilet break at other times too, particularly if working twelve-hour shifts. When going to office meetings, especially with people who may be clients, outside contractors, or colleagues from another department, it's both prudent and polite to warn them that your service dog will be accompanying you. Legally you don't have to, but it pays to be nice.

Mazey and Mina, being Rottweilers, require two substantial walks per day, no matter what the weather is, rain or shine, summer or winter. Therefore I would need to walk them properly both before and after work, plus a little leg stretch at lunchtime, if I had a regular office job. Other service dogs, particularly small toy breeds, may only need two short walks per day in addition to some at-home enrichment activities and would be mortified at the thought of going for a walk in anything but the most pleasant of weather. This excludes most days of the year in Scotland.

If your service dog has sufficient exercise and enrichment activities at home, she probably won't need any bones, chews or toys while she is in the office; she might be quite content to sleep. The chewing, licking noise of a dog with a bone can be quite distressing if you have noise sensitivities or are not keen on dogs. If there are other dogs in the office and she is not crated, make sure none of them are possessive over their toys, lest there be some form of fisticuffs over a favorite toy. A stolen toy is, of course, the best toy. All dogs know this.

Smells. It's time to talk about smells. Bad ones. It's important to ensure that as far as is humanly possible, your service dog is clean and well groomed, with no obvious doggy smell, or worse still, sporting fox poop eau de parfum, beloved by dogs everywhere. Doggy farts are not even appreciated by the dog herself, but it's kind of hard to specify you want a non-farting dog when looking for a service dog prospect, though it has to be said some breeds are "windier" than others. Part of your service dog's risk assessment may involve regular bathing of your dog and her bedding, not to mention completion of a program of suggested vaccinations, in addition to any required preventative treatments for zoonotic diseases/health risks, such as rabies, worms and flea treatments.

Of course, the reality is that having a service dog in the office will provide many benefits. She is not a therapy dog, and no one should be handling her or in any way distracting her without your permission. However, depending on your attitude toward her making friends with your work colleagues, all dogs and, in particular, service dogs do enormously boost morale in the workplace.

Chapter Fifteen

Maintaining a Healthy Service Dog, from Puppyhood to Retirement

Being a service dog is surprisingly hard work, both mentally and physically, so it's essential we look after our service dog's health as best we can. Having taken the time to source, raise and train a service dog, you are almost certainly by now on a first-name basis with your local veterinarian. State laws and/or any charity/organization you are a member of may prescribe that your service dog has specific vaccinations and/or medications regularly administered—for example, vaccinations for rabies.[1]

Even in the absence of specific health concerns or mandatory health treatments, I would still recommend a yearly checkup with your veterinarian just to make sure everything is tickety-boo with your service dog. An annual health check is also a requirement for most pet insurance policies. And if you ever did need to kennel your dog in an emergency, most kennels have minimum requirements as regard vaccinations/titer test results, plus the administration of worming/flea products.

For a young dog going to the veterinarian for an annual checkup, this may simply be a bog-standard clinical examination that checks for any abnormalities or differences from her last clinical exam, plus standard preventative healthcare treatments and vaccinations. If you're not a fan of routine vaccines, you can have a titer test done to determine the presence and level of antibodies she has against certain diseases, though titer tests are not available for every condition she may need protection from via a vaccine. And as they require a blood draw, they tend to be more expensive than just having your dog vaccinated.

Always be led by your veterinarian as regards necessary healthcare for your service dog, remembering much is going to depend on where you live. For example, I live in the UK where testing for heartworm is not standard, unlike in the U.S. where heartworm is a major concern in many states. For an older service dog, don't be surprised if your veterinarian suggests blood and urine tests in addition to a standard clinical examination, plus any additional tests that may be appropriate given your dog's individual circumstances. If you have an older un-spayed bitch, some veterinarians will recommend an annual mammary ultrasound, whereas others will be content just to rely on a careful physical examination.

Having dealt with your dog's physical health, we must now turn to your dog's mental health, which is also of utmost importance since your service dog has a lot of responsibility. Of course, much will depend on how frequently you work your dog and the tasks she does for you, but nevertheless, even though your dog adores her work, it can at times be very stressful for her.

Everyone knows their own individual dog, and we should always be on the lookout for signs of stress. Mazey is the biggest lovebug ever, and is an extremely confident and resilient dog, but even so, like any other dog, Mazey can sometimes get stressed and need a bit of a break. One of the indicators of stress in Mazey is after she has finished work and we have left a shop, she will start picking up pieces of litter with human scents on them, like paper receipts. She then likes to carry them back to the car where she has a little stash. She also enjoys picking up leaves. At times my car can look quite messy, but it's just Mazey and my somewhat feral attitude to housework.

If I see Mazey start to collect litter on consecutive days, then I'll try and give her two or three days totally off work. When we go out, we'll go on fun walks to her favorite places, and not go near any shops or areas she will need to be on best behavior, as befits a service dog. If I need help going shopping, I will either order goods online or have a care worker come out with me. Mazey does do medical alert at home, but a lot of that responsibility has now been taken off her shoulders by Mina. I found that when Mina was old enough to help out in this way, Mazey became less stressed and needed fewer breaks.

On the subject of breaks, I try and give Mazey a total break from her work as my service dog twice a year, usually for one or two weeks each time. I know that this may not be possible for everyone, but if you can, I really do think it does a service dog a world of good. On her holidays I make a special effort to go on Mazey's favorite walks, even if they are not mine(!), and to go to new places none of us have ever been before. Mazey and Mina have nice walks daily anyway, but on Mazey's holidays, we go to Mazey's absolute special places, one of which is a river. She plays with her ball, dunking it under the water. It's a river I've had to wade right into in order to retrieve her when she was younger and a bit of a naughty puppy!

Mazey loves playing in the water and dunking her ball. Photo by the author (2021).

Even apart from scheduled time off on service dog vacation, it's important that your service dog gets plenty of free time and also enrichment in her day-to-day life. We all think of enrichment as making a special effort to do fun things, which is true, but enriching a dog's life goes much deeper than that. Enrichment can be as simple as observing what her preferences are in her daily life and making that as good as it can be for her.

For example, food bowls. Does your dog like metal bowls? Does she prefer ceramic ones, or even plastic? What about her food itself? Some dogs like their food heated up ever so slightly. Or if it's a hot day, many dogs enjoy pupsicles as a treat, which you can either buy or make yourself. All of these things can easily enrich the lives of our service dogs.

In addition to this basic environmental enrichment, I also believe it's good to have specific enrichment activities in addition to your dog's regular walks. Mazey and Mina really enjoy it when I take some of their daily food ration, and instead of using it as training treats as I often do, I scatter it all over the garden. I hide some extra special bits of food in places they need to search for it, and the rest is thrown into the long grass, with some on the lawn. It takes the girls about thirty minutes to sniff out all the hidden food, and it's a game they love.

I also often take the girls on sniffy walks, which are walks where they dictate the pace and the direction of the walk—a challenge with two dogs! Sometimes they're off-lead, but other times they remain on-lead, but are allowed to sniff where they like, go into undergrowth, etc. They don't get sniffy walks every day; I tend to rotate sniffy walks with a food hunt in the garden. These are just examples. Some dogs enjoy environmental enrichment inside the home, with pieces of food hidden around the house or treats using a snuffle mat, puzzle feeders and other toys.

In addition to enrichment activities as I have described above, both Mazey and Mina have two off-lead walks per day: a shorter one in the morning for about twenty to thirty minutes, and a longer one in the evening. The shorter morning walk mainly takes the form of a walk together with both dogs, immediately followed by an individual play session for each dog at the end of the walk, which will generally involve me and that particular dog just hanging out, having fun with each other. We'll play games such as tug, a bit of scent-work, hide and seek, tag, or chasing the ball. It may only be ten minutes of individual time each, but both girls really appreciate having that one-on-one play with me, without the other barging in.

In the evening, when it's cool, we have our main walk of the day on the beach or in the forest, which is fun for all three of us. Due to my autism, we tend to go out late at night, when the world is dark and quiet, and it's just us. This walk is about an hour long, and the girls are off-lead and free to play and run as much as they like. Mazey likes to have a little play with her ball, then carry it around in her mouth. Mina for some reason likes carting what seems like entire tree trunks around with her. Each to their own!

Most days I will also do either a tracking session or an obedience training session with both Mazey and Mina, which is done on an individual basis due to the nature of the activity. They also have regular physiotherapy sessions, which are a bit like Pilates for dogs, in order to keep them supple and to maintain their muscular strength and agility.

Whew! As you can see, my girls and I have very busy, active lives. Being working-line Rottweilers, Mazey and Mina need this sort of lifestyle to be mentally and physically stimulated, content, fit and healthy, but for many dogs, this would be

way too much activity. Each dog needs to be looked at as an individual. Walks and enrichment activities should suit your dog, not just be what you consider to be fun, though ideally both of you should enjoy yourselves.

Alas, time catches up with us all, and our beloved service dogs are no different. One day they're mischievous bundles of fluff; the next, they're going gray around the muzzle. I absolutely dread the idea of Mazey retiring. She adores her job, and I'm not sure how she would cope with being left behind in the house, unable to go out on adventures with me. It breaks my heart to think of her lonely and sad, waiting on the sofa all alone for Mina and I to return. I'm hoping Mazey has many working years left, and although this part of the chapter is a bit of a sad one, it's an important conversation that all service dog owners need to have.

If your service dog is from a service dog charity/organization,

Mazey enjoys her physiotherapy sessions with her bosu ball. Photo by the author (2021).

it may have already set a provisional date for your service dog to retire, solely based on her age. Hopefully this means training a new service dog for you who is ready to step in and take over from your retiree. Check to see if this is the case, and also whether your service dog can stay with you or whether she will be re-homed. You should already know this, but sometimes policies do change.

I'm sure most people's gut instinct will tell them to keep their retired service dog no matter what. That's how I feel about Mazey. All of my dogs and cats come to live with me for better or worse, til death do us part. With Mazey, I have an even stronger bond than with my pets since Mazey has literally saved my life on more than one occasion. We are a team, and I can't imagine life without her.

However, not everyone is in the same position as I am, and I absolutely do not judge or throw shade at anyone who places an older service dog into a retirement home. There are pros and cons to keeping a retired dog, and every case must be looked at on its own merits. I have the luxury of Mazey being my pet first and foremost, but not everyone is able to live that way. Most people who have a service dog are very fond of them, but nevertheless they view their service dog as being in their home to do a job for them. A primary consideration must also be the service dog herself, and how she would cope with retirement in her own home, having to see herself replaced with a newer model and left behind for long periods during the day.

If you do feel your older dog would be happier in a new home, please don't feel that you have let her down in some way. There are many lovely people who are proud to give a retired service dog a new home, and dogs tend to settle very well, though most of us don't like to admit our dogs could ever cope without us. I have seen several re-homed service dogs who all ended up in large houses in the country, with massive gardens to play in, pools to swim in, and woods to frolic in with other canine friends. A doggy heaven really, in many respects.

Most service dogs do not just one day fall over and die; instead they start to gradually slow down. Smaller dogs will have a lot longer working life than larger dogs, with breeds such as Terriers going strong well into their teens. By contrast, larger dogs may be slowing down before they are even nine or ten. Dogs all age differently, and you may find your service dog is perhaps becoming a little stiff after long walks. Maybe she is starting to occasionally miss medical alerts or is struggling with assisting to pull your manual wheelchair, whereas a year ago there was no stopping her.

Milly living her best life after retirement. Photo by Carol Mair, her owner (2022). Reproduced by permission of the photographer.

Where you do feel your service dog is starting to show signs of aging, your first step is to call your veterinarian for a clinical examination and health check, which will probably include a full blood panel and urine analysis. A basic clinical examination for an older dog is much the same as for a younger one, though your veterinarian may spend more time than usual checking certain areas for problems that are more common in older dogs. This would include carefully feeling all over her body for any new or unusual lumps and bumps.

Many older dogs have problems with their teeth, especially smaller breeds, who might have had lifelong dental problems. This is particularly true for brachycephalic breeds. Your veterinarian may recommend your older dog has a scale and polish, plus any necessary extractions. Although lots of dog groomers offer teeth cleaning these days, they cannot go underneath the gumline, which is necessary for a proper clean. This sort of teeth cleaning may be worthwhile as part of your dog's regular oral hygiene, in addition to you brushing her teeth yourself, but it's not a substitute for a proper dental examination, scale, polish and treatment by a veterinarian.

Blood tests may take several days to come back if sent to an outside lab, though some vets now have in-house hematology machines. If there are problems looming on the horizon, and if your veterinarian does not seem particularly proactive in tackling them, or doesn't have much interest in geriatric medicine, I would give serious consideration to consulting with a specialist in this field, in order to give your older service dog the chance to enjoy her job for as long as she can.

If your dog is starting to suffer from age-related diseases, there are a wide range of different treatments to help older dogs these days, depending, of course, on what is wrong. Even something as simple as daily joint supplements can make all the difference to an older dog who has osteoarthritis and is getting a little stiff. An adjustment to her lifestyle may help too, with frequent, shorter walks, and not so much ball chasing or high-impact activities. Dietary management can also be of great help for a range of medical conditions. OK, I'll be honest: put fat dogs on a diet!

With a bit of luck, veterinary intervention should keep your service dog working happily and comfortably for up to ten years, depending on breed. However, it's prudent to plan for her retirement sooner rather than later, including looking into getting a new service dog. Whether your new dog comes from a service dog charity/organization, is a privately purchased dog, or is one you wish to train yourself, it can take months, if not years, to find another dog who you feel can eventually step into your older dog's shoes. Don't leave it until the last minute.

If you have never done so before, and you do end up buying a new service dog prospect, you will find having two dogs is a lot more work than keeping one. If you have two dogs of differing ages, breeds, sizes or temperaments, then you may very well have to walk them separately, in addition to separate training sessions for your new dog. Altogether this can be a real chore if your own health is not great. It's also vastly more expensive to keep two dogs, particularly if you have trained and bought your original service dog privately, and her insurance, veterinarian fees, food, etc., are all paid solely by you. Now multiply that sum by two!

If you do get a new dog, make sure your older service dog still gets plenty of attention, plus peace and quiet away from the interloper whenever she needs it. A younger dog is not all bad news and can give an older dog a new lease on life, including those who are used to being the only dog in the home. Most "only dogs" are slightly horrified with a new puppy in the beginning, but soon settle down into the swing of things and very quickly the two become bosom buddies. Mazey was initially mortified with the arrival of Mina. She formed an alliance with Holly Bengal in the face of a common enemy; they huddled up together on the sofa, both trying to murder Mina with gazes that fully showed their evil intent. However, after a few days, all was well and Mazey, very much considering herself Mina's mother, even regurgitated her food for Mina.

Dogs do mimic each other, and your older service dog can often serve as an example to your younger dog. It may also be possible to work both dogs in tandem, though this could prove to be a handful. I have only done it once with Mazey and Mina, mainly out of necessity. I was on a road trip and desperately needed some medication, and could not leave Mina in the car as it was too hot, so she had to come into the chemist with Mazey and I. It actually went a lot better than I thought it would, and I know working tandem dogs is far more popular in the U.S. than it is in the UK.

It's very much going to be a matter of your own judgment as to when it's time to fully retire your service dog. Some dogs are better off retired gradually from public access work, though they may enjoy still performing small tasks about the home. As with humans, it can be depressing growing old, particularly if there's a new arrival who's getting all the attention. Helping your older dog still feel relevant can be vitally important for her health and mental well-being. Instead of working her as hard as you usually would, perhaps keep to lighter tasks, gradually reducing them until your new service dog has enough experience to fully take over.

I have been so lucky with Mina who has fit into my little family incredibly well. However, as with all best-laid plans, Mina does not look like she will end up as my perfect service dog in the way Mazey is, because Mina's basic nature is super excitable. I did buy Mina when Mazey was four, giving me plenty of time to train her or decide what to do if service dog life turns out not to be for Mina. For now, she is performing medical alert and other tasks at home, but doing very little public access. This is working out great as Mazey loves meeting people and being out and about, but gets a rest in the evenings with Mina taking the helm at home.

Mazey is still going strong, and absolutely adores her job as a service dog. As she ages, I'll leave it up to her as regards when she wants to fully retire. She's a great favorite among the staff in so many shops, and I know Mazey would be devastated to see me leave her behind every day and go gallivanting off with Mina. I'll almost certainly retire her in stages, possibly finding her a new, less stressful job for her. Mazey is the biggest lovebug in the world, so even though the thought of her retiring fills me with dread, it may be possible for her to do a little therapy dog work with children or older people, just for the cuddles and attention.

Chapter Sixteen

So Long, Farewell and All That Jazz

It seems we have come to the end of the book and our adventures in service dog land. Mazey Rottweiler, service dog extraordinaire, your oh-so-glamorous and awe-inspiring host, tells me it's been a great privilege for her to write this book for you, which she hopes you have found both interesting and informative. She has, of course, been accompanied by and had just a small amount of assistance from her not-so-gorgeous sidekick, ahem, me, Nicola.

If you told me ten years ago that I'd be disabled and virtually unemployable, and instead of ministering to dogs I'd be writing about them, I would not have believed you. But life is like the ghost train at a traveling fairground, full of twists and turns, ups and downs, with a habit of taking you by surprise; yes, even those of us who think we've seen and experienced it all before. Rock bottom does not exist; you can always go lower, and lower, and lower. Skeletons leap at you from every direction, and the boogeyman's arms telegraph out to gather you in a tight, unwelcome embrace, a bit like an evil Inspector Gadget.

Some of us have been disabled from birth; others have had it thrust upon them when least expected, leaving them scared and confused, worried about a future that now appears desolate and bleak, without the faintest hint of light, warmth or comfort. That was me until Mazey came into my life. She very much represented a ray of hope in what was otherwise a waiting game, trying to pass time until those I loved had all died, and I could finally take my own leave of this planet without causing any hurt or distress to anyone else.

If you're reading this book in much the same position I was in, or love and care for someone who is, I'm not going to patronize you and tell you all will be well with the simple addition of a service dog into your family. It won't. If you're thinking about a service dog, there's a lot to consider. She is a massive commitment in terms of time, energy and money and it may be years before she can do the actual job you've obtained her for, particularly if self-training.

However, if you *do* bring a service dog into your life, and I hope many of you will be inspired to do so, it's the start of a new and exciting chapter of your life. Admittedly, initially that new chapter is filled with copious amounts of puppy poop and wee on carpets that then need to be cleaned. But then again, there's that oh so sweet puppy breath when you snuggle in close together at night, and even if just for an instant, all is right with the world.

I was brought up to keep a stiff British upper lip, from a generation that did not discuss their emotions or problems, but I'm not afraid or ashamed to tell the entire world that I love Mazey with all my heart, and that, without her, I do not believe I

Feline overlords of the Ferguson household, Izzy and Levi Bengal. Photo by the author (2022).

would be alive today. She gave me a purpose in life when I was at my lowest. She showed me that even though I will never qualify to live the life I feel I was destined for—I wished to be a veterinarian—what I do have is a dog that has given me her heart and her soul. With Mazey, I've experienced a love and a bond that few humans are ever privileged to have with another species. I feel truly blessed to share my life with Mazey, as well as with Mina, Izzy and Levi.

I hope this book has taught you a little about service dogs, and even at times cheered you up a bit. If you're planning on getting your own service dog, hopefully you now have most of the practical information you need to make an informed choice. This book is, of course, written from my own personal experience, and other service dog users may feel very differently on a lot of things. I hope what all of us agree on, however, is that our service dogs are absolutely amazing, the superheroes of the canine world. Keep those tails wagging, and perhaps we'll meet again another day.

Lots of love from Nicola and Mazey, with assistance from Mina Snogweiler, as supervised by feline overlords Izzy and Levi Bengal.

Glossary

ABA—Applied Behavioral Analysis. At its worst, a means of "training" autistic children like an old-fashioned zookeeper armed with a taser.

ADUK—A coalition of UK service dog charities and not-for-profit organizations

assistance dog—The UK term for a service dog; a dog trained to mitigate the disabilities of a disabled person.

balanced training—A dog training methodology that states both positive and negative methods may be used while training dogs.

bashers—Trainers who use physical violence on dogs, such as punching and kicking. Yank-and-crank trainers who use hard leash corrections.

buzzers—Trainers who misuse e-collars, using frequent, high stimulation shocks.

BYB—Insert your own desired expletive here [ ]. Breeders who exploit animals, most often from their own home as a small enterprise, but the term can also include puppy farms.

canicross—A dog sport that involves running with your dog.

Complesso di Giulia Felice—House of Julia Felix. What a letdown in English, ehh?

corrections—Giving a dog a correction is simply telling a dog that what they have done is incorrect.

crazy cat lady—All dictionaries of quality should include a photograph of me under this phrase.

Crypt Keeper—For the woefully undereducated, *Tales from the Crypt* is a TV marvel.

e-collar—An e-collar is a collar that uses electricity to provide a beep, a vibration (like your phone), or an electric stimulation.

F1 cross—An F1 cross is the first genetic cross between two different breeds, such as a Poodle with a Labrador Retriever. An F2 cross could be an F1 Doodle crossed back to a Labrador Retriever or a Poodle, or another breed commonly used when breeding Doodles, such as a Cocker Spaniel.

fab four—The fab four are the Standard Poodle, Collie (though this is a bit broad, there are lots of Collie breeds), Golden Retriever and Labrador Retriever.

force-free/purely positive training—A dog training methodology that states no force is used while training dogs, only reward and positive reinforcement.

Grand Tour—The olde days equivalent to a gap year for rich kids.

green dog—A young dog who is physically reaching maturity but lacks any formal training.

head-collar—A head-collar is a device that is fastened onto a dog's head, and which works by putting pressure directly on the nerves and fascia of said dog's head. Ouchy ouch.

IGP—Internationale Gebrauchshund Pruefung is a dog sport composed of three phases: obedience, tracking and protection.

liger—A liger is a cross between a male lion and a female tiger, and which typically grows much larger than either parent.

martingale collar—A collar that typically is made of one part material/leather, with a chain that tightens around the dog's neck. It can be adjusted so it either fully tightens around the dog's neck, or stops so several fingers can go underneath it.

off-breed—A breed of service dog that is not commonly trained by most service dog charities/organizations.

off-switch—The ability of a dog to settle in the home, quietly sleeping or amusing themselves without constantly looking for human attention.

Old Masters—Geezers of yesteryear who could paint.

play-based training—Scrabble, Snakes and Ladders, Monopoly: no. Scent work, tug, etc.: yes.

PoTS—Postural tachycardia syndrome.

privy—An outside toilet, beloved by Brits well into the 1970s.

prong collar—No, not a device from the dog trainer edition of *Fifty Shades of Grey*, but a collar that is designed for a light touch and to distribute the load evenly around the dog's neck rather than one spot.

proto-service dog—A not-quite-there dog. Not a wolf, but not yet a dog.

rewards—Rewards are something we like. I would like $1 million in my bank account, for example.

service dog—A dog trained to mitigate the disabilities of a disabled person.

service dog charity—An organization with charitable status that either trains service dogs itself or helps disabled people who are owner training their own service dog.

service dog organization—In many cases identical to a service dog charity, except the organization does not have charitable status.

service dog prospect—A service dog in training.

service dog team—A service dog with their disabled owner/handler.

settle mat—A blanket, often slightly weighted to keep its shape, that your dog can use to lie on while she waits for you in public places.

stooge dog—A dog that has calm, relaxed body language around other dogs and that can be used for behavioral modification of dogs with reactivity problems.

TARDIS—Time And Relative Dimensions In Space. It's a time machine, which really exists. Promise.

tasks or task-work—The behaviors a service dog is taught to perform in order to mitigate their owner's/handler's disabilities—for example, emptying the washing machine.

tethering—Tethering is a service dog task, whereby an autistic child is physically tethered to the dog to prevent the child from running away and placing themselves in danger.

white cane laws—Traffic laws to help disabled people.

Chapter Notes

Chapter One

1. Skoglund, P., Ersmark, E., Palkopoulou, E. & Dalén, L. "Ancient Wolf Genome Reveals an Early Divergence of Domestic Dog Ancestors and Admixture Into High-latitude Breeds." *Current Biology* 25, 1515–1519 (2015). Accessed 02/17/2022 at: https://www.sciencedirect.com/science/article/pii/S0960982215004327.

2. Handwerk, B. "How Accurate Is the Theory of Dog Domestication in 'Alpha'?" *Smithsonian Magazine*, August 15, 2018. Accessed 02/17/2022 at: https://www.smithsonianmag.com/science-nature/how-wolves-really-became-dogs-180970014/.

3. Anderson, A. "Dire Wolves Were Real and Even Stranger Than We Thought." *National Geographic*, January 13, 2021. Accessed 02/17/2022 at: https://www.nationalgeographic.com/animals/article/dire-wolf-dna-study-reveals-surprises.

4. UC Museum of Paleontology, University of California at Berkeley. "What Is a Sabretooth?" Accessed 02/11/2022 at: https://ucmp.berkeley.edu/mammal/carnivora/sabretooth.html#:~:text=It%20went%20extinct%20about%2010%2C000,arthritis%20and%20other%20degenerative%20diseases.

5. Naveed, S. "Why Did Neanderthals Go Extinct?" *Psychology Today*. Accessed 02/17/2022 at: https://www.psychologytoday.com/us/blog/the-red-light-district/202102/why-did-neanderthals-go-extinct.

6. Dunn, J. and Dunn, B. "Pompeii in Pictures." Accessed 02/17/2022 at: http://pompeiinpictures.com/pompeiinpictures/R2/2%2004%2003.htm.

7. Rembrant, H. "A Blind Beggar with a Boy and a Dog." Accessed 02/18/2022 at: https://commons.wikimedia.org/wiki/File:Rembrandt_Harmensz_van_Rijn,_%27A_blind_beggar_with_a_boy_and_a_dog%27.jpg.

8. Gaugain, T. "A Shoeless Blind Girl Is Led by a Dog on a Path." Sepia stipple engraving by T. Gaugain, 1785, after J. Northcote. Welcome Collection. Accessed 02/18/2022 at: https://wellcomecollection.org/works/teuz3pwg.

9. International Guide Dog Federation. "History of Guide Dogs." Accessed 02/18/2022 at: https://www.igdf.org.uk/guide-dogs/history-of-guide-dogs/.

10. Smith, T.J. "A Legless Man Sitting on a Wooden Cart, Presumably Begging." Accessed 02/18/2022 at: https://wellcomecollection.org/works/fxktfavj.

11. Engelmann, after M.S. Baptiste. "A Troupe of Blind Musicians and Their Dogs Confronting a Rival Street Musician and His Dog." Lithograph by Engelmann, 1828. Accessed 03/27/2022 at: https://wellcomecollection.org/works/cmmxmmvc/items.

12. Guide Dogs for the Blind. "The History of Guide Dogs." Accessed 02/19/2022 at: https://www.guidedogs.org.uk/about-us/what-we-do/the-history-of-guide-dogs/.

13. *Ibid.*

14. History.com. "Salem Witch Trials." Accessed 02/19/2022 at: https://www.history.com/topics/colonial-america/salem-witch-trials.

15. Ellen Castelow. "Witches in Britain." Accessed 02/11/2022 at: https://www.historic-uk.com/CultureUK/Witches-in-Britain/.

16. The Pendle Witch Company. "The Story of the Pendle Witches." Accessed 02/21/2022 at: https://www.pendlewitchcompany.com/about-pendle-witches.

17. Winsham, W. "Familiar Spirits and Devilish Imps." Accessed 21/02/2022 at: https://www.liverpoolmuseums.org.uk/stories/familiar-spirits-and-devilish-imps.

18. Age Up. "A Brief History of Human Longevity." Accessed 21/02/2022 at: https://learn.age-up.com/blog/a-brief-history-of-human-longevity/.

19. Sutherland, G. "The Murder of Charles Walton on Meon Hill in 1945 Is Linked with Witchcraft, but What Are the Facts?" *Stratford-upon-Avon Herald*. Accessed 02/21/2022 at: https://www.stratford-herald.com/news/witchcraft-and-murder-on-meon-hill-9223403/.

20. Local History, BBC Home. "Uncovering Warwickshire's Sinister Secret." Accessed 02/21/2022 at: https://www.bbc.co.uk/coventry/features/weird-warwickshire/1945-witchcraft-murder.shtml.

Chapter Two

1. U.S. Department of Justice. "ADA Requirements, Service Animals." Accessed 02/22/2022 at: https://www.ada.gov/service_animals_2010. htm#:~:text=A%20service%20animal%20must%20 be,safe%2C%20effective%20performance%20 of%20tasks.
2. Legislation: The Equality Act 2010. Accessed 02/22/2022 at: at: https://www. legislation.gov.uk/ukpga/2010/15/contents.
3. Cornell Law School, Legal Information Institute. "Supremacy Clause." Accessed 02/22/2022 at: https://www.law.cornell.edu/wex/ supremacy_clause.
4. ADA National Network. "What Is the Definition of Disability Under the ADA?" Accessed 02/22/2022 at: https://adata.org/ faq/what-definition-disability-under-ada.
5. Psychiatric Service Dog Partners. "How Many Service Dog Tasks Are Required?" Accessed 02/22/2022 at: https://www.psychdogpartners. org/resources/work-tasks/number-of-tasks.
6. Kretinick, J. "Service Dogs 101: All You Need to Know." The American Kennel Club. Accessed 02/02/2022 at: https://www.akc.org/expert-advice/ training/service-dog-training-101/.
7. Gibeault, S. "All You Need to Know About Emotional Support Animals." The American Kennel Club. Accessed on 02/21/2022 at: https:// www.akc.org/expert-advice/news/everything-about-emotional-support-animals/.
8. Wisch, R. "Table of State Service Animal Laws." Accessed 05/04/2022 at: https://www. animallaw.info/topic/table-state-assistance-animal-laws.
9. Legislation: The Equality Act 2010. Accessed 02/22/2022 at: https://www.legislation. gov.uk/ukpga/2010/15/part/12/chapter/1.
10. UK Gov. "Definition of Disability Under the Equality Act 2010." Accessed 02/22/2022 at: https://www.gov.uk/definition-of-disability-under-equality-act-2010.
11. Equality and Human Rights Commission. "Assistance Dogs: A Guide for All Businesses." Accessed 03/22/2022 at: https://www. equalityhumanrights.com/sites/default/files/ assistance-dogs-a-guide-for-all-businesses.pdf.
12. CPS. "Dangerous Dogs Offenses." Accessed on 05/13/2022 at: https://www.cps.gov.uk/legal-guidance/dangerous-dog-offences.

Chapter Four

1. The Guardian (online). "German Police Dogs Sent Off Duty After Ban on 'Pulling Collars.'" Accessed 03/22/2022 at: https://www.theguardian. com/world/2022/jan/06/german-police-dogs-sent-off-duty-after-ban-on-pulling-collars.

Chapter Five

1. American Kennel Club. "Answer These 5 Questions to Find the Right Dog for You." Accessed 02/22/2022 at: https://www.akc. org/expert-advice/lifestyle/answer-5-questions-find-right-dog/.
2. UK Kennel Club. "Breeds A to Z." Accessed 02/23/2022 at: https://www.thekennelclub.org. uk/search/breeds-a-to-z/.
3. Parsemus Foundation. "Hormone-Sparing Sterilization." Accessed on 05/03/2022 at: https:// www.parsemus.org/pethealth/hormone-sparing-sterilization/#:~:text=Hormone%2Dsparing %20methods%20%E2%80%94%20like%20 hysterectomy,who%20offers%20hormone%2 Dsparing%20sterilization.
4. The Smart Dog U Blog. "Why Great Danes for Service Work?" Accessed on 02/25/2022 at: https://smartdog.typepad.com/smart_dog/ 2009/06/why-great-danes-for-service-work. html.
5. Diebelius, G. "Dog Rescued from Streets Becomes One of UK's First Police Staffies." Accessed on 02/25/2022 at: https://metro.co.uk/ 2018/11/19/dog-rescued-from-streets-becomes-one-of-uks-first-police-staffies-8157347/.
6. Revesz, R. "U.S. Police Departments Are Training and Adopting Pit Bulls Instead of Pure Breed Dogs to Save Money." Accessed on 02/25/2022 at: https://www.independent.co.uk/ news/world/americas/police-departments-adopting-pit-bull-dogs-save-money-euthanised-training-a7367821.html.
7. Murugesu, J. "French Bulldogs are the Shortest-Lived Dog Breed in the UK." Accessed on 05/02/2022 at: https://www.newscientist. com/article/2318084-french-bulldogs-are-the-shortest-lived-dog-breed-in-the-uk/ #ixzz7S97AiuxI.
8. Time Magazine (online). "Greyhound Racing Is Nearing Its End in the U.S." Accessed on 05/03/2022 at: https://time.com/6172581/ greyhound-dog-racing-end/.

Chapter Six

1. Lead Academy. "How Much Does It Cost to Train a Guide Dog?" Accessed on 04/07/2022 at: https://lead-academy.org/how-much-does-it-cost-to-train-a-guide-dog/.
2. U.S. Department of Justice. "Frequently Asked Questions About Service Animals and the ADA." Accessed on 04/07/2022 at: https:// www.ada.gov/regs2010/service_animal_ qa.html#:~:text=A.,related%20to%20the%20 person's%20disability.

Chapter Seven

1. Erb, H. "Puppy Temperament Tests: A Tool to Help with Placement." Accessed on 05/10/2022 at: https://www.akc.org/expert-advice/dog-breeding/puppy-temperament-tests-tool-help-placement/.

2. OFA online. Accessed on 05/10/2022 at: https://www.ofa.org/.

3. The Kennel Club. "Health Tests Results Finder." Accessed on 05/10/2022 at: https://www.thekennelclub.org.uk/search/health-test-results-finder/.

4. Australian Labradoodle Association Inc. Accessed on 05/10/2022 at: https://www.laa.org.au/.

Chapter Ten

1. American Kennel Club. "Puppy Fear Periods: Why Is My Puppy Suddenly Afraid?" Accessed on 04/18/2022 at: https://www.akc.org/expert-advice/training/dont-panic-training-through-and-around-puppy-fear-periods/.

2. American Kennel Club. "Creativity & Critical Timing Are Key to Puppy Socialization." Accessed on 04/18/2022 at: https://www.akc.org/expert-advice/puppy-information/creativity-and-timing-key-to-puppy-socialization/.

Chapter Eleven

1. Access card. Accessed 04/17/2022 at: https://www.accesscard.org.uk/.

Chapter Thirteen

1. NY subway. "Service Animals and the New York Subway." Accessed on 04/20/2022 at: https://nysubway.com/service-animals-ny-subway/.

2. Spectrum News NY 1. "NYPD: Pit Bull in Subway Attack Was a Service Dog, Owner Still Facing Charges." Accessed on 04/20/2022 at: https://www.ny1.com/nyc/all-boroughs/news/2018/04/26/pit-bull-owner-arrested-in-subway-attack-caught-on-video-#.

3. UK Civil Aviation Authority. "Traveling with an Assistance Dog." Accessed on 04/20/2022 at: https://www.caa.co.uk/Passengers/PRM/Travelling-with-an-assistance-dog/#:~:text=Airlines%20must%20accept%20all%20assistance,usually%20a%20little%20more%20space).

4. U.S. Department of Transportation. "U.S. Department of Transportation Service Animal Air Transportation Form." Accessed on 04/20/2022 at: https://www.transportation.gov/sites/dot.gov/files/2021-01/U.S.%20DOT%20Service%20Animal%20Air%20Transportation%20Form.pdf.

5. British Airways. "Traveling with a Service Dog." Accessed on 04/20/2022 at: https://www.britishairways.com/en-gb/information/disability-assistance/travelling-with-your-assistance-dog.

Chapter Fifteen

1. American Veterinary Medical Association. "Administration of Rabies Vaccination State Laws." Accessed on 05/15/2022 at: https://www.avma.org/advocacy/state-and-local-advocacy/administration-rabies-vaccination-state-laws.

Bibliography

I include a list of books that you may find of interest. A few of these books may surprise you, as some of the information is really quite opposite to my own beliefs. However, it's important to concede that not everyone is right all of the time (except for Mazey, naturally) and we all have a great deal that we can learn from each other. Therefore, only certain parts of these books will be useful or of interest. I will leave you to separate the raw meaty bones from the kibble. Enjoy!

Aiello, Susan E., and Michael A. Moses. *The Merck Veterinary Manual*. 11th ed. Hoboken, NJ: Wiley, 2016. (ISBN-13: 978–0911910612).

Arden, Jane. *Mission Control: How to Train the High Drive Dog*. Tucson, AZ: First Stone Publishing, 2020. (ISBN 10:1910488577).

Bailey, Gwen. *The Perfect Puppy*. Rev. ed. Richmond Hill, Canada: Firefly Books, 2017. (ISBN 13: 9781770859111).

Balabanov, Ivan, and Karen Duet. *Advanced Schutzhund*. New York: Howell Reference Books, 1999. (ISBN 13: 978–0876057308).

Barnes, Stuart. *The Way of the Dog: Training by Instinct*. CreateSpace Independent Publishing Platform, 2015. (ISBN-13: 978–1512078688).

Burch, Mary, and Jon Bailey. *How Dogs Learn*. New York: Howell Book House, 1999. (ISBN-13: 978–1630260392).

Case, Linda. *Dog Smart: Evidence Based Training with the Science Dog*. CreateSpace Independent Publishing Platform, 2018. (ISBN 13: 9781979380317).

Charles River Editors. *The Domestication of Dogs: The History of Dogs' Genetic Divergence from Wolves and the Origins of Their Relationship with Human*. Independently published, 2020. (ISBN-13: 979–8645367978).

The Complete Dog Breed Book: Choose the Perfect Dog for You. London: Dorling Kindersley, 2020. ISBN-13: 978–0241412732.

Cusack, Carmen. *Laws, Policies, Attitudes & Processes That Shape the Lives of Puppies in America: Assessing Society's Needs, Desires, Values & Morals*. East Sussex, UK: Sussex Academic Press. 2000. (ISBN-13: 978–1845197810).

Eschenweber, Sina. *Mental Exercise for Dogs: The 101 Best Dog Games for More Agility, Intelligence & Fun*. Independently published, 2020. (ISBN-13: 979–8566060880)

Fogle, Bruce. *The Dog's Mind*. New York: Howell Book House, 1992. (ISBN-13: 978–072 0719642).

Gay, Barry. *Balanced Training: Obedience for Dogs and Their Owners*. Altona, Canada: Friesen Press, 2017. (ISBN 13: 9781525507984).

Goody, Peter. *Dog Anatomy: A Pictorial Approach to Canine Structure*. Ingatestone, UK: Allen, 1999. (ISBN-13: 978–0851316369).

Gutteridge, Sally. *Enrichment through Scentwork for Highly Aroused Dogs*. Independently published, 2018. (ASIN: B07KCNB9PS).

Käufer, Mechtild. *Canine Play Behaviour: The Science of Dogs at Play*. Wenatchee, WA: Dogwise Publishing, 2011. (ISBN-13: 978–1617812712).

Kay, Debby. *Super Sniffer Handbook: A Guide to Scent Training for Medical Alert Dogs*. Wenatchee, WA: Dogwise Publishing, 2013.

Krohn, Larry. *Everything You Need to know about E-Collar Training*. Independently published, 2017. (ISBN-13: 978–1521126554).

Mackinnon, Pam. *Detector Dog: A Talking Dogs Scentwork® Manual*. Dorset, UK: Hubble & Hattie, 2017. (ISBN-13: 978–1845849634).

Mann, Steve. *Easy Peasy Doggy Squeezy: Even More of Your Dog Training Dilemmas Solved*. London: Blink, 2020. (ISBN-13: 978–1788703413).

Mann, Steve. *Easy Peasy Puppy Squeezy*. London: Blink, 2019. (ISBN-13: 978–1788701600).

Millis, Darryl, and David Levine, eds. *Canine Rehabilitation and Physical Therapy*. 2nd ed. Philadelphia: Saunders, 2013. (ISBN-13: 978–1437703092).

Scott, John Paul, and John L. Fuller. *Dog Behavior: Genetics and the Social Behavior of the Dog*. University of Chicago Press, 1998. (ISBN-13: 978–0226743387)

Walkowicz, Chris, and Bonnie Wilcox. *Successful Dog Breeding: The Complete Handbook of Canine Midwifery*. 2nd ed. Hoboken, NJ: Wiley, 1994. (ISBN-13: 978–0876057407).

Wycherley, Jeannie. *Losing My Best Friend: Thoughtful Support for Those Affected by Dog Bereavement or Pet Loss*, Devon, UK: Bark at the Moon Books, 2018. (ISBN-13: 978–0995781825).

Zinc, Chris, and Janet B. Van Dyke. *Canine Sports Medicine and Rehabilitation*. Hoboken, NJ: Wiley-Blackwell, 2018. (ISBN-13: 978–1119380382).

Index

www.ingramcontent.com/pod-product-compliance
Lightning Source LLC
Chambersburg PA
CBHW080554270326
41929CB00019B/3305